AMERICAN POLITICAL, ECONOMIC, AND SECURITY ISSUES

WHISTLEBLOWERS

PROTECTION, PRACTICES AND DISCLOSURE

AMERICAN POLITICAL, ECONOMIC, AND SECURITY ISSUES

Additional books and e-books in this series can be found on Nova's website under the Series tab.

American Political, Economic, and Security Issues

Whistleblowers

Protection, Practices and Disclosure

Isabelle Guertin
Editor

snova
New York

NOTICE TO THE READER

Additional color graphics may be available in the e-book version of this book.

Library of Congress Cataloging-in-Publication Data

ISBN: 978-1-53616-310-0

Published by Nova Science Publishers, Inc. † New York

CONTENTS

PREFACE

Whistleblowing is "the act of reporting waste, fraud, abuse and corruption in a lawful manner to those who can correct the wrongdoing." Safeguarding confidentiality to the maximum extent possible is essential for encouraging whistleblowers to report wrongdoing without fear of reprisal. This book discusses the practices and programs that protect whistleblowers.

Chapter 1 - Safeguarding confidentiality to the maximum extent possible is essential for encouraging whistleblowers to report wrongdoing without fear of reprisal. In fiscal year 2018, DODIG received over 12,000 contacts from potential whistleblowers related to fraud, waste, abuse, employee misconduct, or other violations. The National Defense Authorization Act for Fiscal Year 2017 included a provision for GAO to review the integrity of DOD's whistleblower program. This chapter assesses the extent to which DODIG and the military service IGs (1) met and took steps to achieve key fiscal year 2018 timeliness and quality goals, (2) established processes to protect whistleblower confidentiality, and (3) are able to safeguard sensitive information necessary to handle whistleblower complaints. It also evaluates (4) the extent to which select cases involving certain senior DOD civilian officials met key requirements. GAO assessed fiscal year 2018 IG performance data, surveyed all 108 DODIG employees who directly handle whistleblower complaints, reviewed IT security controls, and analyzed all 125 cases involving civilian DOD Presidential appointees with Senate confirmation dismissed by DODIG in fiscal years 2013-2017.

Chapter 2 - Whistleblowing is "the act of reporting waste, fraud, abuse and corruption in a lawful manner to those who can correct the wrongdoing." Intelligence community (IC) whistleblowers are those employees or contractors working in any of the 17 elements of the IC who reasonably believe there has been a violation of law, rule, or regulation; gross mismanagement; waste of resources; abuse of authority; or a substantial danger to public health and safety. The IC has publicly recognized the importance of whistleblowing, and supports protections for whistleblowers who conform to guidelines to protect classified information. The Director of National Intelligence (DNI) whistleblowing policy and guidance is publicly available and specifically addresses the process for making protected disclosures and whistleblower protections for IC contractors, members of the Armed Forces, and federal employees. There are differing opinions, however, on whether the IC's internal processes have the transparency necessary to ensure adequate protections against reprisal, and whether protections for IC contractors are sufficient. IC whistleblower protections have evolved in response to perceptions of gaps that many believed left whistleblowers vulnerable to reprisal. The first whistleblower legislation specific to the IC was limited to specifying a process for IC whistleblowers to make a complaint but offered no specific protections. Subsequent legislation included only general provisions for protecting IC whistleblowers with no additional guidance on standards for implementation. Presidential Policy Directive (PPD)-19, signed in 2012, provided the first specific protections against reprisal actions for making a complaint. The Intelligence Authorization Act for Fiscal Year 2014 codified these provisions, which were further supported with IC implementation policy. Separate legislation under Title 10 of the U.S. Code, along with DOD implementing guidance, provides protections for members of the Armed Forces, including those assigned to elements of the IC. In early 2018, Congress passed legislation to address perceived gaps in protections for IC contractors.

Chapter 3 - On February 21, 2018, the Supreme Court decided in *Digital Realty Trust, Inc. v. Somers* that the anti-retaliation protections in the Dodd-Frank Wall Street Reform and Consumer Protection Act of 2010 (Dodd-Frank) apply only to whistleblowers who report suspected securities law violations to the Securities and Exchange Commission (SEC or Commission). In so doing, the Court rejected a more expansive reading of Dodd-Frank that would have extended its whistleblower protections to those who report securities violations internally within their organization and suffer retaliation, even if they did not take the additional step of reporting to the SEC. The ruling not only has potentially important implications for the nature and quantity of potential whistleblower actions brought under federal securities law, but *Digital Realty* also provides broader insights into the Supreme Court's current approach toward statutory interpretation.

Chapter 4 - Federal whistleblowers—employees who report violations of law, agency mismanagement or ethical violations—help to safeguard the federal government against waste, fraud, and abuse. Whistleblowers can report to various entities, including the Congress. While these reports are a key source of information for federal oversight, whistleblowers can risk reprisal. Therefore, it is important to appropriately handle whistleblowers' information and identity. The House Committee on Appropriations Report 115-696 included a provision for GAO to identify congressional avenues, resources, and best practices for working with whistleblowers. This chapter describes (1) how the Congress receives whistleblower information, (2) the policies and training currently available to congressional staff, and (3) key practices that the Congress could consider for receiving and referring information from whistleblowers. GAO interviewed congressional staff, officials from the Office of Special Counsel (OSC) and the Council of the Inspectors General on Integrity and Efficiency (CIGIE), and selected advocacy groups that have experience working with whistleblowers. GAO analyzed congressional websites and queried congressional staff regarding policies and training on whistleblowers for congressional staff. To develop key practices, GAO reviewed literature, existing procedures, and standards. GAO is not making recommendations, but is available to assist the Congress with practices for working with whistleblowers. OSC and CIGIE provided technical comments that were incorporated as appropriate.

Chapter 5 - NASA obligated over $18 billion in contracts and more than $1 billion in grants in fiscal year 2016, and it relies on a significant number of contractor and grantee employees to accomplish its work. These employees are legally protected from reprisal—such as demotion or firing—for whistleblowing. GAO was asked to review NASA's whistleblower reprisal protections for contractor and grantee employees. This chapter addresses, among other things, the extent to which (1) NASA's Inspector General investigated contractor and grantee whistleblower reprisal complaints; (2) NASA's Administrator reviewed reprisal complaints in a timely manner; and (3) NASA communicated the applicable whistleblower reprisal protections to contractors. GAO reviewed NASA and its Inspector General's policies and guidance; reviewed a generalizable sample of 100 contracts from all NASA centers with contracts in fiscal year 2016; and interviewed relevant officials and contractors, grantees, and advocacy groups.

Chapter 6 - OSC is responsible for safeguarding the merit system in federal employment by protecting employees and applicants, including whistleblowers. Consequently, OSC must ensure its case processes are adequate to protect the federal workforce, including its own employees. GAO was asked to review OSC case processes and procedures for whistleblower disclosures and PPPs. For both types of cases, this chapter among other things (1) examines trends in cases received and closed from fiscal year 2011 to 2016, (2) examines timeliness of cases closed from fiscal year 2011 to 2016, and (3) assesses the extent to which safeguards are in place for OSC employees who make allegations. GAO reviewed OSC case guidance, processes, controls, and the latest available OSC data from fiscal year 2016. GAO also assessed whether OSC's processes adhered to *Standards for Internal Control in the Federal Government*; and surveyed and interviewed OSC employees.

Chapter 7 - Tax whistleblowers who report on the underpayment of taxes by others have helped IRS collect $3.6 billion since 2007, according to IRS. IRS pays qualifying whistleblowers between 15 and 30 percent of the proceeds it collects as a result of their information. However, until February 9, 2018, IRS did not pay whistleblowers for information that led to the collection of FBAR penalties. GAO was asked to review how often and to what extent whistleblower claims involve cases where FBAR penalties were also assessed. Among other objectives, this chapter (1) describes the extent to which FBAR penalties were included in whistleblower awards prior to the statutory change in definition of proceeds; (2) examines how IRS used whistleblower information on FBAR noncompliance, and how IRS responded to the statutory change in definition of proceeds; and (3) describes the purposes for which IRS collects and uses FBAR penalty data, and assesses controls for ensuring data reliability. GAO reviewed the files of 132 claims closed between January 1, 2012, and July 24, 2017, that likely included FBAR allegations; analyzed IRS data; reviewed relevant laws and regulations, and IRS policies, procedures and publications; and interviewed IRS officials.

In: Whistleblowers
Editor: Isabelle Guertin

ISBN: 978-1-53616-310-0

Chapter 1

WHISTLEBLOWER PROTECTION: ANALYSIS OF DOD'S ACTIONS TO IMPROVE CASE TIMELINESS AND SAFEGUARD CONFIDENTIALITY*

United States Government Accountability Office

ABBREVIATIONS

CIGIE	Council of the Inspectors General on Integrity and Efficiency
D-CATS	Defense Case Activity Tracking System
D-CATSe	Defense Case Activity Tracking System enterprise
DOD	Department of Defense
DODIG	Department of Defense Office of Inspector General
IG	Office of Inspector General

---

* This is an edited, reformatted and augmented version of United States Government Accountability Office; Report to Congressional Committees; Accessible Version, Publication No. GAO-19-198, dated March 2019.

IT	Information Technology
NIST	National Institute of Standards and Technology
PAS	Presidential Appointee with Senate Confirmation

WHY GAO DID THIS STUDY

Safeguarding confidentiality to the maximum extent possible is essential for encouraging whistleblowers to report wrongdoing without fear of reprisal. In fiscal year 2018, DODIG received over 12,000 contacts from potential whistleblowers related to fraud, waste, abuse, employee misconduct, or other violations. The National Defense Authorization Act for Fiscal Year 2017 included a provision for GAO to review the integrity of DOD's whistleblower program. This chapter assesses the extent to which DODIG and the military service IGs (1) met and took steps to achieve key fiscal year 2018 timeliness and quality goals, (2) established processes to protect whistleblower confidentiality, and (3) are able to safeguard sensitive information necessary to handle whistleblower complaints. It also evaluates (4) the extent to which select cases involving certain senior DOD civilian officials met key requirements.

GAO assessed fiscal year 2018 IG performance data, surveyed all 108 DODIG employees who directly handle whistleblower complaints, reviewed IT security controls, and analyzed all 125 cases involving civilian DOD Presidential appointees with Senate confirmation dismissed by DODIG in fiscal years 2013-2017.

WHAT GAO RECOMMENDS

GAO is making 12 recommendations, including that the IGs take additional actions to improve timeliness, develop additional procedures to protect whistleblower confidentiality, and take steps to further limit IG employee access to sensitive whistleblower information. DOD concurred with all of the recommendations.

WHAT GAO FOUND

The Department of Defense Office of Inspector General (DODIG) and military service offices of inspector general (IG) met some but not all fiscal year 2018 timeliness and quality goals for handling whistleblower complaints. For example, DODIG met its goals related to referring complaints to the appropriate agency within a certain number of days. All IGs also generally met goals related to the quality of investigations. However, about 85 percent of DODIG reprisal and senior official misconduct investigations exceeded statutory and internal timeliness goals. Further, military service IGs did not meet most goals for handling cases within prescribed timeframes. For example, the service IGs averaged between 17 and 84 days to notify DODIG of their receipt of whistleblower reprisal allegations, exceeding the 10-day goal. The IGs have various initiatives underway to improve timeliness, such as a Naval IG program to reduce timeframes for initial credibility determinations. However, additional actions could provide a more targeted approach to improving performance against unmet timeliness goals—such as for senior official misconduct investigations and better assure whistleblowers that their cases will be handled expeditiously.

DODIG and the military service IGs have policies to protect whistleblower confidentiality, but some gaps exist. For example, DODIG guidance for protecting whistleblowers who report internal DODIG misconduct does not specify key steps investigators should take to protect confidentiality, such as not identifying complainants during interviews with case subjects. Also, Air Force, Naval, and Marine Corps IG guidance does not specify when whistleblower identities can be disclosed without consent. Without updated guidance, the IGs cannot ensure the consistent implementation of confidentiality protections.

The IGs have taken steps to safeguard whistleblower information in their information technology (IT) systems and applications, such as by restricting access to case information through unique user permissions and by taking actions to follow DOD's IT risk management process. However, between 2016 and 2018, employees in all of the IGs have been able to access sensitive whistleblower information without a need to know. For example, DODIG determined that numerous restricted whistleblower records in its document repository were accessible to DODIG personnel without a need to know. Similarly, the Air Force IG's application did not restrict users from other DOD components from viewing Air Force IG case descriptions and complainant identities, while the Army IG's application and the Naval IG's system did not restrict personnel within those IGs from viewing allegations or investigations involving other personnel within those IGs. Additionally, employees in Marine Corps IG offices were able to see whistleblower cases assigned to other IG offices without a need to know. While some actions have been taken to address these issues, additional steps are needed to restrict access to case information in order to mitigate ongoing risks to whistleblower confidentiality.

DODIG generally met key documentation requirements for the 125 cases it dismissed without investigation involving civilian DOD Presidential appointees with Senate confirmation.

March 7, 2019

The Honorable James M. Inhofe
Chairman

The Honorable Jack Reed
Ranking Member
Committee on Armed Services
United States Senate

The Honorable Adam Smith
Chairman

The Honorable Mac Thornberry
Ranking Member
Committee on Armed Services
House of Representatives

The integrity of the Department of Defense (DOD) whistleblower program is paramount to establishing a culture that encourages the reporting of potential fraud, waste, abuse, misconduct, and other complaints.[1] DOD offices of inspector general (IG)—including the DOD Office of Inspector General (DODIG) and the IGs of the Air Force, the Army, the Navy, and the Marine Corps—rely in part on whistleblowers to help improve government operations.[2] Because whistleblowers also risk reprisal—such as demotion, reassignment, and firing—IGs have a special responsibility to protect whistleblower identity to the greatest extent possible, and to investigate allegations in a timely, confidential, independent, and objective manner.[3]

Congress and the former administration established a statutory and policy framework which defines responsibilities for investigating whistleblower allegations of DOD employee misconduct and for protecting DOD whistleblowers from reprisal. Under this framework, DODIG is responsible for investigating and overseeing the investigation of misconduct and reprisal allegations from certain DOD civilian employees, contractors, and military servicemembers, while the IGs of the military services are responsible for investigating and reporting allegations involving military servicemembers to DODIG. In recent years, members of

---

[1] For the purposes of this report, the DOD whistleblower program is defined as the administrative investigative components of the Department of Defense Office of Inspector General and the military services' offices of inspector general that handle whistleblower allegations of misconduct and reprisal.

[2] The IGs of the Air Force, the Army, the Navy, and the Marine Corps are hereafter collectively referred to as military service IGs. We use the term "Naval IG" to refer to the Navy's Office of Inspector General, separate from the Marine Corps' Office of Inspector General.

[3] Section 7(b) of the Inspector General Act of 1978, as amended, codified at 5 U.S.C., Appendix § 7(b), states that IGs shall not, after the receipt of a complaint or information from an employee, disclose the identity of the employee without the consent of the employee, unless the IG determines such disclosure is unavoidable during the course of the investigation. Pub. L. No. 95-452 (1978).

Congress and the public have expressed concerns regarding the integrity of misconduct and reprisal investigations, including those involving senior DOD officials and DODIG employees. Further, DODIG has designated ensuring ethical conduct as a top management challenge for the department.[4] In fiscal year 2018, DOD's Hotline received 12,470 complaints from potential whistleblowers.[5]

We have previously reported on DOD's whistleblower reprisal program. In February 2012, May 2015, and September 2017, we found that DOD faced challenges in overseeing its program and made 25 recommendations to help improve the timeliness, quality, independence, and performance measurement of military, civilian, and contractor investigations, among other things.6 DOD concurred with all of our recommendations, and as of November 2018, has implemented 18 of them.[7]

Section 536 of the National Defense Authorization Act for Fiscal Year 2017 included a provision for us to review the integrity of DOD's whistleblower program.[8]

This chapter assesses the extent to which DODIG and the military service IGs (1) met and took steps to achieve key fiscal year 2018

---

[4] Department of Defense Office of Inspector General, *Top DOD Management Challenges, Fiscal Year 2018* (Nov. 20, 2017).

[5] The DOD Hotline provides a confidential, reliable means to report violations of laws, rules, or regulations; mismanagement; gross waste of funds; abuse of authority; and serious security incidents that involve DOD.

[6] GAO, *Whistleblower Protection: Actions Needed to Improve DOD's Military Whistleblower Reprisal Program*, GAO-12-362 (Washington, D.C.: Feb. 22, 2012); *Whistleblower Protection: DOD Needs to Enhance Oversight of Military Whistleblower Reprisal Investigations*, GAO-15-477 (Washington, D.C.: May 7, 2015); and Whistleblower Protection: Opportunities Exist for DOD to Improve the Timeliness and Quality of Civilian and Contractor Reprisal Investigations, GAO-17-506 (Washington, D.C.: Sept. 29, 2017).

[7] DOD has not yet fully addressed our 2015 recommendation to standardize the investigation process across the military services or our 2017 recommendations to assess the feasibility of collecting key workload data, and including such data in a future personnel requirements assessment; document threats to independence and incorporate such information into an evaluation of independence threats; establish and communicate a declination policy for nondiscretionary cases; revise its internal controls checklist to include all key case file documentation and investigative events; develop a process to fully implement requirements related to the oversight of defense intelligence component cases; and develop quality performance measures and enhance existing timeliness measures to reflect key attributes of successful performance measures.

[8] See Pub. L. No. 114-328 §536, (2016) as amended by Pub. L. No. 115-91, §578 (2017).

timeliness and quality goals related to the handling of whistleblower complaints, (2) established processes to protect the confidentiality of whistleblowers, and (3) are able to access and safeguard classified and sensitive information necessary to handle whistleblower complaints. It also evaluates (4) the extent to which select misconduct and reprisal cases involving certain senior DOD civilian officials met key documentation and reporting requirements.[9]

For the first objective, we reviewed documentation and interviewed officials on DODIG and military service IG timeliness and quality goals, performance measures, and associated performance data for fiscal year 2018, along with ongoing and planned efforts to improve performance. We selected data from this period because they constituted the most complete and recent performance data available. Using the data, we assessed the extent to which DODIG and the military service IGs met timeliness and quality goals defined by statute and internal IG policy.[10] To identify factors affecting timeliness and quality, we interviewed IG officials and reviewed performance documentation. We also compared DODIG and military service IG efforts to improve timeliness and quality, both planned and completed, against Council of the Inspectors General on Integrity and Efficiency (CIGIE) standards for federal IGs[11] related to establishing

---

[9] Civilian Presidential appointees with Senate confirmation (PAS) include cabinet secretaries, agency heads, and undersecretary-level posts.

[10] Under 10 U.S.C. § 2409, as amended, investigations of contractor and subcontractor whistleblower reprisal complaints are required to be completed in 180 days or fewer, or DODIG must notify the complainant and obtain permission to extend the investigation for no more than an additional 180 days. Also, in military whistleblower reprisal cases under 10 U.S.C. § 1034 if, during the course of the investigation, the IG determines that it is not possible to submit the report of investigation to the Secretary of Defense and the secretary of the military department concerned within 180 days after the receipt of the allegation, the IG shall provide to the Secretary of Defense, the military department secretary, and the servicemember making the allegation a notice of a description of the current progress of the investigation and an estimate of the time remaining until the completion of the investigation and when the report will be submitted to the servicemember.

[11] See CIGIE, *Quality Standards for Federal Offices of Inspector General* (August 2012). CIGIE was statutorily established as an independent entity within the executive branch by the Inspector General Reform Act of 2008, Pub. L No. 110-409 (2008) and codified at 5 U.S.C. Appendix. Primarily comprised of inspectors general, CIGIE's mission is to address integrity, economy, and effectiveness issues that transcend individual government agencies and develop policies, standards, and approaches to aid in the establishment of a well-trained and highly skilled workforce in the offices of IGs.

performance plans with goals and performance measures, as well as *Standards for Internal Control in the Federal Government* related to assessing and improving performance.[12] We assessed the reliability of DODIG and military service IG data by administering questionnaires on data collection, storage, and compilation; interviewing cognizant officials; and reviewing case management system documentation and quality assurance procedures. We determined that these data were sufficiently reliable for the purpose of assessing the extent to which DODIG and military service IGs met fiscal year 2018 timeliness and quality performance goals related to the handling of whistleblower complaints.

For the second objective, we assessed DODIG and military service IG policies[13] and procedures for handling whistleblower allegations against DOD policy, CIGIE standards for federal IGs,[14] and statutory protections related to safeguarding whistleblower confidentiality.[15] We also reviewed the results of DODIG's quality assurance reviews of the Air Force (2017), Army (2018), and Naval (2016) IGs, and surveyed all 108 DODIG employees directly involved with the handling of whistleblower cases to ascertain whether, in their view, confidentiality processes are being implemented in accordance with guidance and standards, identify potential confidentiality issues, and to gather perceptions on the integrity of the internal process for reporting misconduct, among other things. The survey achieved an 80 percent response rate. For the third objective, we reviewed documentation and interviewed officials on the extent to which DODIG and the military service IGs have developed, implemented, and assessed key information technology (IT) security controls, and authorized the IT systems and applications used to process, store, and transmit sensitive

---

[12] GAO, *Standards for Internal Control in the Federal Government*, GAO-14-704G (Washington, D.C.: September 2014).

[13] For example, see DOD Instruction 7050.01, *DOD Hotline Program* (Oct. 17, 2017); Air Force Instruction 90-301, *Inspector General Complaints Resolution* (Aug. 27, 2015); Army Assistance and Investigations Guide (January 2016); Secretary of the Navy Instruction 5370.5B, *DON Hotline Program* (Nov. 24, 2004); Secretary of the Navy Instruction 5430.57G, *Mission and Functions of the Naval Inspector General* (Dec. 29, 2005); and Marine Corps Order 5430.1A, *Marine Corps Inspector General Program* (Aug. 1, 2018).

[14] See CIGIE *Quality Standards for Federal Offices of Inspector General* (August 2012) and *Quality Standards for Inspections* (Nov. 15, 2011).

[15] See 5 U.S.C., Appendix § 7(b).

whistleblower information. These reviews were based on requirements and standards prescribed by DOD,[16] the Office of Management and Budget,[17] and the National Institute of Standards and Technology (NIST).[18] We also reviewed documentation and interviewed cognizant officials on the development and implementation of the Defense Case Activity Tracking System enterprise (D-CATSe)—DOD's future system for managing whistleblower information across DODIG and the military service IGs. Separately, we reviewed data and information on the number and percentage of DODIG and military service IG classified cases closed in fiscal year 2017, and the number and allocation of DODIG and military service IG staff possessing security clearances. We also reviewed the processes and procedures for storing and accessing classified information within DODIG and the military service IGs against DOD policy related to establishing controls to ensure access to classified information is limited to authorized persons.[19]

To determine the extent of substantiated and potential confidentiality violations and retaliatory investigations involving DODIG employees, we also obtained and analyzed fiscal years 2013–2018 data on known or perceived violations of confidentiality standards and retaliatory investigations from DODIG, the service IGs, the Office of Special Counsel,[20] and the CIGIE Integrity Committee.[21] We selected the data

---

[16] DOD Instruction 8510.01 *Risk Management Framework for DOD Information Technology* (Mar. 12, 2014) (Incorporating change 2, Jul. 28, 2017).

[17] Office of Management and Budget, Circular No. A-130, *Managing Federal Information as a Strategic Resource*, (July 28, 2016).

[18] See National Institute of Standards and Technology, *Assessing Security and Privacy Controls in Federal Information Systems and Organizations: Building Effective Assessment Plans*, Special Publication 800-53A, Revision 4 (December 2014); *Security and Privacy Controls for Federal Information Systems and Organizations*, Special Publication 800-53, Revision 4 (April 2013); and *Guide for Applying the Risk Management Framework to Federal Information Systems: A Security Life Cycle Approach*, SP 800-37, Revision 1 (February 2010). At the conclusion of our work, NIST published a new version of Special Publication 800-37. See National Institute of Standards and Technology, *Risk Management Framework for Information Systems and Organizations: A System Life Cycle Approach for Security and Privacy*, Special Publication 800-37, Revision 2 (December 2018).

[19] DOD Manual 5200.01, Vol.3, *DOD Information Security Program: Protection of Classified Information* (Feb. 24, 2012) (Incorporating change 2, Mar. 19, 2013).

[20] The Office of Special Counsel is an independent agency within the executive branch established under the Whistleblower Protection Act of 1989 to investigate whistleblower reprisal and other federal personnel action complaints.

covering this period of time because they were the most recent and reliable data available. We assessed the reliability of these data by administering questionnaires, interviewing cognizant officials, and reviewing the methods used to query IG case management systems for the data. We determined the data to be sufficiently reliable for the limited purpose of identifying potential confidentiality violations and retaliatory investigations.

For the fourth objective, we reviewed all 125 administrative misconduct and reprisal cases involving civilian DOD PAS subjects that were dismissed by DODIG in fiscal years 2013 through 2017. We chose to review cases from this period because they constituted the most recent and complete data in DODIG's case management system and because they would most accurately reflect the extent to which the majority of DODIG's cases included required documentation. To conduct this review, we developed and used a data collection instrument to capture information regarding general case characteristics and the presence of information and documentation required by DOD policies and CIGIE best practices. Core elements of this instrument were shared with DODIG officials to ensure alignment with the policies and practices in place when the cases were dismissed.

To help ensure the accuracy of the information we collected, two analysts reviewed each casefile and coded for the presence of required information using the data collection instrument. In the event that disagreement between the two analysts occurred, the analysts discussed and resolved the disagreement by identifying and reviewing supporting database information or documentation, and obtained the input of a third analyst, if necessary. We reviewed all cases dismissed during this period; as a result, the dismissed case data in this chapter do not have a sampling error.[22]

---

[21] The CIGIE Integrity Committee receives, reviews, and refers for investigation whistleblower complaints made against Inspectors General, designated staff members of an IG, and the Special Counsel and Deputy Special Counsel of the Office of Special Counsel.

[22] During the course of our review, we removed five out-of-scope cases, reducing the number of cases reviewed from 130 to 125. Four cases were removed because the related allegations were investigated, and one case was removed because it was a record used to track an

Separately, we also reviewed documentation from DODIG on civilian DOD PAS official allegations and investigation results reported to the Secretary of Defense and Congress since fiscal year 2013. Appendix I provides additional details about our scope and methodology.

We conducted this performance audit from October 2016 to March 2019 in accordance with generally accepted government auditing standards. Those standards require that we plan and perform the audit to obtain sufficient, appropriate evidence to provide a reasonable basis for our findings and conclusions based on our audit objectives. We believe that the evidence obtained provides a reasonable basis for our findings and conclusions based on our audit objectives.

While this audit was initiated in October 2016, work was suspended from December 2016 until September 2017 due to other engagement work.

BACKGROUND

DOD Personnel Misconduct

The Inspector General Act of 1978, as amended, provides that the IG may receive and investigate complaints or information from an employee concerning the possible existence of an activity constituting a violation of law, rules or regulations; gross mismanagement; gross waste of funds; abuse of authority; or a substantial and specific danger to public health or safety.[23] Violation of the law may also include a violation of a provision of criminal law, including the Uniform Code of Military Justice, which is codified in Title 10 of the United States Code.[24]

---

investigation occurring at a military service IG. See appendix I for more details on our file review methodology.

[23] See 5 U.S.C. § 7(a), Appendix.

[24] Chapter 47 of Title 10, United States Code.

Whistleblower Protections for DOD Personnel

Whistleblowers are protected from reprisal as a result of making a protected disclosure through various statutes, regulations, and presidential policy covering different DOD personnel groups.

Table 1. Whistleblower Protections for Department of Defense (DOD) Civilians, Contractors, and Military Servicemembers

DOD personnel group	Authority	Selected protected disclosures	Selected prohibited personnel actions
Appropriated-fund civilians	5 U.S.C. §§ 2301 and 2302	Violation of any law, rule, or regulation, or mismanagement. Gross waste of funds. Abuse of authority. Substantial and specific danger to public health or safety.	Detail, transfer, or reassignment. Decision concerning pay, benefits, or awards. Any other significant change in duties, responsibilities, or working conditions.
Non-appropriated-fund instrumentality employees	10 U.S.C. § 1587	Violation of any law, rule, or regulation, or mismanagement. Gross waste of funds. Abuse of authority. Substantial and specific danger to public health or safety.	Disciplinary or corrective action. Any other significant change in duties or responsibilities inconsistent with the employee's salary or grade level.
Employee of a contractor, subcontractor, grantee, subgrantee, or personal services contractor	10 U.S.C. § 2409	Violations of any law, rule, or regulation related to a DOD contract or grant. Abuse of authority relating to a DOD contract or grant. Gross mismanagement of a DOD contract or grant.	Discharging, demoting, or otherwise discriminating against the employee.
Defense Civilian Intelligence Personnel System employees and employees with eligibility for access to classified information	Presidential Policy Directive (PPD) 19 50 U.S.C. § 3234	Violation of any law, rule, or regulation. Gross waste of funds. Abuse of authority. Substantial and specific danger to public health or safety. Gross mismanagement.	Termination. Reassignment. Demotion. Taking or withholding, or threatening to take or withhold, any action affecting an employee's eligibility for access to classified information.
Military service members	10 U.S.C. § 1034	Violation of any law, rule, or regulation. Gross waste of funds. Abuse of authority. Substantial and specific danger to public health or safety. Gross mismanagement.	Taking or withholding, or threatening to take or withhold, a personnel action. Any other significant change in duties or responsibilities not commensurate with the servicemember's grade.

Source: GAO analysis of whistleblower statutes and Presidential Policy Directive 19. | GAO-19-198.

Table 1 summarizes the statutory and policy authorities covering DOD personnel, along with selected protected disclosures and prohibited personnel actions—which are two required elements of the test for determining whether there was reprisal against a complainant for whistleblowing. A protected disclosure is a disclosure of wrongdoing by a whistleblower to a party that is an eligible recipient of that disclosure, while prohibited personnel actions include those actions that are taken or threatened in response to a protected disclosure, such as termination, reassignment, or a significant change in duties, responsibilities, or working conditions.

DODIG and Military Service IG Roles and Responsibilities for Investigating Whistleblower Reprisal Complaints

DODIG and the military service IGs share responsibility for investigating misconduct and whistleblower reprisal complaints. Allegations of misconduct and other whistleblower complaints, including those involving senior officials, may be investigated by DODIG or a military service IG depending on the nature of the allegation or the DOD employees involved. Responsibilities for investigating whistleblower reprisal complaints differ according to DOD personnel type.

Specifically, DODIG is responsible for investigating and overseeing DOD component investigations[25] of complaints alleging reprisal against

---

[25] Under the Intelligence Authorization Act for Fiscal Year 2014 and the Intelligence Authorization Act for Fiscal Year 2010, the defense intelligence component IGs—the IGs of the Defense Intelligence Agency, the National Geospatial-Intelligence Agency, the National Reconnaissance Office, and the National Security Agency—have independent statutory authority to conduct investigations of reprisal complaints brought by Defense Civilian Intelligence Personnel System employees. See Intelligence Authorization Act for Fiscal Year 2014, Pub. L. No. 113-126, § 412 (2(A)-(B)) (2014) and Intelligence Authorization Act for Fiscal Year 2010, Pub. L. No. 111-259, § 431(a) (2010) (codified at 5 U.S.C., Appendix §§ 8G and 12). The roles and responsibilities of DODIG and the component IGs are enumerated in Presidential Policy Directive-19 (PPD-19), *Protecting Whistleblowers with Access to Classified Information* (Oct. 10, 2012), and DOD Directive-Type Memorandum 13-008, *DoD Implementation of Presidential Policy Directive 19* (July 8, 2013) (Incorporating change 3, Feb. 9, 2016).

certain DOD civilian employees,[26] and for investigating complaints alleging reprisal against DOD contractor, subcontractor, grantee, and subgrantee employees.[27] For complaints alleging reprisal against a military servicemember, DODIG has the authority to either investigate the complaint or refer it to a military service IG for action.[28] Most reprisal cases involving military servicemembers are investigated by the military services IGs, with DODIG oversight.

In order to carry out its responsibilities, DODIG has established several directorates to facilitate the handling and investigation of misconduct and reprisal complaints. Figure 1 provides a high-level depiction of the DODIG and military service IG processes for handling reprisal, senior official misconduct, and internal DODIG employee complaints, along with the basic roles of the DODIG directorates.

---

[26] DOD investigates all reprisal complaints from civilian *non-appropriated fund* employees under 10 U.S.C. § 1587. Under the Inspector General Act of 1978, as amended, DODIG may retain for investigation those civilian *appropriated-fund* complaints filed with DODIG that are of particular interest to DODIG, although the Office of Special Counsel has primary jurisdiction to investigate the majority of civilian whistleblower reprisal cases across the federal government, including those involving most DOD appropriated-fund civilians. The Office of Special Counsel is an independent agency established under the Whistleblower Protection Act of 1989 to investigate whistleblower reprisal and other prohibited personnel practices.

[27] Under 10 U.S.C. § 2409, DODIG is responsible for investigating all complaints of reprisal involving DOD contractor employees.

[28] Department of Defense Directive 7050.06, *Military Whistleblower Protection* (Apr. 17, 2015).

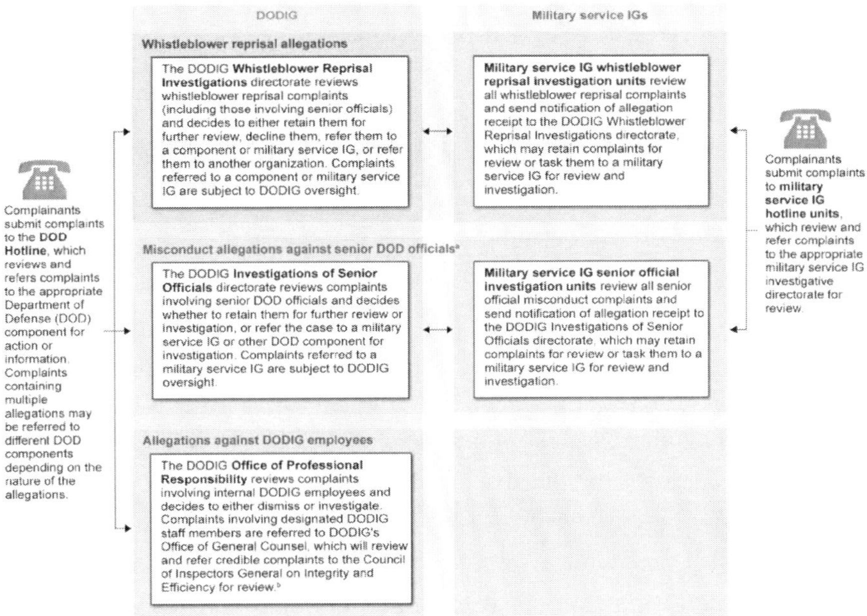

Source: GAO analysis of Department of Defense Office of Inspector General (DODIG) and military services office of Inspector General (IG) information. | GAO-19-198.

Note: This graphic depicts the interaction of DODIG and military service IGs in handling whistleblower reprisal and senior DOD official misconduct complaints. Military service IGs include the Air Force, Army, Navy, and Marine Corps IGs.

[a]Senior officials are those current or former military personnel in the grade of O-7 and above, those selected for promotion to O-7, members or former members of the senior executive service and Defense Intelligence senior executive service, and current or former presidential appointees. The grade of O-7 is a Brigadier General in the Army, Air Force, and Marine Corps, and a Rear Admiral (lower half) in the Navy.

[b]Section 11 (d)(4)(C) of title 5, U.S. Code, Appendix, requires IGs to annually submit to the CIGIE Integrity Committee a list of designated OIG staff members who report directly to an IG. In addition, each IG must designate any positions with significant responsibilities such that, in the judgment of the IG and depending on the size and organization of the particular OIG, there is a heightened risk that an internal investigation of them would lack objectivity in fact or appearance. DODIG's most recent designated staff member memorandum was submitted in May 2018 and includes nine designated staff members.

Figure 1. DOD Processes for Handling Whistleblower Complaints.

Protecting Whistleblower Confidentiality

Whistleblowers confidentiality protections are codified in federal law. The Inspector General Act of 1978, as amended, restricts DODIG and military service IGs from disclosing a whistleblower's identity without the consent of the whistleblower unless the IG determines that such disclosure is unavoidable during the course of the investigation.[29] For example, if a complaint includes information that poses a personal or public safety concern, disclosing the identity of the complainant may be unavoidable. Additionally, the Privacy Act of 1974 prohibits the disclosure of records on any person to another agency without the consent of the person the record relates to, but allows for the disclosure of an employee's identity if the purpose is for routine use—that is, a use that is disclosed for a purpose compatible with the purpose for which it was collected.[30] For example, referring an allegation from an IG hotline to an appropriate investigative unit would be considered routine use.

Federal Law and Standards Establish Information Security Requirements to Protect Federal Systems

The Federal Information Security Modernization Act of 2014 is intended to provide a comprehensive framework for ensuring the effectiveness of information security controls over information resources that support federal operations.[31] The law requires each agency to develop, document, and implement an agency-wide information security program to provide risk-based protections for the information and information systems that support the operations and assets of the agency. The law also requires agencies to comply with NIST standards and the Office of Management

---

[29] See 5 U.S.C., Appendix § 7(b).

[30] See 5 U.S.C. § 552a(b).

[31] The Federal Information Security Modernization Act of 2014, Pub. L. No. 113-283 (2014), partially superseded the Federal Information Security Management Act of 2002, enacted as title III, E-Government Act of 2002, Pub. L. No. 107-347 (2002).

and Budget requires agencies to comply with NIST guidelines for protecting federal IT systems.

Among other things, NIST defines how agencies should determine the security category of their information and information systems based on the potential impact or magnitude of harm that could occur should there be a loss in the confidentiality, integrity, or availability of the information or information system. NIST also prescribes an array of activities associated with the selection, implementation, and assessment of IT security controls—and the authorization to operate federal IT systems and other products.

DOD Instruction 8510.01, *Risk Management Framework for DOD Information Technology*,[32] established a risk management framework for DOD information technology that is consistent with the principles established in NIST Special Publication 800-37. This framework includes requirements and procedures for identifying, implementing, assessing, and managing security controls.

Council of the Inspectors General on Integrity and Efficiency (CIGIE) Standards

CIGIE's *Quality Standards for Investigations and Quality Standards for Federal Offices of Inspectors General* collectively provide a set of overarching principles that IGs should adhere to in conducting their operations. They also provide a framework for conducting high-quality investigations through the definition of general and qualitative standards.[33] General standards, among other things, address the qualifications of investigators, independence, and the concept of due professional care and confidentiality protections throughout the course of an investigation. Qualitative standards focus on the establishment of policies, procedures,

---

[32] DOD Instruction 8510.01, *Risk Management Framework for DOD Information Technology* (Mar. 12, 2014) (Incorporating Change 2, Jul. 28, 2017).

[33] CIGIE, *Quality Standards for Investigations* (Nov.15, 2011) and *Quality Standards for Federal Offices of Inspectors General* (August 2012).

and instructions for confidentially handling and processing complaints, along with investigative planning, execution, reporting, and information management.

The CIGIE Integrity Committee receives, reviews, and refers for investigation allegations of wrongdoing made against Inspectors General, designated staff members of an IG, and the Special Counsel and Deputy Special Counsel of the Office of Special Counsel.[34] Each Inspector General, including the DODIG, is required to submit a list of designated staff members to the CIGIE Integrity Committee Chairperson annually.

IGs Met Some Timeliness and Many Quality Goals, but More Actions Could Improve Performance against Unmet Goals

DODIG Met Some, but Not All, Fiscal Year 2018 Timeliness Goals

DODIG met some but not all internal timeliness goals for fiscal year 2018 related to the intake and referral of whistleblower allegations, as well as the oversight of DOD component investigations. DODIG also did not meet internal goals related to the timeliness of senior official misconduct investigations or internal and statutory goals related to the timeliness of reprisal investigations. Intake is the initial process to determine whether a complaint contains a prima facie allegation[35] of whistleblower reprisal or a credible allegation of misconduct by senior officials.[36]

---

[34] A staff member is an employee within a federal inspector general office who reports directly to an IG or is designated as a staff member in the annual submission to the CIGIE chairperson. See 5 U.S.C. Appendix § 11(d)(4)(B).

[35] Black's Law Dictionary, 10th ed. (2014), defines prima facie as "sufficient to establish a fact or raise a presumption unless disproved or rebutted, based on what seems to be true on first examination, even though it [may] later be proved to be untrue."

[36] Senior officials are those current or former military personnel in the grade of O-7 and above, those selected for promotion to O-7, members of the senior executive service and Defense Intelligence senior executive service, and presidential appointees. The grade of O-7 is a

Oversight reviews are conducted by the DODIG whistleblower reprisal and senior official investigations directorates to ensure the quality of DOD component investigations.

DODIG officials cited several reasons for not meeting timeliness goals, including a backlog of cases and a lengthy report review process. Further, DODIG officials noted that the number of whistleblower reprisal cases increased from 1,013 to 2,002 (98 percent) over the past 5 years, while an internal DODIG fiscal year 2018 performance report cited other reasons for not meeting timeliness goals, including the assumption of responsibility for all sexual assault victim reprisal cases by the whistleblower reprisal investigations unit, the number of high-priority senior official cases concurrently open, and the increasing scope and complexity of investigations.

Timeliness of DODIG Intake and Oversight Reviews

By comparison, DODIG met its fiscal year 2017 targets related to the percentage of intakes and oversight reviews meeting timeliness goals, but it did not meet its goals for the average days of reprisal and senior official misconduct intakes.

DODIG met its fiscal year 2018 timeliness goals for civilian and contractor case intakes and senior official misconduct oversight reviews goals, but did not meet goals related to the average days of senior official misconduct and military reprisal intakes, and the average days for reprisal oversight reviews (see Figure 2). In fiscal year 2018, DODIG resolved and closed 631 senior official misconduct cases during the intake review process and it performed intake reviews for 1,032 whistleblower reprisal cases. It also conducted oversight reviews for 157 senior official misconduct cases and 995 reprisal cases.

Brigadier General in the Army, the Air Force, and the Marine Corps, and a Rear Admiral (lower half) in the Navy.

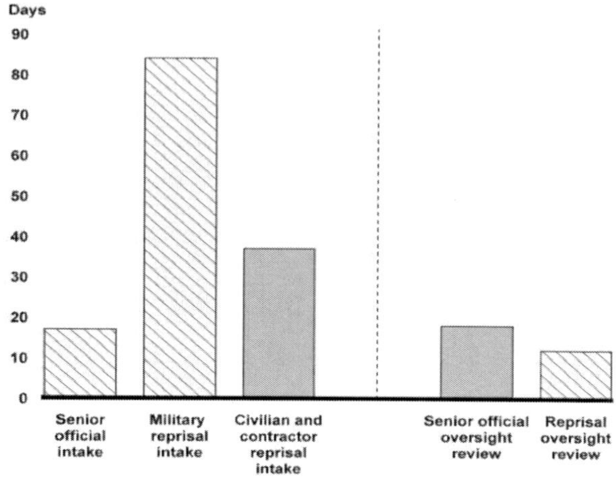

	Senior official intake	Military reprisal intake	Civilian and contractor reprisal intake	Senior official oversight review	Reprisal oversight review
Timeliness goal (days)	15	30	45	30	10
Average number of days	17	84	37	18	12
Percentage meeting goal (Target)	73% (51%)	61% (51%)	81% (51%)	87% (51%)	63% (51%)

Met goal — Did not meet goal

Source: GAO analysis of the Department of Defense Office of Inspetor General (DODIG) data. | GAO-19-198.

Note: Intake is the initial process to determine whether a complaint contains a prima facie allegation of whistleblower reprisal or credible allegation of misconduct by senior officials. Oversight reviews are conducted by the DODIG whistleblower reprisal and senior official investigations directorates to ensure the quality of DOD component investigation.

Figure 2. Timeliness of Fiscal Year 2018 DODIG Senior Official Misconduct Cases Resolved During Intake, Reprisal Intakes, and Oversight Reviews.

Timeliness of DODIG Senior Official Misconduct and Reprisal Investigations

DODIG did not meet internal or statutory timeliness goals related to the percentage or average days for senior official or reprisal investigations (see Figure 3).[37]

---

[37] The timeliness of investigations in fiscal year 2018 varied in comparison to fiscal year 2017. For example, the timeliness of senior official misconduct investigations improved from fiscal year 2017, during which none met the goal of 210 days or less, and the average days for investigations was 455 days. However, the average days to complete military and contractor reprisal investigations increased between fiscal years 2017 and 2018 from 394 days to 541 days, and the average days for civilian reprisal investigations also increased from 461 days to 596.

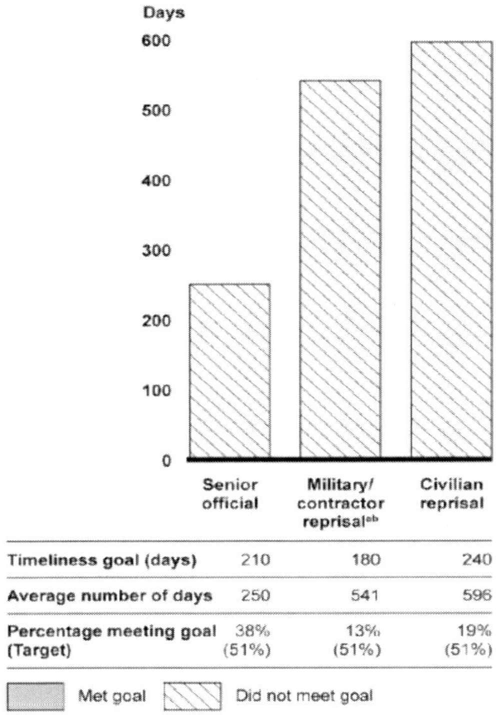

Source: GAO analysis of the Department of Defense Office of Inspector General (DODIG) data. | GAO-19-198.

[a]Under 10 U.S.C. § 1034 if, during the course of the investigation, the IG determines that it is not possible to submit the report of investigation to the Secretary of Defense and the service Secretary within 180 days after the receipt of the allegation, the IG shall provide to the Secretary of Defense, the service Secretary concerned, and the servicemember making the allegation a notice of that determination including the reasons why the report may not be submitted within that time and an estimate of the time when the report will be submitted.

[b]Under 10 U.S.C. § 2409, as amended, investigations of contractor and subcontractor whistleblower reprisal complaints are required to be completed in 180 days or fewer, or DODIG must notify the complainant and obtain permission to extend the investigation.

Figure 3. Timeliness of Fiscal Year 2018 DODIG Senior Official Misconduct and Reprisal Investigations.

DODIG closed 73 investigations in fiscal year 2018, including 13 senior official misconduct cases and 60 military, contractor, and civilian reprisal cases. Overall, about 85 percent of all investigations did not meet the timeliness goal.

DODIG similarly did not meet its investigation timeliness goals for senior official misconduct and reprisal investigations in fiscal year 2017. However, DODIG officials noted that the record closure of 60 reprisal investigations in fiscal year 2018 was a significant improvement over the 37 closed in fiscal year 2017, and DODIG data showed that the average age of closed and open investigations peaked in April 2018 and June 2018, respectively, and that both were lower as of January 1, 2019. Additionally, DODIG officials stated that they expected to eliminate the case backlog and reach a sustainable state of timeliness during fiscal year 2019.

Timeliness of DOD Hotline Referrals and Completion Report Reviews

In fiscal year 2018, the DOD Hotline referred 3,872 cases[38] to other entities for inquiry, and it performed oversight of 945 completion reports from DOD components.[39] As shown in Figure 4, the DOD Hotline met its timeliness goals, except for the percentage of referrals meeting the goal for priority 1 complaints.

Comparatively, in fiscal year 2017, the DOD Hotline did not meet timeliness goals for the average days or percentage of referrals, but did meet its goal for completion reports.

---

[38] This number represents initial referrals. According to DODIG officials, the Hotline referred a total of 6,655 cases, with multiple referrals sometimes being made from a single Hotline complaint.

[39] A Hotline contact becomes a case when the Hotline opens and refers the case for action or information to a DODIG component, military service IG, DOD agency or field activity, or other agency outside of DOD. Hotline completion reports are completed by DOD components and submitted to DOD Hotline for oversight upon the completion of an investigation that was referred to the component by DOD Hotline.

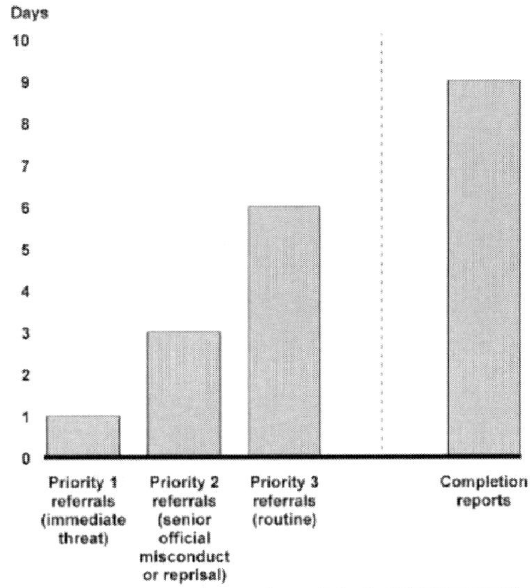

	Priority 1	Priority 2	Priority 3	Completion reports
Timeliness goal (days)	1	3	10	45
Average number of days	1	3	6	9
Percentage meeting goal (Target)	76% (80%)	91% (80%)	94% (80%)	96% (75%)

Met goal Did not meet goal

Source: GAO analysis of the Department of Defense Office of Inspector General (DODIG) data. | GAO-19-198.

Note: Completion reports are submitted by DOD components upon the completion of an investigation referred to the component by DOD Hotline.

Figure 4. Timeliness of Fiscal Year 2018 DOD Hotline Referrals and Oversight of Completion Reports.

DODIG Generally Met Fiscal Year 2018 Internal Quality Goals

Quality goals can enhance the ability of organizations to provide reasonable assurance that they are exercising appropriate safeguards for federal programs, as demonstrated by our prior work.[40] DODIG generally met its fiscal year 2018 internal quality goals related to the thoroughness

[40] GAO, *DOD Personnel Clearances: Comprehensive Timeliness Reporting, Complete Clearance Documentation, and Quality Measures Are Needed to Further Improve the Clearance Process*, GAO-09-400 (Washington, D.C.: May 19, 2009).

and completeness of senior official misconduct and whistleblower reprisal investigations, as well as the completeness and accuracy of information in DOD Hotline referrals.[41] DODIG's internal quality goals for senior official misconduct and reprisal investigations pertain to the thoroughness of required case-file documentation and the integrity and completeness of data in its case management system. Criteria for assessing these goals include whether or not key documentation of the investigation—such as the incoming complaints and required notifications—are present in the proper folders in the case file, and whether start, end, or milestone dates have been recorded in the case management system. Criteria for assessing the completeness and accuracy of information in DOD Hotline referrals include checks on whether whistleblower consent is accurately documented and whether correspondence is addressed to the correct recipient. According to DOD Hotline officials, a weighted checklist was created in June 2018 that has greater focus on those criteria associated with protecting confidentiality.

In fiscal year 2018, DODIG reported that it conducted quality reviews for 59 whistleblower reprisal cases and 13 senior official misconduct cases. DODIG further reported conducting reviews related to the quality of DOD component investigations for 80 whistleblower reprisal cases and 80 senior official misconduct cases, while the Hotline reviewed the thoroughness of 1,954 referrals. As shown in Table 2, DODIG either met or partially met its quality goals except for the data integrity and completeness goal for senior official investigations and the documentation goal for senior official oversight reviews.

While we have reported DODIG's performance against its quality measures, we recommended in September 2017 that DODIG develop quality performance measures and enhance then-existing timeliness measures to reflect key attributes of successful performance measures, and DODIG concurred.

---

[41] Hotline manages the receipt and referral of DOD misconduct reports.

Table 2. Extent to Which DODIG Met Fiscal Year 2018 Quality Goals for Investigations, Oversight Reviews, and Hotline Activities

Activity goal	Target	Number/Percent of compliant assessment criteria	Percent of cases compliant	Goal met?
Reprisal investigations: Thoroughness and documentation	≥ 81 percent	562/633 (89 percent)	100	Yes
Reprisal investigations: Data integrity and completeness	≥81 percent	625/767 (81 percent)	78	Partially
Senior official investigations: Thoroughness and documentation	≥ 81 percent	113/132 (86 percent)	100	Yes
Senior official investigations: Data integrity and completeness	≥81 percent	135/182 (74 percent)	69	No
Oversight reviews: Thoroughness	≥ 81 percent	*Senior official–976/989 (99 percent)* *Reprisal –1038/1119 (93 percent)*	100100	Yes Yes
Oversight reviews: Documentation	≥ 81 percent	*Senior official –65/94 (69 percent)* *Reprisal–89/102 (87 percent)*	6684	No Yes
Hotline quality control: Referral thoroughness	≥80 percent	1092/1131 (97 percent)[a]	88	Yes

Source: GAO analysis of Department of Defense Office of Inspector General (DODIG) information. | GAO-19-198.

Note: A goal was partially met if only one of the targets for the percent of compliant assessment criteria or percent of cases compliant was met.

[a]The number of compliant criteria reflect only June through September 2018.

In November 2018, DODIG officials stated that DODIG is currently using the quality measures it had in place prior to fiscal year 2017, and noted that DODIG had developed DOD-wide quality performance measures for 2018 that measure the thoroughness of military service investigations. As a result, we continue to believe that our 2017 recommendation is valid in that DODIG's performance measures should reflect key attributes of successful performance measures.

Military Service IGs Generally Did Not Meet Fiscal Year 2018 Timeliness Goals

Military service IGs generally did not meet internal and statutory timeliness goals related to the notification of receipt of allegations of reprisal and misconduct, intake reviews, or senior official misconduct and reprisal investigations.[42]

Military service IG officials provided several reasons for not meeting the internal and statutory timeliness goals for notifications, intake reviews, and investigations. Specifically, officials cited an increasing number of complaints; the increasing complexity of complaints, such as those that include multiple allegations and subjects; staffing challenges, such as training related to the rotation of military staff; and the use of reservists, who only work part-time. In addition, a senior official from one military service IG noted that service IGs should be provided greater latitude in dismissing complaints without DODIG review and approval, such as for reprisal complaints where there is no protected communication or personnel action.

Timeliness of Military Service IG Notifications and Intake Reviews

The military service IGs did not meet fiscal year 2018 timeliness goals for notifying DODIG of allegation receipts, or conducting intake reviews for reprisal cases (see Figure 5).[43] In fiscal year 2018, the military service IGs sent 141 senior official misconduct notifications and 876 reprisal notifications to DODIG, and performed 618 reprisal intake reviews.

---

[42] Our assessment of military service IG timeliness is based on performance data provided by DODIG. As noted in figure 6, the Marine Corps did meet its senior official investigation timeliness goal.

[43] According to DODIG officials, DODIG does not assess the timeliness of military service IG intake reviews for senior official misconduct cases.

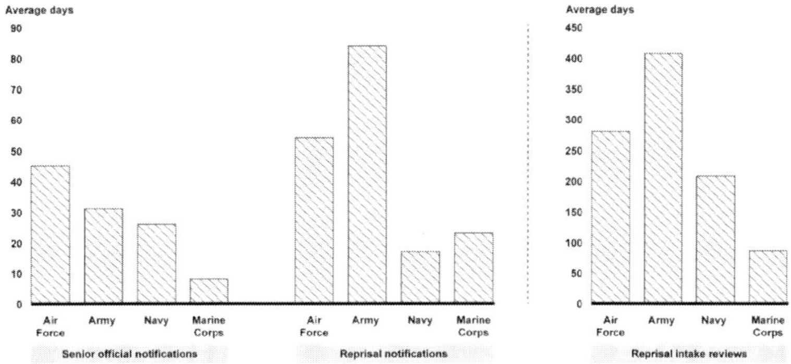

	Days	Average days			
	Timeliness goal	Air Force	Army	Navy	Marine Corps
Senior official notifications	5	45	31	26	8
Reprisal notifications	10	54	84	17	23
Reprisal intake reviews	30	280	407	208	86

Met goal | Did not meet goal

Source: GAO analysis of Department of Defense Office of Inspector General (DODIG) data. | GAO-19-198.

Note: DODIG data on reprisal intake reviews included two non-military reprisal cases, for which the timeliness goal is 45 days. However, DODIG data do not specify which military service IGs handled the cases.

Figure 5. Timeliness of Fiscal Year 2018 Military Service IG Senior Official Misconduct Notifications, Reprisal Notifications, and Reprisal Intake Reviews.

Timeliness of Military Service IG Senior Official Misconduct and Reprisal Investigations

The military service IGs did not meet statutory or internal timeliness goals for senior official misconduct and whistleblower reprisal investigations, with exception of the Marine Corps IG—which met its goal for senior official misconduct investigations (see Figure 6). In fiscal year 2018, the military service IGs closed 424 investigations, including 347 reprisal investigations, and 77 senior official misconduct investigations.[44]

[44] DODIG data on military service IG reprisal intakes includes intake reviews for both military reprisal cases and an indeterminate number of Presidential Policy Directive-19 cases.

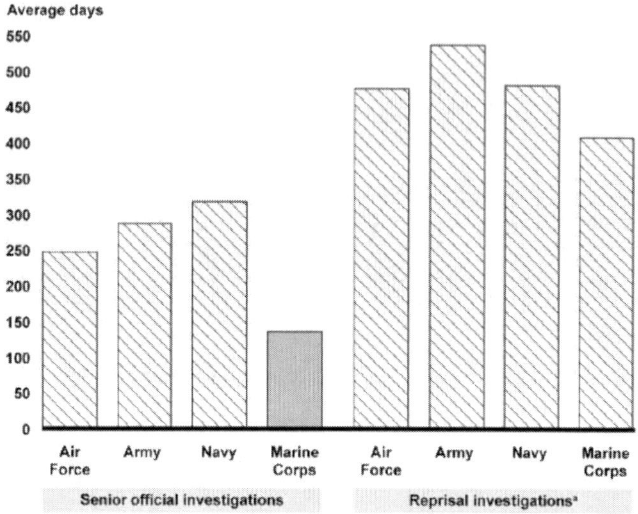

	Air Force	Army	Navy	Marine Corps	Air Force	Army	Navy	Marine Corps
Timeliness goal (days)	180	180	180	180	180	180	180	180
Average days	247	287	318	136	476	537	481	408

Met goal / Did not meet goal

Source: GAO analysis of Department of Defense Office of Inspector General (DODIG) data. | GAO-19-198.

[a]Reprisal investigations include military reprisals and may include Presidential Policy Directive-19 reprisals, which have a 240-day goal. Under 10 U.S.C. § 1034 if, during the course of the investigation, the IG determines that it is not possible to submit the report of investigation to the Secretary of Defense and the service Secretary within 180 days after the receipt of the allegation, the IG shall provide to the Secretary of Defense, the service Secretary concerned, and the servicemember making the allegation a notice of that determination including the reasons why the report may not be submitted within that time, and an estimate of the time when the report will be submitted.

Figure 6. Timeliness of Military Service IG Senior Official Misconduct and Reprisal Investigations.

Military Service IGs Met DODIG and Internal Quality Goals for Investigations

Military service IGs met fiscal year 2018 quality goals established by DODIG related to the thoroughness of investigations conducted by the service IGs. Specifically, 89 percent of DODIG's thoroughness criteria were met in the 93 senior official misconduct investigations conducted by the military service IGs and other DOD components, exceeding the 81 percent goal established by DODIG.[45] Similarly, 85 percent of DODIG's thoroughness criteria were met in the 310 whistleblower reprisal investigations conducted by the military service IGs and other DOD components, exceeding the 81 percent goal established by DODIG. DODIG has established six criteria for assessing the thoroughness of senior official investigations, including whether all allegations were addressed, whether the complainant and subject were interviewed, and whether relevant documents were obtained. DODIG has seven criteria for assessing the thoroughness of reprisal investigations, including whether protected communications and personnel actions were identified, and whether the report of investigation was approved.

The Army, the Air Force, and the Marine Corps IGs also met internal quality goals for fiscal year 2018 related to the percentage of cases returned by DODIG for rework due to quality issues. Specifically, Army IG officials stated that they met their goal of having no more than 5 percent of the investigations they submitted to DODIG for review returned by DODIG due to quality issues, and Air Force IG officials stated that they met their goals of obtaining DODIG concurrence on all of the senior official investigations they submitted for review, and having no more than 5 percent of reprisal investigations returned for rework. Similarly, the Marine Corps IG achieved its goal of having no investigations returned for rework, according to a senior Marine Corps IG official. The Naval IG did not provide us with any internal quality goals.

Aside from the quality goals, DODIG also conducted quality assurance reviews for the Air Force (2017), Army (2018), and Naval (2016) IGs, in which the quality of a sample of case files was examined. The reviews concluded that the military service IGs reviewed were generally complying with internal regulations and CIGIE standards for quality. In addition, in

---

[45] Military service quality data presented in this report include data related to other DOD components, such as the defense intelligence components. DODIG data on the quality of military service IGs were available only in aggregate form, covering all DOD components.

accordance with recommendations made in the quality assurance reviews, each of the service IGs reviewed by DODIG has developed or plans to develop checklists to help ensure that all required documentation is present in their case files, according to service IG officials and documentation.

IGs Have Implemented and Planned Initiatives to Improve Timeliness, but Initiatives Do Not Target All Aspects of Timeliness

DODIG and the military service IGs have implemented and planned various initiatives to improve the timeliness of their processing of senior official misconduct and reprisal complaints. Table 3 shows examples of recent DODIG and military service IG initiatives.[46]

While these initiatives are positive steps, given that the performance of some measures is far below the goals, additional efforts could be made to improve performance against unmet timeliness goals—including those pertaining to senior official misconduct investigations conducted by the military service IGs, military service IG notifications made to DODIG, and military service IG intake reviews for reprisal cases. Additionally, DODIG and some of the military service IGs do not agree on the timeframes prescribed by DOD policy for military service IGs to notify DODIG of the receipt of a complaint, thereby complicating achievement of these goals. For example, officials from the Air Force IG stated that they notify DODIG of the receipt of misconduct allegations only after making a credibility determination, instead of within the five working days of receipt prescribed by DOD policy for senior official allegations.[47] Similarly, Marine Corps IG officials stated that senior official allegations should be reported to DODIG within five days of a credibility determination.

---

[46] See appendix II for additional examples of timeliness improvements provided by DODIG.

[47] See Department of Defense Directive 5505.06, *Investigations of Allegations Against Senior DOD Officials* (June 6, 2013) and Department of Defense Directive 7050.06, *Military Whistleblower Protections* (Apr. 17, 2015).

Table 3. Examples of Recent DODIG and Military Service IG Initiatives to Improve Timeliness

DODIG	Military service IGs
DODIG has increased the number of staff in its whistleblower directorates from 114 to 147 full-time equivalents (about a 29 percent increase) since fiscal year 2016.[a]	The Air Force IG is developing a proposal to centralize its investigation function for reprisal cases instead of conducting these investigations at the local IG level. According to Air Force officials, centralizing this function would produce efficiencies by shortening the current review process for investigations and mitigating the effects of turnover at the local IG level.
DODIG is in the process of assessing its staff workload associated with different types of misconduct and reprisal cases, in response to our 2017recommendation. This effort is intended to help inform its resource allocation.[b]	The Army IG reassigned internal staff to better assist with whistleblower reprisal caseload, and in November 2018 changed how reprisal case numbers are assigned to expedite the assignment process, according to an Army IG official.
DODIG and the military service IGs established a working group in August 2018 comprised of reprisal and senior official investigations representatives to identify efficiencies for military reprisal investigations, according to DODIG officials.	The Naval IG has implemented a pilot program which would meet the 30 day requirement to make a credibility determination, in part by eliminating prescribed preliminary analysis steps that went beyond the standard intake credibility determination.
DODIG implemented an alternative dispute resolution process in September 2017 to mediate reprisal complaints. According to DODIG officials, this process is a quicker alternative to an investigation, and it has provided significant relief to investigator caseloads by resolving many complaints that would have otherwise gone through the intake process, and potentially been investigated.[c]	The Marine Corps IG has hired an additional investigator and will hire a supervisory investigator, according to Marine Corps IG. These officials stated that they have also implemented procedures to more thoroughly intake and review complaints, along with an immediate credibility determination for all senior official complaints, thus speeding the timeline for doing so.

Source: GAO analysis of DODIG and military service IG information. | GAO-19-198.

[a]Specifically, full-time equivalents increased in the senior official investigations unit from 29 to 33, the whistleblower reprisal investigations unit from 50 to 72, and the DOD Hotline from 35 to 42.

[b]In September 2017, we recommended that DODIG assess the feasibility of collecting additional workload data, such as the amount of direct and indirect labor hours associated with each case, and include such data in future personnel requirements assessments, as appropriate. See GAO-17-506.

[c]According to DODIG officials, the alternative dispute resolution unit reviews all contractor and subcontractor cases and non-appropriated fund civilian cases, as well as other select reprisal complaints.

Standards for Internal Control in the Federal Government state that management should complete and document corrective actions to remediate internal control deficiencies in a timely manner.[48] Expanding initiatives to target unmet goals related to military service senior official investigations, notifications, and intakes could provide DODIG and the military service IGs a more comprehensive approach to improving timeliness and better position the IGs to improve upon the timeliness goals prescribed by DOD policy. In addition, resolving disagreements related to notification timeliness could improve the military service IGs' ability to achieve those goals. Further, additional initiatives could provide greater assurance to potential whistleblowers that their cases will be handled expeditiously.

IGs Have Processes to Protect Whistleblower Confidentiality, but Some Gaps Exist

DODIG Has Policies and Procedures to Protect DOD Whistleblower Confidentiality

DODIG has established policies and procedures to implement key statutory requirements[49] and CIGIE standards[50] for protecting the confidentiality of whistleblowers from the receipt of a whistleblower complaint through its investigation. The Inspector General Act of 1978, as amended, states that the Inspectors General shall not, without consent from the employee, disclose the identity of an employee who reports misconduct or provides information, unless the Inspector General determines that such disclosure is unavoidable during the course of the investigation. Further, CIGIE's *Quality Standards for Investigations* states that policies,

---

[48] GAO-14-704G.

[49] Inspector General Act of 1978 (as amended) (codified at 5 U.S.C., Appendix § 7(b)) and 5 U.S.C. § 552a.

[50] CIGIE, *Quality Standards for Federal Offices of Inspector General* (August 2012) and *Quality Standards for Investigations* (Nov.15 2011).

procedures and instructions for handling and processing complaints should be in place to ensure that basic information is recorded, held confidential, and tracked to final resolution.

Table 4. Examples of Confidentiality Protections Included in DODIG Policies and Procedures for Hotline Activities and Senior Official Misconduct and Reprisal Investigations

Category	Category information
DOD Hotline	DOD Hotline staff are required to obtain verbal or written consent from whistleblowers to disclose their identity outside of DOD Hotline on a need-to-know basis. The whistleblower's decision to consent or not must be documented in the case record.
DOD Hotline	Select complaints—such as those involving DODIG employees—are to be restricted in the DOD Hotline's case management system.
DOD Hotline	Cases involving whistleblowers that do not consent to the release of their identity are to undergo a quality control review prior to referral to ensure the complaints are properly redacted.
DOD Hotline	Release of reports of investigation pursuant to the Freedom of Information Act[a] or DODIG's proactive release policy are redacted and reviewed prior to release by either the DODIG Freedom of Information Act Office or the DODIG Office of General Counsel, as appropriate.[b]
Senior official misconduct and reprisal investigations	Investigators are to exercise caution when contacting whistleblowers and conducting whistleblower clarification interviews, especially in their workplace, so as not to compromise identity.
Senior official misconduct and reprisal investigations	Investigators are to inform witnesses that DODIG is committed to protecting their confidentiality to the maximum extent possible within the law, and obtain witness acknowledgement of recording interviews at the outset of any interview.
Senior official misconduct and reprisal investigations	Information shared with subjects at the conclusion of an investigation, such as a copy of the draft record of investigation, is to be redacted in order to protect the whistleblower and other sources of information.
Senior official misconduct and reprisal investigations	Reports of investigation and underlying documentation supporting the reports, such as witness information, maybe redacted to protect confidentiality, should circumstances warrant.

Source: GAO analysis of Department of Defense Office of Inspector General (DODIG) policies and procedures. | GAO-19-198.

[a]See 5 U.S.C. § 552. The Freedom of Information Act requires federal agencies to provide the public with access to certain government information on the basis of the principles of openness and accessibility in government.

[b]DODIG's proactive release policy aims to release in a timely fashion, and to the extent possible, final reports and other records and information related to DODIG's performance of its statutory duties to Congress, other government agencies, the news media, and the public.

Table 4 shows examples of key confidentiality protections included in DOD Hotline and senior official misconduct and whistleblower reprisal investigation policies.

DODIG officials stated that they routinely emphasize the importance of protecting whistleblower confidentiality and that confidentiality policies and procedures are addressed through internal training, staff meetings, and on-the-job instruction. Further, 69 of 86 (80 percent) DODIG respondents to our survey reported believing that the guidance they received on protecting confidentiality is sufficient to maintain the confidentiality of individuals involved in IG investigations, citing many of the processes identified in Table 4 above as examples of guidance they have received.[51]

DODIG Guidance for Protecting the Confidentiality of Whistleblowers Who Report Internal DODIG Misconduct Lacks Sufficient Detail

The DODIG Office of Professional Responsibility's investigations manual[52] on handling misconduct complaints against internal DODIG employees requires that complainant information be strictly controlled in order to protect the integrity of the investigative process and to avoid potential harm to the privacy and reputation of the employee.[53] This guidance also includes some steps to protect whistleblower information such as redacting substantiated reports of investigation to be provided to investigation subjects. As previously noted, DOD Hotline guidance also includes steps to protect the confidentiality of internal DODIG

[51] Notably, 72 survey respondents (84 percent) also stated that they will seek direction from a supervisor for guidance on how to maintain the confidentiality of all individuals involved in the records they handle.

[52] The investigations manual consists of seven chapters updated at different points between July 2009 and July 2013.

[53] The DODIG Office of Professional Responsibility reported receiving 415 complaints from fiscal year 2013 through fiscal year 2018, of which 84 complaints were investigated (50 were substantiated) and 199 were provided to other DODIG components for further consideration and action, as appropriate. Of the 415 complaints received, 123 (about 30 percent) were referred to the office from the DOD Hotline.

whistleblowers. However, the Office of Professional Responsibility guidance does not include several key steps and procedures that some DODIG officials reported taking to protect whistleblower confidentiality, such as excluding complainant information from notifications sent to subjects and not identifying complainants during interviews with case subjects. In addition, DODIG's Office of General Counsel does not have documented procedures for controlling access to cases involving designated DODIG staff members subject to review by the CIGIE Integrity Committee.[54] DODIG designated staff members include the Principal Deputy Inspector General, Deputy Inspectors General, General Counsel, and Senior Advisor to the Inspector General, among other staff members.

Guidance on handling complaints alleging internal DODIG misconduct is also outdated and does not reflect recent organizational changes. In particular, the Office of Professional Responsibility's investigations manual does not reflect its updated roles and responsibilities since splitting from the Quality Assurance and Standards directorate in October 2016, and certain chapters do not recognize that it now reports directly to the Inspector General.[55] Further, sections of the manual have been revised at different points in time and do not align with the office's current functions. For example, the section covering the office's organization, mission, and authorities has not been updated since July 2009. Similarly, the section detailing investigation policies and procedures has not been updated since November 2012.

Some of the DODIG employees we surveyed reported concern that DODIG's process for reporting employee misconduct and resolving

---

[54] Section 11 (d)(4)(C) of 5 U.S.C., Appendix, requires IGs to annually submit to the CIGIE Integrity Committee a list of designated OIG staff members who report directly to an IG. In addition, each IG must designate any positions with significant responsibilities such that, in the judgment of the IG and depending on the size and organization of the particular OIG, there is a heightened risk that an internal investigation of them would lack objectivity in fact or appearance. DODIG's most recent designated staff member memorandum was submitted in May 2018 and includes nine designated staff members.

[55] Prior to October 2016, the Quality Assurance and Standards directorate was responsible for investigating internal DODIG employee misconduct and performing quality inspections and audits of DODIG components. According to DODIG officials, separating the two functions was intended to make the Office of Professional Responsibility a separate and independent office.

internal complaints may not protect whistleblower confidentiality. For example, 14 (16 percent) survey respondents reported believing that DODIG's internal process for reporting misconduct did not protect DODIG employee confidentiality or only protected it slightly. Also, 36 (42 percent) survey respondents reported not knowing whether or not DODIG's internal process for reporting misconduct protects confidentiality, and 36 (42 percent) reported believing that it protects confidentiality somewhat or very well.[56] Additionally, 14 of 86 (16 percent) and 9 of 86 (10 percent)[57] employees surveyed reported having considered but ultimately choosing not to resolve an issue through the Office of the Ombuds—which may receive some internal misconduct complaints—or report misconduct through DODIG's internal process on or after October 1, 2016, respectively, because they feared that their confidentiality could be compromised.[58] Table 5 shows the distribution of these responses.

---

[56] According to the 2018 Federal Employee Viewpoint Survey, about 16 percent of DOD survey respondents and 15 percent of DODIG respondents disagreed or strongly disagreed with their ability to disclose a suspected violation of law, rule, or regulation without fear of reprisal, and about 16 percent of DOD respondents and 13 percent of DODIG respondents neither agreed nor disagreed. See *United States Office of Personnel Management, 2018 Federal Employee Viewpoint Survey: Report by Agency*. The Office of Personnel Management administers the survey annually to measure employee perceptions of conditions that contribute to their organization's success.

[57] In commenting on a draft of this report, DODIG officials expressed concern that we were not reporting the more substantial number of respondents that responded to our survey questions positively. However, the number of employees surveyed that reported considering but ultimately choosing to not resolve an issue through the Office of the Ombuds or report misconduct through DODIG's internal process because they feared their confidentiality could be compromised represent subsets of those employees who responded that they chose to not do so for one reason or another (e.g., concern about length of process, issue resolved through another avenue). As a result, it cannot be reported that 84 percent or 90 percent of respondents did not fear their confidentiality would be compromised. See appendix IV for additional information on our survey.

[58] The Office of the Ombuds functions as an independent, impartial, and confidential resource for employees to resolve conflict among DODIG employees. During the course of performing its duties, the Office of Ombuds may receive allegations of DODIG employee misconduct, which are to be forwarded to the Office of Professional Responsibility for review. According to DODIG guidance, the Ombuds shall not disclose the identity of any individual contacting the Office of the Ombuds or reveal information provided in confidence that could lead to the identification of any individual contacting the office without the individual's explicit permission. DODIG employees may consent to the disclosure of their identity when they elect to participate in resolution with management, according to DODIG officials.

Survey respondents identified some concerns related to the confidentiality, objectivity, and independence of DODIG's internal process for reporting misconduct and suggested some related improvements.[59] For example, although it has separated from the Quality Assurance and Standards directorate, the Office of Professional Responsibility continues to share office space with the directorate and hold complainant and witness interviews in the shared space.[60] Also, it was suggested that an online form could be used so that internal complaints are routed directly to the Office of Professional Responsibility instead of through the DOD Hotline. DODIG officials told us that there are record-keeping and performance measure-related bases for continuing to use the DOD Hotline to receive complaints of internal misconduct, but that they would carefully evaluate the suggestion.

Table 5a. Survey Responses on Confidentiality during Internal DODIG Processes

Extent that respondents believed DODIG's internal process for reporting misconduct protected the confidentiality of DODIG employees.		
Not at all/slightly	Somewhat/very well	I don't know
14	36	36

Source: GAO survey of Department of Defense Office of Inspector General (DODIG) employees. | GAO 19 198.

---

[59] We presented these examples because they aligned with other information obtained during our review. For example, a DODIG employee that we interviewed similarly noted that holding complainant and witness interviews in the shared space was problematic. These examples were provided by one or more different respondents.

[60] According to DODIG officials, Office of Professional Responsibility personnel take reasonable and prudent measures to protect confidentiality, including by using private offices and a separate conference room for meeting with complainants, witnesses, and subjects. DODIG officials also stated that Office of Professional Responsibility personnel use white noise machines for conversations with complainants and others, and noted that all DODIG personnel must have personal swipe access or request entrance to every suite in DODIG, so the presence of an "unknown" or unfamiliar person in any suite, including the Office of Professional Responsibility, is neither significant nor noteworthy. Additionally DODIG officials stated that it was not clear whether separating the Office of Professional Responsibility would improve confidentiality, and that DODIG employees could observe who walks into a separate office and have more certainty that the employee was going to see the Office of Professional Responsibility rather than the Quality Assurance and Standards directorate.

Table 5b. Survey Responses on Confidentiality during Internal DODIG Processes

Extent that respondents who considered reaching out to the DODIG Office of Ombuds, but ultimately chose not to, indicated that fear that confidentiality would be compromised influenced their decision to not reach out.[a]		
Slightly	Somewhat	Very much
1	3	10

Source: GAO survey of Department of Defense Office of Inspector General (DODIG) employees. | GAO-19-198.

Table 5c. Survey Responses on Confidentiality during Internal DODIG Processes

Extent that respondents who considered reporting misconduct against a DODIG employee through DODIG's internal processon or after October 1, 2016, but ultimately chose not to, indicated that fear that confidentiality could be compromised influenced their decision not to report through that process.[b]		
Slightly	Somewhat	Very much
0	1	8

Source: GAO survey of Department of Defense Office of Inspector General (DODIG) employees. | GAO-19-198.

[a,b]These questions included response options of "not at all" and "don't recall," neither of which was selected by survey respondents.

CIGIE Quality Standards for Federal Offices of Inspector General state that IGs should establish and follow policies and procedures for receiving and reviewing allegations and ensure that whistleblower identities are not disclosed without consent, unless the IG determines that such disclosure is unavoidable during the course of the investigation. CIGIE *Quality Standards for Investigations* also state that policies and procedures should be revised regularly to align with current laws and regulations. DODIG officials told us in November 2018 that the Office of Professional Responsibility investigations manual is in the process of being updated but were unable to provide a timetable for the completion of these updates, and stated that all of the provisions—including the confidentiality protections—are subject to changes and updates. In addition, in January 2019 DODIG officials noted, after discussion with GAO, that they intended to implement guidance for making referrals to the CIGIE Integrity Committee. Until DODIG develops guidance that incorporates procedures to protect confidentiality and documents how to maintain whistleblower confidentiality throughout the CIGIE referral process, it will lack reasonable assurance that its process for investigating internal misconduct allegations can fully protect the confidentiality of whistleblowers.

Military Service IGs Have Guidance for Protecting Whistleblower Confidentiality, but It is Not Comprehensive

Military service IG guidance identifies confidentiality as a core tenet of handling and investigating whistleblower complaints.[61] For example, military service IG guidance states that consent should generally be obtained from complainants before each military service IG can share a complainant's identity with officials who will investigate the allegations, and provides that complaints may be redacted or summarized to omit personally identifiable information—such as when consent is not given or for other purposes. In addition, military service IG guidance state that a complainant's identity may only be disclosed without consent when an authorized official has determined that such disclosure is unavoidable in order to investigate an allegation.

Aside from these shared provisions, each of the military service IGs' guidance includes additional precautions aimed at protecting whistleblower confidentiality. For example, Air Force Instruction 90-301 instructs Hotline personnel to coordinate communication between the complainant and investigator if a complainant does not give consent to disclose his or her identity. In addition, Army and Marine Corps IG guidance stipulate

---

[61] Air Force Instruction 90-301, *Inspector General Complaints Resolution* (Aug. 27, 2015); Army Regulation 20-1, *Inspector General Activities and Procedures* (July 3, 2012, revised on Feb. 13, 2018); Secretary of the Navy Instruction 5370.5B, *DON Hotline Program*, (Nov. 24, 2004);Department of the Navy, *Hotline Program Standard Operating Procedure,* (November 2016); Inspector General of the Marine Corps, *Marine Corps Inspectors General Program Concepts and Systems Guide* (August 2009); Inspector General of the Marine Corps, *Marine Corps Inspector General Program Investigations Guide* (August 2009).

that whistleblowers will be notified if it becomes necessary to disclose their identity without their consent, and Naval IG guidance requires investigators to inform complainants that although the use of their testimony may be necessary under administrative action procedures, their identity will be released as a witness, not a complainant, to safeguard their identity.

While all military service IGs acknowledge the need to preserve confidentiality, we found gaps in confidentiality protections in Air Force, Naval, and Marine Corps IG guidance, but not Army IG guidance. For example, we found that Air Force, Naval, and Marine Corps IG guidance did not include requirements outlined in DOD Instruction 7050.01 related to the specific conditions under which information disclosures may be made without complainant consent.[62] According to DOD Instruction 7050.01, these include circumstances when a complainant has made it known outside IG channels that he or she submitted the complaint, there is an emergency situation or health or safety issue, or the allegation is being transferred outside of DOD to another IG. Air Force, Naval, and Marine Corps IG guidance predate DOD Instruction 7050.01, updated in October 2017, and reference an older instruction that omits this disclosure guidance.[63]

Additionally, DODIG's 2016 and 2017 quality assurance reviews of the Naval IG and Air Force IG concluded that confidentiality protections could be improved. Specifically, DODIG found that the Air Force IG did not have written procedures for handling and restricting IG employee access to complaints against individuals with access to the Air Force IG's whistleblower database, including both IG employees and contractors that support the database.

In addition, DODIG found that the Naval IG Hotline program instruction needed to be updated and that it did not have a hotline standard

---

[62] DOD Instruction 7050.01, *DOD Hotline Program* (Oct. 17, 2017).

[63] Specifically, Air Force Instruction 90-301, *Inspector General Complaints Resolution,* was updated in August 2015; Marine Corps IG Investigations Guide and Concepts and Systems Guide were both updated in August 2009; and the Secretary of the Navy Instruction 5370.5B, *DON Hotline Program*, which provides guidance to both Naval IG and Marine Corps IG Hotlines, was updated in November 2004.

operating procedure with guidance to redact complainant identities before releasing investigation reports to installation commanders or other military officials.[64]

Air Force, Naval, and Marine Corps IG officials stated that they are currently in the process of updating their guidance to better incorporate confidentiality protections. For example, Naval IG officials told us that the Naval IG is updating its Hotline instruction, which will provide guidance to obtain consent from complainants prior to releasing investigation reports to installation commanders or other military officials, or redact the complainant's name. According to Naval IG officials, the updated instruction should be finalized in the first quarter of fiscal year 2019.

CIGIE *Quality Standards for Federal Offices of Inspector General* state that IGs should establish and follow policies and procedures for receiving and reviewing allegations and ensure that whistleblower identities are not disclosed without consent, unless the IG determines that such disclosure is unavoidable during the course of the investigation. Further, *CIGIE Quality Standards for Investigations* state that policies and procedures should be revised regularly to align with current laws and regulations, and that confidentiality should be considered throughout an investigation, to include drafting reports, validating contents, and submitting the final report. Without updated policies and procedures that fully implement confidentiality standards for complaint handling and investigation, the Air Force IG, the Naval IG, and the Marine Corps IG may not be able to ensure the consistent implementation of confidentiality protections within their offices.

---

[64] SECNAVINST 5370.5B.

IGs Are Able to Access Whistleblower Information to Perform Their Duties and Have Taken Some, but Not All, Required Steps to Safeguard It

IGs Are Able to Access Information Needed to Handle Whistleblower Complaints, and Have Taken Steps to Safeguard Classified Information

DODIG and military service IGs do not experience significant challenges in accessing sensitive or classified information necessary to handle whistleblower complaints, according to cognizant IG officials. Such information includes documentary evidence or witness statements. Similarly, 79 of 86 (92 percent) DODIG respondents to our survey reported that they are generally able to access all types of unclassified information necessary to perform the duties of their position, while 82 of 86 (95 percent) respondents stated that they are either able to access classified information as necessary or do not require access to classified information.

DODIG and the military service IGs have also taken steps to safeguard physical and electronic classified whistleblower information in accordance with DOD policy, which requires that DOD components establish a system of technical, physical, and personnel controls to ensure access to classified information is limited to authorized persons.[65] Cases including classified information constituted a small percentage of cases closed by DODIG and the military service IGs in fiscal year 2017, with the percentage of those closed by DODIG directorates—including the DOD Hotline and the whistleblower reprisal and senior official investigations— ranging from

[65] DOD Manual 5200.01 Vol.3, *DOD Information Security Program: Protection of Classified Information* (Feb. 24, 2012) (Incorporating change 2, Mar. 19, 2013).

0.2 percent to 0.5 percent, according to DODIG officials.[66] Officials from each of the military service IGs reported closing no classified cases in fiscal year 2017. In addition, DODIG and military service IG officials reported having an adequate number of staff with clearances at the requisite levels (e.g., SECRET) to handle classified case information, along with processes for physically and electronically storing and accessing information at different classification levels.

Most IGs are Following DOD's IT Risk Management Process

DODIG and most military service IGs are following DOD's IT risk management process, which involves the assessment of and authorization to operate IT used to manage DOD information—including sensitive but unclassified whistleblower information.[67] The Naval IG has not authorized its case management system in accordance with DOD policy, which implements NIST[68] and Office of Management and Budget[69] federal IT security guidelines related to IT systems and applications, including those used by the IGs.[70] However, it is taking steps to do so. DODIG and the Naval IG use IT systems to manage sensitive whistleblower information, while the Air Force, Army, and Marine Corps IGs use IT applications—

---

[66] Cases closed by DODIG could include reprisal or misconduct cases involving military service or defense intelligence component personnel for which DODIG has chosen to exercise its discretionary authority to investigate.

[67] See DOD Instruction 8510.01.

[68] See National Institute of Standards and Technology, *Assessing Security and Privacy Controls in Federal Information Systems and Organizations: Building Effective Assessment Plans*, Special Publication 800-53A, Revision 4 (December 2014); *Security and Privacy Controls for Federal Information Systems and Organizations*, Special Publication 800-53, Revision 4 (April 2013); and *Guide for Applying the Risk Management Framework to Federal Information Systems: A Security Life Cycle Approach*, Special Publication 800-37, Revision 1 (February 2010).

[69] Office of Management and Budget, Circular No. A-130, *Managing Federal Information as a Strategic Resource*, (July, 2016).

[70] An information system is a discrete set of information resources organized for the collection, processing, maintenance, use, sharing, dissemination, or disposition of information. An application is a software program hosted by an information system. See Committee on National Security Systems Instruction No. 4009, *Committee on National Security Systems (CNSS) Glossary* (Apr. 6, 2015).

which are not subject to the full IT risk management authorization process, as discussed below.

DODIG and Naval IG IT Systems

DODIG has followed the DOD IT risk management process by authorizing the Defense Case Activity Tracking System (D-CATS)—its whistleblower case management system—to operate in accordance with DOD policy and federal IT security guidelines. DOD's risk management process requires that IT systems be authorized to operate using a multistep process that entails the identification, implementation, and assessment of system security controls, along with the corresponding development and approval of a system security plan, security assessment report, and plan of action and milestones.[71] The process requires systems to be reassessed and reauthorized every 3 years in order to ensure the continued effectiveness of security controls, and allows for ongoing authorizations through a system-level strategy for the continuous monitoring of security controls employed within or inherited by the system. The strategy should include a plan for annually assessing a subset of system security controls. DOD policy states that component heads may only operate systems with a current authorization to operate, and that authorization termination dates must be enforced.

DODIG last authorized D-CATS to operate in May 2017, determining that overall system security risk was acceptable based on a review of the system security plan, security assessment report, and plan of action and milestones. Our review of DODIG's system authorization documents also found that they addressed key, required content elements. For example, the

---

[71] An authorization to operate is issued when a system's authorizing official reviews the system authorization package and deems the risks associated with the system acceptable. The security authorization package documents the results of the security control assessment and provides the authorizing official with information needed to make a risk-based decision on whether to authorize operation of an information system. The authorization package includes a (1) security plan that provides an overview of security requirements, a description of agreed-upon security controls, and other supporting security-related documents; (2) security assessment report that provides the security control assessment results and recommended corrective actions for control weaknesses; and (3) plan of action and milestones that describes the measures planned to correct weaknesses or deficiencies and to reduce or eliminate known vulnerabilities.

system security plan specified the security controls intended to be in place based on the system's risk classification, and the security assessment report documented findings of compliance and the methods used by the assessor to evaluate security controls when implementing DODIG's continuous monitoring strategy.[72] Additionally, the plan of action and milestones identified tasks needed to mitigate identified vulnerabilities along with resources and milestones to accomplish the tasks.

However, as of December 2018, the Naval IG had not authorized its case management system in accordance with the DOD risk management process, and the system remained in operation.[73] The Naval IG was issued an interim authorization to operate its case management system in March 2017 by the Commander, U.S. Fleet Cyber Command. The interim authorization—which expired in January 2018—required the Naval IG to transition from the department's prior IT risk management process to the current process by the time of its expiration, noting that the overall risk of the system was high due to incomplete testing.[74] Subsequently, in June 2018, the Naval IG requested and was eventually granted, in September 2018, a conditional authorization to continue operating the case management system through October 2018.

In early December 2018, the Naval IG requested another conditional authorization to operate the case management system until September 2019. According to Naval IG officials, the conditional authorization is needed because the whistleblower case management system's host environment is not expected to attain its authorization until September 2019. As a result, the Naval IG was taking steps beyond the conditional authorization request to manage IT security risks as it works towards compliance with the new DOD risk management process. For example, Naval IG officials stated that new leadership was put in place to oversee

---

[72] DODIG included these procedures in a separate document. We did not assess the sufficiency of the evaluation methods.

[73] The Naval IG is the only military service IG that operates a case management system instead of an application under the DOD IT risk management process categorization rules.

[74] DOD Instruction 8510.01 requires that DOD components transition to the current DOD risk management process within two-and-a-half years from the component's last authorization under the prior DOD Information Assurance Certification and Accreditation Process, which could be used until October 2016.

the case management system; that a senior system administrator would be hired to help maintain IT security; and that the case management system was undergoing regular scans to assess security risks, with any resultant issues being remediated.[75]

NIST guidelines state that organizations should design and prioritize activities to mitigate security risks, and that alternative strategies may be needed when an organization cannot apply controls to adequately reduce or mitigate risk.[76] As noted, the Naval IG's case management system was not authorized as of December 2018 and it was not yet able to transition to the current DOD risk management process. However, if completed, the actions planned and underway—including the conditional authorization and security scans—should help to mitigate system security risks and provide greater assurance that existing system security controls safeguard sensitive whistleblower information.

Air Force, Army, and Marine Corps IG IT Applications

The IGs of the Air Force, the Army, and the Marine Corps are following DOD's IT risk management procedures for their primary case management applications, which are not subject to the full IT risk management authorization process. According to DOD Instruction 8510.01, *Risk Management Framework (RMF) for DOD Information Technology (IT)*, DOD IT such as applications must be securely configured in accordance with applicable DOD policies, and application security controls must undergo special assessment of their functional and security-related capabilities and deficiencies. The results of such assessments are to be documented within an application-level security assessment report and reviewed by a security manager to ensure that the product does not introduce vulnerabilities into its host system.

---

[75] Naval IG officials stated that the ongoing efforts to reauthorize the case management system would not have been required if the enterprise case management system being developed by DODIG had been released according to its original schedule. As discussed later in this report, the enterprise system will replace the IT systems and applications currently used by the military service IGs, but its incremental release schedule has been delayed.

[76] National Institute of Standards and Technology, Special Publication 800-53, Revision 4.

We found that while the Army, Air Force, and Marine Corps IGs have not produced the required application-level security assessment reports for their primary applications, they have met the intent of these requirements through other actions. Specifically, we noted that the Air Force and Army IGs' primary case management applications reside in host systems that were authorized to operate under the risk management process within the last 3 years, and that the assessments associated with the host system authorizations included a review of application-level security controls, according to IG officials.[77] Similarly, the Marine Corps IG's case management application was exempted from assessment by its authorizing official because it was determined that the application did not introduce additional risk into its authorized host system.

DODIG Does Not Fully Restrict Employee Access to Sensitive Whistleblower Information

DODIG's Case Management System Does Not Include Some Controls to Restrict Internal Employee Access

As previously discussed, DODIG has taken steps to restrict employee access to whistleblower information, such as by restricting access to cases in which a complainant has not consented to releasing his or her identity. DOD Hotline also applies additional restrictions to all cases involving internal misconduct referrals to the Office of Professional Responsibility and CIGIE Integrity Committee, and it has the capability to further restrict records, according to DODIG officials.

---

[77] The Air Force's case management application resides in a system that was granted a conditional authorization to operate in March 2018. The conditional authorization was contingent on the implementation of all system baseline security controls, monthly updates to the plan of action and milestones, and the submission of an approved continuous monitoring strategy. As of August 2018, these conditions had generally not been met, according to Air Force officials. However, these same officials stated that the Air Force IG was working with the authorizing official to address shortfalls and that a denial to operate had not been issued. Additionally, these officials noted that the application's host system would also be moving to a new environment by December 2018, at which point a new assessment would be needed.

Beyond restricting records, the case management system also includes user roles, which govern users' view of information. However, employees at the three DODIG directorates that are principally responsible for handling whistleblower information are generally able to access sensitive whistleblower information belonging to other directorates in both the Defense Case Activity Tracking System (D-CATS)–DODIG's whistleblower case management system—and an associated document repository, that is not necessary to accomplish assigned tasks. NIST Special Publication 800-53, *Security and Privacy Controls for Federal Information Systems and Organizations*, states that organizations should employ the core security principle of *least privilege*, which allows only authorized access for users that is necessary to accomplish assigned tasks in accordance with organizational missions and business functions.[78]

DODIG employees in the DOD Hotline, senior official investigations directorate, and whistleblower reprisal investigations directorate are able to access whistleblower information belonging to other DODIG directorates in both D-CATS and its associated document management repository because DODIG has not developed sufficient system controls needed to restrict access across the three directorates. For example, a DODIG employee in either the senior officials or reprisal investigations directorates can access Hotline records in D-CATS that the employee does not have a need to access, with the exception of cases specifically restricted by the DOD Hotline to prevent unauthorized access. According to an August 2018 internal DODIG memo, the lack of controls to restrict access to information across the three directorates has been known since the system was established in 2012.

DODIG plans to establish controls to restrict access among the DODIG directorates in a new enterprise system (D-CATSe), which will eventually replace D-CATS and the case management systems used by the military service IGs. D-CATSe is intended to provide a common case activity tracking system capable of supporting mandatory reporting requirements and collecting, storing, and exchanging IG records related to

---

[78] National Institute of Standards and Technology, Special Publication 800-53, Revision 4.

complaints and administrative investigations throughout a complaint's lifecycle.

According to DODIG officials, D-CATSe will restrict access both within and among user IGs, including the DODIG directorates and military service IGs, each of which may have unique access requirements based on their different types of user groups. According to DODIG officials, this will be accomplished through the establishment of unique business units at different organizational levels, teams, and user roles, which will collectively determine what information a user can access. However, as shown in Figure 7 below, the incremental release schedule for D-CATSe has been delayed, and the IGs are not expected to fully transition to the new system until fiscal year 2021.

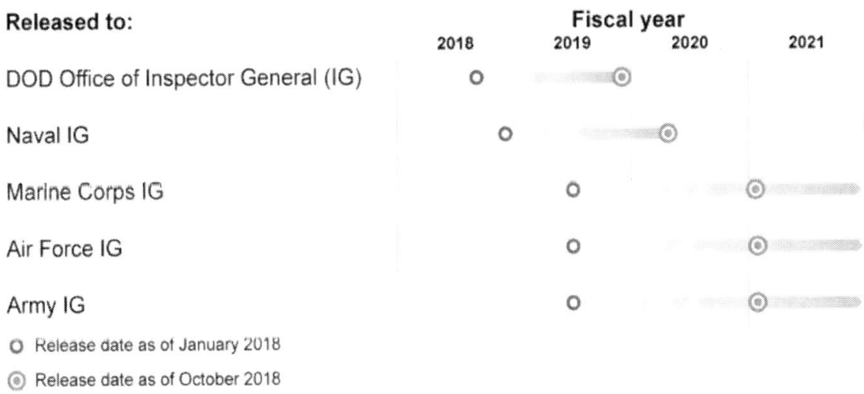

Source: GAO analysis of Department of Defense Office of Inspector General (DODIG) information. | GAO-19-198.

Figure 7. Change in Defense Case Activity Tracking System enterprise Projected Release Dates Between January and October 2018.

NIST guidelines state that organizations should design and prioritize activities to mitigate security risks, and that alternative strategies (such as plans) may be needed when an organization cannot apply controls to adequately reduce or mitigate risk.[79]

[79] National Institute of Standards and Technology, Special Publication 800-53, Revision 4.

Further, NIST guidelines state that addressing assurance-related controls[80] during system development can help organizations obtain sufficiently trustworthy information systems and components that are more reliable and less likely to fail.[81] However, DODIG does not plan to take other actions to address the lack of cross-directorate controls before the advent of the enterprise system.

Additionally, while DODIG is designing such controls and plans for each system release to provide a requirements basis for subsequent releases, it has not developed an assurance plan for testing controls, according to DODIG officials, or fully defined the system requirements needed to implement these controls and ensure it has achieved least privilege both within and across the user IGs. Without considering interim actions to address the lack of D-CATS cross-directorate access controls, DODIG may be unable to sufficiently mitigate security risks while D-CATSe is developed. Also, without developing a plan with assurance controls for achieving least privilege in D-CATSe, DODIG may be unable to ensure the confidentiality and integrity of sensitive whistleblower information during its implementation.

DODIG Has Identified Instances Involving Improper Employee IT Access Rights to Whistleblower Information

Separate from the lack of cross-directorate controls, DODIG has identified multiple instances in which sensitive but unclassified whistleblower information in the DODIG Administrative Investigations directorate whistleblower case management system and document repository was accessible to DODIG personnel who did not have a need to know this information. These instances involve DOD Hotline records that are specifically restricted to protect complainants requesting confidentiality, along with records belonging to DODIG's Office of

---

[80] Assurance is the grounds for justified confidence that a security or privacy claim has been or will be achieved. See National Institute of Standards and Technology, Special Publication 800-37, Revision 2.

[81] National Institute of Standards and Technology, Special Publication 800-53, Revision 4.

Professional Responsibility—which handles internal DODIG misconduct complaints.

Table 6 shows examples of recent instances in which DODIG determined that sensitive whistleblower records were accessible to DODIG personnel without a need to know. According to DODIG officials, as of January 2019, there were no known instances of anyone without a need to know actually accessing these records.[82] These officials also stated that corrective action had been taken for each instance in table 6, including by blocking access to information while the underlying issues were resolved; that at no time was information available to the public; and that the instances did not result in any disclosure outside of DODIG.

Table 6. Select Accessibility Issues Identified by DODIG from November 2017 through May 2018

Instance
Numerous restricted records in DODIG's whistleblower document repository were accessible to DODIG administrative investigations personnel without a need to know, including through an intranet search.
946 folders in DODIG's document repository were accessible to DODIG employees formerly with DOD Hotline and the senior officials and whistleblower reprisal investigations directorates.[a]
Restricted DOD Hotline records were accessible to unauthorized DODIG employees in the DODIG's document repository.
Two case records belonging to DODIG's Office of Professional Responsibility were accessible to DOD Hotline staff in the case management system.[b]

Source: GAO analysis of Department of Defense Inspector General (DODIG) after-action report and information memorandum to the DODIG Chief of Staff. | GAO-19-198.

[a]DODIG officials stated that any DODIG employees formerly with the DOD Hotline or senior officials or whistleblower reprisal investigations directorates would likely not have known how to actually access these files because such files are typically accessed through links in D-CATS and because the files would not have been part of the employees' default view in the document repository.

[b]DODIG officials stated that the case records were briefly visible to DODIG employees responsible for handling Hotline complaints, and that DODIG immediately began remediation steps.

NIST guidelines state that the need for certain user privileges may change over time, necessitating the periodic review of assigned user privileges in order to determine if the rationale for assigning such

[82] However, DODIG did not provide documentation that improper access was thoroughly investigated in all instances.

privileges remains valid.[83] DODIG has determined that its user access issues are broadly attributable to system administration and application problems, including permission changes resulting from system updates. To address such issues, DODIG has taken several remedial actions and identified additional recommended steps, including:

- reconciling user accounts and validating permissions related to restricted records;
- reviewing policies related to protecting complainant confidentiality and conducting awareness training with personnel, as appropriate; and
- developing enhanced user management procedures and internal controls related to establishing user accounts, reconciling current user permissions, and controlling access to restricted records.

In addition, in October 2018, DODIG instituted a process whereby user privileges associated with its case management system and document repository will be reviewed, validated, and corrected, if necessary, on a quarterly basis. If fully implemented, this process, along with the proposed actions, should help ensure that assigned user privileges are periodically validated and aligned with business needs. However, DODIG's process does not include steps to test document repository permissions after case management system updates, which were determined by DODIG to be the cause of some permission issues.[84] Without including such steps in its process, DODIG lacks assurance that system permissions will align with business needs on an ongoing basis, and therefore may not be able to appropriately control user accounts to prevent unauthorized access by system users.

---

[83] National Institute of Standards and Technology, Special Publication 800-53, Revision 4.

[84] A May 2018 internal DODIG after action-report recommended that document repository permissions be thoroughly tested after each case management system update.

Sensitive Whistleblower Information Has Been Accessible to Military Service IG Employees without a Need to Know

The military service IGs' case management systems and applications incorporate IT controls, such as authenticated user accounts and unique permissions, to protect certain whistleblower information. However, service IG systems and applications do not fully restrict employee access to sensitive whistleblower information only to information that is necessary to accomplish assigned tasks. As previously discussed, NIST guidelines state that organizations should only provide authorized access to users which is necessary to accomplish assigned tasks in accordance with organizational missions and business functions.[85] As shown in Table 7, DODIG's quality assurance reviews and our work identified issues related to IG employee access restrictions.

At the time of our review, the military service IGs had not taken steps to fully address the identified access issues. Specifically, Air Force officials stated that they did not plan to address the application access issues because they did not have funding to continue developing their existing application prior to transitioning to D-CATSe, although they would explore whether solutions were possible within current fiscal constraints during the next system maintenance evaluation. Similarly, Army IG officials stated that while the Army IG had resources to further develop its existing case management application, they had elected to not use those resources to remedy the identified access issue in light of the future arrival of D-CATSe. In addition, Naval IG officials reported taking action to restrict senor official investigations, but did not provide information to us on actions taken to address DODIG's recommendation to restrict cases involving internal Naval IG personnel. Finally, Marine Corps IG officials stated that access restrictions would be implemented as part of an application redesign scheduled to be complete by the end of 2018.

However, these officials also noted that they have not identified the root of the access problem or developed a plan to ensure that needed access

[85] National Institute of Standards and Technology, Special Publication 800-53, Revision 4.

restrictions are implemented and functioning properly, raising questions as to whether the redesign will fully restrict access on a continuing basis. As mentioned previously, the Marine Corps' case management application is also exempt from testing under the DOD IT risk management process, and therefore is not subject to routine security assurance testing.

Table 7. Employee Access Issues Involving Military Service IG Information Systems and Applications

Military service IG	Description of access issue
Air Force	DODIG found in its 2017 quality assurance review that the Air Force IG's application allowed users from other DOD component IGs (such as the Defense Contract Audit Agency IG) to view case descriptions and complainant identities for cases belonging to the Air Force IG, and that it did not restrict the system support contractor from viewing cases that involved its employees.
Army	DODIG found in its 2018 quality assurance review that the Army IG's application did not restrict Army IG personnel without a need to know from accessing allegations involving Army IG personnel.
Marine Corps	Marine Corps IG officials told us in August 2018 that employees in Marine Corps IG offices were able to see cases assigned to other Marine Corps IG offices without a need to know, and that the application contained other similar malfunctions, such as returning search results for a user other than the user performing the search, within the same IG office.
Naval	DODIG found in its 2016 quality assurance review that the Naval IG's system did not prevent Naval IG personnel from viewing investigations involving other internal Naval IG personnel, and that it did not adequately restrict employee access to senior official investigations.

Source: GAO analysis of Department of Defense Office of Inspector General (DODIG) and military service IG information. | GAO-19-198.

Federal Standards for Internal Control state that management should analyze and respond to risks, and evaluate and remediate internal control deficiencies on a timely basis, including those related to audit findings.[86]

Further, NIST guidelines state that organizations should design and prioritize activities to mitigate security risks, and that alternative strategies, such as plans, may be needed when an organization cannot apply controls to adequately reduce or mitigate risk. These guidelines also encourage

---

[86] GAO-14-704G.

organizations to obtain assurance-related evidence on an ongoing basis in order to maintain the trustworthiness of information systems.[87] As previously discussed, D-CATSe is being implemented incrementally, with releases for the Naval IG and the Air Force and Army IGs not scheduled to occur until fiscal years 2020 and 2021, respectively. By considering actions prior to the advent of D-CATSe, the Air Force, Army, and Naval IGs could mitigate existing risks to whistleblower confidentiality by reducing the potential for unauthorized employee access of whistleblower records. Also, by developing a plan to ensure that access restrictions function properly, the Marine Corps IG could better ensure the confidentiality and integrity of sensitive whistleblower information in its redesigned case management application on a continuing basis.

IGs Report Few Instances of Confidentiality Violations but IT Access Issues Create This Potential

Potential violations of whistleblower confidentiality may be reported to DODIG, the service IGs, the Office of Special Counsel, or CIGIE. IGs identified some substantiated violations of whistleblower confidentiality between fiscal years 2013 and 2018. Specifically, DODIG identified 8 substantiated violations of whistleblower confidentiality between fiscal years 2013 and 2018, representing approximately .01 percent of the 95,613 contacts handled by DODIG during that timeframe, according to DODIG officials.[88]

Army IG identified 6 substantiated violations of whistleblower confidentiality between these years. These violations include the improper release of IG information, disclosures made to individuals who do not have a need to know, and unauthorized access to whistleblower records by IG personnel. DODIG officials noted that in some instances, violations were

[87] National Institute of Standards and Technology, Special Publication 800-53, Revision 4.

[88] DODIG officials stated that they manually reviewed case data in order to identify potential violations, but that a future release of DODIG's case management system will include an automated capability to track allegations of compromising IG source identities with a specific field checkbox.

determined not to result from employee misconduct because the complainant's identify was disclosed unwittingly. According to DODIG and Army IG officials, disciplinary or corrective action was taken in all but one of the 14 substantiated violations because the DODIG employee involved resigned prior to action being taken. Officials from the Air Force, Naval, and Marine Corps IGs stated that they were unaware of any substantiated incidences of confidentiality violations between fiscal years 2013 and 2018 and that they were unable to specifically track such incidents in their case management systems.[89] Similarly, CIGIE Integrity Committee and Office of Special Counsel officials stated that they were unaware of and do not specifically track confidentiality violations, and we did not identify any confidentiality violations in the fiscal year 2013-2018 data they provided to us that involved DODIG employees.[90]

Respondents to our survey of DODIG employees separately reported potential violations of whistleblower confidentiality.[91] Specifically, 15 of the 86 respondents (about 17 percent) reported being aware of at least one instance since June 1, 2017, where the identity of a complainant or source was avoidably disclosed by a DODIG employee to an organization or individual without a need to know, and nine of these 15 were aware of more than one instance.

These responses are not intended to be a count of separate instances because respondents may have recalled the same instance(s), including one or more of the 8 substantiated violations reported to us by DODIG. The most common avoidable disclosure described by survey respondents involved distributing whistleblower materials to the wrong official or

---

[89] A senior Marine Corps official recalled one potential violation of confidentiality, wherein IG staff provided a protected communication to the alleged subject. According to this official, the potential violation was not fully investigated because the IG staff that allegedly shared the information was terminated from his or her position.

[90] To address our mandate, we also asked DODIG about the extent of retaliatory investigations involving DODIG employees between fiscal years 2013 and 2018. DODIG officials stated that there were no known incidences of retaliatory investigations, and we did not identify any such instances in the fiscal years 2013-2018 data we reviewed on cases involving DODIG employees from DOD Hotline, the DODIG Office of Professional Responsibility, the CIGIE Integrity Committee, or the Office of Special Counsel.

[91] As noted, these are potential violations of whistleblower confidentiality. We did not independently assess the specifics of the avoidable disclosures reported by survey respondents.

agency. Survey respondents reported that in such instances corrective action included recalling the complaint and deleting the erroneously sent record, or, in some cases, sending a complaint to DODIG's Office of Professional Responsibility for the investigation of possible misconduct.

While the number of known violations is small, IT access issues related to the case management systems and applications used by DODIG and the military service IGs create the potential for additional violations of whistleblower confidentiality.[92] As previously discussed, issues such as the absence of cross-directorate access controls within DODIG's case management system and the ability for non-Air Force IG users of the Air Force IG case management system to view IG case information allow for the improper access of sensitive whistleblower information. Recognizing this potential, a senior DODIG official noted concern regarding the possible extent of confidentiality violations stemming from these and the other access issues previously discussed in this chapter. Additionally, DODIG requested that the Defense Criminal Investigative Service investigate the April 2018 incident involving 946 case folders to determine who accessed the identified records. Without steps to address these ongoing IT access issues, the potential for additional violations of whistleblower confidentiality will persist.

---

[92] DOD's privacy program defines lost, stolen or compromised information or a breach of information as an actual or possible loss of control, unauthorized disclosure, or unauthorized access of personal information where persons other than authorized users gain access or potential access to such information for an other than authorized purpose where one or more individuals will be adversely affected. See DOD 5400.11-R *Department of Defense Privacy Program* (May 14, 2007).

DODIG Generally Met Documentation Requirements in Senior Official Cases that GAO Reviewed and Reported Most Credible Allegations

DODIG Dismissed Most Cases Involving Civilian DOD Presidential Appointees with Senate Confirmation and Generally Included Required Data and Documentation

DODIG closed 129 misconduct and reprisal cases in fiscal years 2013 through 2017 with complaints involving a civilian DOD Presidential appointee with Senate confirmation (PAS)[93] subject.[94] Of the 129 cases closed, DODIG dismissed without investigation 125 cases and investigated the remaining four. Figure 8 shows the number of cases closed in each fiscal year, by case disposition.

Our review of the 125 case files for dismissed misconduct and reprisal cases found that key documentation and data needed to demonstrate compliance with significant aspects of the case-handling process were generally present. Key documentation and data for dismissed cases include the case open and close dates, the incoming complaint, disposition of the case, and the dismissal approval and rationale.[95] CIGIE standards state that the degree to which an organization efficiently achieves its goals is affected by the quality and relevance of information that is collected, stored, retrieved, and analyzed, and that the results of investigative activities should be accurately and completely documented in the case file.[96]

---

[93] PAS positions include cabinet secretaries, agency heads, and undersecretary-level posts.

[94] Appendix III presents data on the characteristics of the 129 closed cases, including closure dates, allegation types, and organizational source.

[95] See appendix I for a more detailed description of our casefile review methodology.

[96] CIGIE, *Quality Standards for Investigations* (Nov.15, 2011).

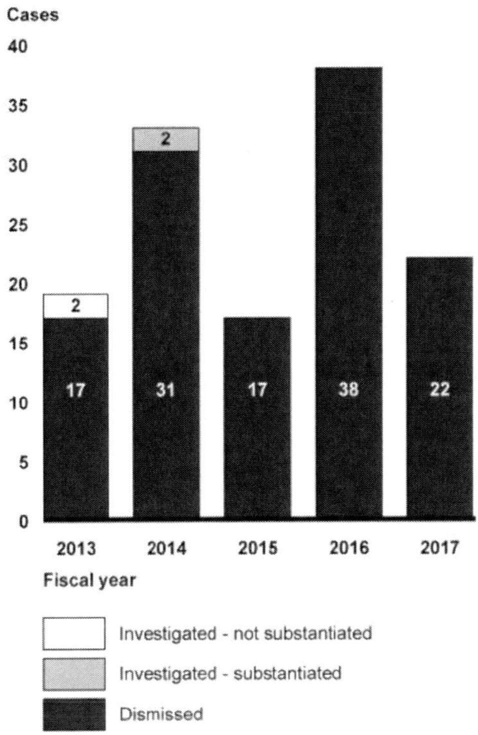

Source: GAO analysis of Department of Defense Office of Inspector General (DODIG) data. | GAO-19-198.

Figure 8. Disposition of DODIG Closed Misconduct and Reprisal Cases Involving Civilian DOD Presidential Appointees with Senate Confirmation, Fiscal Years 2013–2017.

Examples of Data and Documentation Consistently Present

Our review of 125 case files for dismissed cases closed in fiscal years 2013 through 2017 found that key documentation and data were generally present. For example:

- 100 percent of the cases we reviewed included the incoming complaint.

- Approximately 99 percent of the dismissed misconduct cases included a dismissal rationale that aligned with dismissal criteria in DODIG policy.[97]
- 100 percent of the dismissed reprisal cases that involved a closure letter informing the complainant of case dismissal listed a rationale for dismissal in the closure letter.
- 100 percent of the dismissed reprisal cases that did not involve a closure letter to the complainant had a rationale for dismissal elsewhere in the case file.
- Approximately 99 percent of dismissed misconduct cases included a required entry recording the intake disposition.[98]

Documents or Data That Were Not Material

Our review of case files for dismissed cases closed in fiscal years 2013 through 2017 found that some other documentation or data that are needed to demonstrate compliance with DODIG policy were missing. The deficiencies we found were not material to case outcomes. For example, approximately 77 percent of dismissed misconduct cases did not include a recording of case dismissal approval by IG supervisory staff. However, DODIG officials told us that the presence of the required entry recording the intake disposition indicated that the case dismissal had been approved by the appropriate authority. Similarly, approximately 55 percent of dismissed misconduct cases did not include a notification letter to the appropriate military service IG in the case file. DODIG officials stated that while there is guidance to send these letters, it is not a required practice.[99]

---

[97] DODIG dismissal criteria for not investigating cases involving senior official subjects include a determination of whether the allegations are credible and whether the allegations, if proven true violate criminal law. See Office of the Deputy Inspector General for Administrative Investigations, *AI Investigations Manual* (2012) and *AI Investigations Manual* (Mar. 29, 2016).

[98] Intake disposition includes the decisions to accept, decline, or refer a case as well as approval and rationale for dismissals, among other things.

[99] DODIG, *Investigations of Senior Officials Defense Case Activity Tracking System User Guide* (October 2015).

DODIG Has Reported Most Credible Misconduct Allegations to the Secretary of Defense and Some Investigation Results to Congress

DODIG reported most credible allegations concerning civilian DOD PAS officials to the Secretary of Defense as required. DODIG also reported some investigation results involving these officials to Congress prior to the enactment of the Inspector General Empowerment Act of 2016, which required the reporting of results of substantiated investigations involving DOD senior officials.[100] DODIG investigated four of the 129 cases closed in fiscal years 2013 through 2017, with two of those investigations leading to substantiated allegations of misconduct.

DODIG generally met DOD requirements to report credible allegations of misconduct against civilian DOD PAS officials to the Secretary of Defense. DOD Directive 5505.06 requires that DODIG notify the Secretary of Defense of all credible allegations or investigations involving presidential appointees and others of significance, including Senate-confirmed civilian officials.[101] We found documentary evidence that DODIG notified the Secretary of credible allegations in three of the four misconduct and reprisal investigations closed from fiscal years 2013 through 2017, and the secretary of a military service was notified in the fourth case. In addition, DODIG officials stated that the Principal Deputy IG provides the Secretary of Defense periodic updates on current investigations and other periodic updates of incoming allegations, as necessary and appropriate.

Separately, the Inspector General Empowerment Act of 2016 requires that DODIG report in its semiannual reports to Congress on all substantiated allegations of misconduct involving senior officials. Prior to

---

[100] The Inspector General Empowerment Act of 2016, Pub. L. No. 114-317 (2016) amended the Inspector General Act of 1978, at 5 U.S.C. Appendix by requiring that IG semi-annual reports to Congress include a report on each investigation conducted by the office involving a senior government employee where allegations of misconduct were substantiated, and including in the report a detailed description of the facts and circumstances of the investigation and the status and disposition of the matter, including whether the matter was referred to the Department of Justice.

[101] DOD Directive 5505.06.

2016, there was no requirement to notify Congress of substantiated allegations of misconduct involving senior officials. We found evidence that DODIG communicated investigation results to Congress in two of the four civilian DOD PAS official investigations closed between fiscal years 2013 and 2017, but not in the other two because it was not required.[102] For one investigated case, a report of investigation was provided to Congress upon request, and for another investigation, which had a substantiated allegation, the results of the investigation were published in narrative detail in a semi-annual report to Congress. DODIG now reports in its semi-annual reports to Congress summary results of substantiated and unsubstantiated cases closed during the corresponding period, but it has not closed any civilian DOD PAS official allegations since the statutory requirement to report to Congress on all substantiated cases was established.

CONCLUSION

Maintaining a program that instills trust and confidence for potential whistleblowers to come forward is critical to minimizing fraud, waste, abuse, and personnel misconduct in the federal government. Important components of a credible whistleblower program are timeliness of case processing and safeguarding confidentiality to the maximum extent possible. It is encouraging that DODIG and the service IGs have met some key goals and have policies that address whistleblower confidentiality. In addition, DODIG generally met key documentation and data requirements for the 125 cases dismissed by DODIG involving civilian DOD PAS officials, and reported most credible allegations, as required.

However, the IGs face challenges in addressing unmet timeliness goals and updating guidance to ensure full alignment with current confidentiality

[102] DODIG officials stated that all four cases were included in summary statistics reported to Congress in semiannual reports, and that DODIG's Office of Legislative Affairs and Communication may have received and responded to Congressional requests related to one or more of the four cases.

requirements. By pursuing more targeted, collective efforts with additional initiatives aimed at improving performance against unmet timeliness goals, the IGs can better assure current and potential whistleblowers that their complaints will be processed expeditiously. Additionally, without formal guidance documenting procedures for protecting the confidentiality of whistleblowers reporting potential internal DODIG employee misconduct, those employees lack assurance that DODIG can fully protect their identities. Similarly, without updated policies and procedures, the Air Force, Naval, and Marine Corps IGs may not be able to fully ensure whistleblower confidentiality in their organizations.

The integrity of a whistleblower program also extends to ensuring that sensitive information in IT systems remains secure and inaccessible by employees without a need to know. The IGs have existing controls for safeguarding whistleblower information, but additional efforts are warranted. Specifically, without further steps—such as considering interim actions to mitigate the lack of cross-directorate access controls, developing a plan, along with the military service IGs for achieving least privilege in the future enterprise case management system, and enhancing the process for periodically validating user privileges—DODIG may not be able to ensure that access controls in its existing and future case management systems align with business needs on an ongoing basis. Similarly, without considering actions to further restrict IG employee access in existing IT, the Air Force, Army, and Naval IGs may be unable to mitigate ongoing risks to whistleblower confidentiality. Finally, without a plan for ensuring that access restrictions in its redesigned case management system function properly, the Marine Corps IG may be unable to fully ensure whistleblower confidentiality.

RECOMMENDATIONS FOR EXECUTIVE ACTION

We are making a total of 12 recommendations to DOD. Specifically:

The DOD Inspector General should coordinate with the IGs of the military services to take additional actions to improve performance against unmet timeliness goals. This includes steps to improve performance of senior official misconduct investigations and military service reprisal intakes, and to resolve disagreement on notifications. (Recommendation 1)

The DOD Inspector General should issue formal guidance documenting procedures for protecting the confidentiality of whistleblowers throughout its internal misconduct investigation process. (Recommendation 2)

The Air Force Inspector General should establish procedures to fully reflect and implement DOD policy on the protection of whistleblower confidentiality. (Recommendation 3)

The Marine Corps Inspector General should establish procedures to fully reflect and implement DOD policy on the protection of whistleblower confidentiality. (Recommendation 4)

The Naval Inspector General should establish procedures to fully reflect and implement DOD policy on the protection of whistleblower confidentiality. (Recommendation 5)

The DOD Inspector General should consider interim actions as the whistleblower enterprise case management system is being developed to help ensure that access to sensitive whistleblower information in the current case management system and associated document repository is limited to information that is necessary to accomplish assigned tasks. (Recommendation 6)

The DOD Inspector General should coordinate with the IGs of the military services to develop a plan to fully restrict case access in the future whistleblower enterprise case management system so that user access is limited to information necessary to accomplish assigned tasks in accordance with organizational missions and business functions. (Recommendation 7)

The DOD Inspector General should enhance its process for periodically reviewing whistleblower case management system and document repository user privileges by including steps to ensure that such privileges remain valid after system updates, as appropriate. (Recommendation 8)

The Air Force Inspector General should consider interim actions as the whistleblower enterprise case management system is being developed to help ensure that access for users of existing applications is limited to information that is necessary to accomplish assigned tasks in accordance with organizational missions and business functions. (Recommendation 9)

The Army Inspector General should consider interim actions as the whistleblower enterprise case management system is being developed to help ensure that access for users of existing applications is limited to information that is necessary to accomplish assigned tasks in accordance with organizational missions and business functions. (Recommendation 10)

The Marine Corps Inspector General should develop a plan to ensure that its redesigned whistleblower case management application restricts user access to information based on what is needed to accomplish assigned tasks in accordance with organizational missions and business functions. (Recommendation 11)

The Naval Inspector General should consider interim actions as the whistleblower enterprise case management system is being developed to help ensure that access for users of existing applications is limited to information that is necessary to accomplish assigned tasks in accordance with organizational missions and business functions. (Recommendation 12)

AGENCY COMMENTS AND OUR EVALUATION

We provided a draft of this chapter to DODIG and the military service IGs for review and comment. In written comments, DODIG and the military service IGs concurred with each of our 12 recommendations. Comments from DODIG and the Air Force, Army, and Marine Corps IGs are reproduced in appendix V; the Naval IG concurred in an email. These IGs also provided technical comments, which we have incorporated as appropriate.

In its comments, DODIG stated that it will seek to implement the recommendations. In addition to highlighting recent and planned improvements, DODIG provided additional comments on some of the report's findings and statements. In particular, DODIG noted that the report understated its improvements in timeliness, such as by stating that DODIG did not meet timeliness goals related to average days of senior official and military reprisal intakes, and average days for reprisal oversight reviews. Citing figure 2, DODIG further stated that it met its timeliness goals in more than 60 percent of all senior official and reprisal intake cases, including 87 percent of senior official oversight review cases, and that it met its 15-day goal in more than 70 percent of senior official intakes. We agree that DODIG achieved these percentages and present the associated data in figure 2. However, as described in the report, and shown in figure 2, DODIG did not meet its goals for the average days of senior official misconduct and military reprisal intakes, and the average days for reprisal oversight reviews. Nonetheless, it is encouraging that DODIG has taken and planned actions to improve timeliness as its caseload has increased, including by increasing its staff by about 29 percent since fiscal year 2016, during which time it reported that its caseload similarly increased by about 26 percent.

DODIG also noted that the report presented some information in a manner that could create an incomplete impression of the agency's commitment to protecting whistleblower confidentiality. Specifically, DOD stated that the report's presentation of survey data related to DODIG employee concerns about internal DODIG processes may give a misleading impression because of the focus on the small number of respondents who had a negative impression. In particular, DODIG noted that more than 80 percent of respondents either believed that DODIG's internal process for reporting misconduct protected confidentiality somewhat or very well, or did not know if it did so. However, a positive perspective cannot be inferred from the respondents that reported not knowing whether or not DODIG's internal process protects confidentiality (42 percent). Also, it should be recognized that the respondents that held negative views on DODIG's process for reporting internal misconduct (16 percent) accounted for a substantial proportion of respondents (28 percent) that held either positive or negative views on this issue. Importantly, these and other survey information presented in the report also provide valuable information on the degree to which DODIG employees have confidence in the integrity of these important internal processes, and, as mentioned, align with other information obtained during our review. As such, this information may help to inform DODIG's efforts in addressing our recommendation to issue formal guidance documenting procedures for protecting the confidentiality of whistleblowers throughout its internal misconduct process, along with any future efforts to instill employee confidence in internal misconduct reporting mechanisms.

DODIG also noted that portions of the report addressing restrictions on DODIG employee access to sensitive whistleblower records need further context, stating specifically that no DODIG employees outside of the Administrative Investigations directorate, Office of Professional Responsibility, and Office of General Counsel had access to any of the records, and that there was no evidence that any person without a need to know accessed any such records. However, information provided to us by DODIG does not show that accessibility was limited in all instances to employees within one of those DODIG offices. Also, the ability of any employee to access records that were specifically restricted to protect complainant identities or internal records belonging to the Office of Professional Responsibility is problematic given the increased sensitivity of such records. Further, while DODIG did not identify instances in which anyone without a need to know accessed the records, DODIG did not provide evidence that all cases of improper access were thoroughly investigated, as we state in our report, and the instances included in the report are examples and not inclusive of all instances of improper access identified by the DODIG. Nevertheless, it is positive that DODIG has reported taking corrective action to address instances of improper accessibility. It is also encouraging that DODIG plans to implement our recommendations, as the potential for unauthorized access will persist until it establishes cross-directorate controls in the case management system and enhances its processes for periodically reviewing user privileges for its whistleblower case management system and document repository.

All of the military service IGs concurred with the recommendations directed to them. The Air Force and the Army IGs also provided comments on some of the report findings. In particular, the Air Force IG noted in relation to our third recommendation that language in Air Force Instruction 90-301, updated in December 2018, is essentially the same as 5 U.S.C. Appendix § 7, and that this language precludes Air Force officials at any level from waiving the requirement to inform complainants and employees of the requirement to not disclose their identities without their consent, unless the Inspector General determines such disclosure to be unavoidable. However, as stated in our report, Air Force guidance did not include requirements outlined in DOD Instruction 7050.01 related to the specific conditions under which information disclosures may be made without complainant consent. These include circumstances wherein a complainant has made it known outside IG channels that he or she submitted the complaint, there is an emergency situation or health or safety issue, or the allegation is being transferred outside of DOD to another IG. As a result, we continue to believe that without updated policies and procedures that fully implement confidentiality standards, the Air Force IG may not be able to ensure the consistent implementation of confidentiality protections.

Separately, in relation to IG employee access of information, the Army IG stated that the processes it has in place provide judicious access and control of whistleblower information to achieve an appropriate balance between efficient operations and minimized risk. As stated in our report, DODIG's 2018 quality assurance review of the Army IG found that the Army IG's application did not restrict personnel without a need to know from accessing allegations involving Army IG personnel, contrasting with NIST guidelines, which predicate user access on the need to accomplish assigned tasks. Army IG officials acknowledged this issue, but stated that the Army IG had elected to not use existing resources to further develop its case management application in light of the enterprise system being developed by DODIG. As a result, we continue to believe that by considering actions prior to the advent of the enterprise system—which is not expected to be released to the Army IG until fiscal year 2021—the Army IG could mitigate risks to whistleblower confidentiality by reducing the potential for unauthorized IG employee access of whistleblower records.

We are sending copies of this chapter to congressional committees; the Acting Secretary of Defense; the Department of Defense Principal Deputy Inspector General performing the duties of the Inspector General; the Inspectors General of the Air Force, the Army, the Navy, and the Marine Corps; the Office of Special Counsel; and other interested parties.

Brenda S. Farrell
Director
Defense Capabilities and Management

APPENDIX I: SCOPE AND METHODOLOGY

To determine the extent to which the Department of Defense Office of Inspector General (DODIG) and the military service offices of inspector general (IG) met and took steps to achieve key fiscal year 2018 timeliness and quality goals related to the handling of whistleblower complaints, we reviewed performance documentation and interviewed officials on DODIG and military service IG timeliness and quality goals, performance measures, and associated performance data for fiscal year 2018, along with ongoing and planned efforts to improve performance. We also reviewed fiscal year 2017 performance data for comparison purposes. We selected data from this period because they constituted the most complete and recent performance data available. Using the data, we assessed the extent to which DODIG and the military service IGs met timeliness and quality goals defined by statute and internal IG policy. Specifically, we assessed the timeliness of DOD Hotline referrals and completion reports against its internal goals, along with DODIG senior official misconduct and whistleblower reprisal intakes, investigations, and oversight reviews against internal and statutory goals. We also assessed the timeliness of military service IG senior official and reprisal notifications, intakes, and investigations against DOD and statutory goals, and reviewed the results of DODIG quality assessments for DOD Hotline referrals, military service investigations, and DODIG senior official and whistleblower reprisal investigations.

We assessed the reliability of DODIG and military service IG data by administering questionnaires, interviewing cognizant officials, and reviewing case management system documentation and quality assurance procedures. We also compared select electronic data to fiscal years 2013 through 2017 case file documentation associated with our review of case files to determine whether dates had been properly recorded in the system. We determined that these data were sufficiently reliable for our purposes.

To identify factors affecting timeliness and quality, we interviewed IG officials and reviewed relevant documentation including strategic plans, briefing materials, and semiannual reports to Congress. We also compared DODIG and military service IG completed and planned efforts to improve timeliness and quality against Council of the Inspectors General on Integrity and Efficiency (CIGIE) standards for federal IGs[103] related to establishing performance plans with goals and performance measures, and *Standards for Internal Control in the Federal Government* related to assessing performance and improving performance.[104]

To determine the extent to which DODIG and the military service IGs have established processes to protect the confidentiality of whistleblowers, we assessed DOD and military service IG policies and procedures for handling whistleblower allegations against DOD policy, CIGIE standards for federal IGs,[105] and statutory protections related to safeguarding

---

[103] See CIGIE *Quality Standards for Federal Offices of Inspector General* (August 2012).

[104] GAO, *Standards for Internal Control in the Federal Government*, GAO-14-704G (Washington, D.C.: September 2014).

[105] CIGIE was statutorily established as an independent entity within the executive branch by the *Inspector General Reform Act of 2008*, Pub. L. No. 110-409 (2008) and codified at 5 U.S.C. Appendix. Primarily comprised of inspectors general, CIGIE's mission is to address integrity, economy, and effectiveness issues that transcend individual government agencies and develop policies, standards, and approaches to aid in the establishment of a professional, well-trained, and highly skilled workforce in the offices of IGs. See CIGIE, *Quality Standards for Federal Offices of Inspector General* (August 2012) and *Quality Standards for Investigations* (Nov. 15, 2011).

whistleblower confidentiality.[106] We also reviewed the results of DODIG's quality assurance reviews of the Air Force (2017), Army (2018), and Naval (2016) IGs. We performed a web-based survey of the entire population of 108 DODIG Administrative Investigations directorate employees directly involved with the handling of whistleblower cases to ascertain whether, in their view, confidentiality processes are being implemented in accordance with guidance and standards, identify potential confidentiality violations, and to gather perceptions on the integrity of the internal process for reporting misconduct, among other things. We removed four employees from our initial population of 112 employees because two employees left DODIG prior to the initiation of our survey and two employees were new to the organization and therefore likely not familiar with the issues covered by the survey.

To conduct the survey, we developed 27 questions covering (1) access to and protection of sensitive and classified whistleblower information; (2) confidentiality guidance, safeguards and identity disclosures; (3) resolving internal conflict through DODIG's Office of the Ombuds; and (4) reporting misconduct through the internal DODIG process for DODIG employees to report misconduct. A survey specialist helped to develop these questions, and another survey specialist provided independent feedback on the questions to ensure that content necessary to understand the questions was included and that the questions could be answered accurately and completely. To minimize errors that might occur from respondents interpreting our questions differently than we intended, we pretested our survey with seven DODIG employees to ensure the clarity and reasonableness of the questions.[107] During the pretests, conducted in person and by phone, DODIG employees read the instructions and each question out loud and told us whether (1) the instructions and questions were clear and unambiguous, (2) the terms we used were accurate, and (3) they could

---

[106] See the Inspector General Act of 1978, as amended, which states that IGs shall not, after the receipt of a complaint or information from an employee, disclose the identity of the employee without the consent of the employee, unless the IG determines such disclosure is unavoidable during the course of the investigation. See 5 U.S.C., Appendix § 7(b).

[107] The pretests were conducted with one investigative support specialist, one investigator, two senior investigators, and three supervisory investigators.

offer a potential solution to any problems identified. We also asked them for a mock answer to ensure that the questions were understood as intended. We noted any potential problems identified by the reviewers and through the pretests and modified the questionnaire based on the feedback received. A full listing of survey questions is provided in appendix IV.

We conducted the survey between June 14, 2018, and July 6, 2018. To maximize our response rate, we sent reminder emails and contacted non-respondents by telephone to encourage them to complete the survey. In total, we received responses from 86 DODIG employees, achieving a response rate of 80 percent. Although not required, we assessed the potential for non-response bias by analyzing differences in the percent of DODIG employees per directorate and job position (e.g., investigator) that responded to our survey and the percent of potential DODIG respondents in each directorate and position. We found no meaningful differences between respondents and our population of potential respondents, indicating no evidence for non-response bias.[108] Also, we took steps in the development of the survey, data collection, and data analysis to minimize nonsampling errors and help ensure the accuracy of the answers that were obtained.[109] For example, a social-science survey specialist helped to design the questionnaire, in collaboration with analysts having subject-matter expertise. Then, as noted earlier, the draft questionnaire was pretested to ensure that questions were relevant, clearly stated, and easy to comprehend, and it was also reviewed by another specialist with expertise in survey development.

We calculated the frequency of responses to our closed-ended survey questions and performed content analysis on the open-ended questions to identify common themes from across the responses and to determine their frequencies. The quantitative analysis was performed by one analyst and independently reviewed by another analyst. For the qualitative analysis, a

---

[108] All respondents to the survey answered two of the four most-sensitive survey questions, and no more than two did not respond to the other two questions.

[109] The practical difficulties of administering any survey may introduce errors, commonly referred to as nonsampling errors. For example, differences in how a particular question is interpreted, the sources of information available to respondents, how the responses were processed and analyzed, or the types of people who do not respond can influence the accuracy of the survey results.

standard coding scheme was developed to identify common themes and determine their frequencies. We also used professional judgment to identify other themes that were determined to be important based on our review of case files, discussions with DODIG management, and review of guidance and relevant standards.

To determine the extent to which DODIG and the military service IGs are able to access and safeguard classified and sensitive information necessary to handle whistleblower complaints, we reviewed documentation and interviewed officials on the extent to which DODIG and the military service IGs have developed, implemented, and assessed key information technology (IT) security controls, and authorized the systems and applications used to process, store, and transmit sensitive whistleblower information per requirements and standards prescribed by DOD,[110] the Office of Management and Budget,[111] and the National Institute of Standards and Technology.[112] Collectively, these documents delineate an array of documentary and procedural requirements related to the assessment of IT security controls and the authorization to operate IT systems and applications. We also reviewed plans and interviewed cognizant officials on the development and implementation of the Defense Case Activity Tracking System enterprise (D-CATSe)—DOD's future system for managing whistleblower information across DODIG and the military service IGs, and reviewed DODIG's quality assurance reviews of the Air Force (2017), Army (2018), and Naval IGs (2016). Separately, we reviewed data and information on the number and percentage of DODIG and military service IG classified cases[113] closed in fiscal year 2017, the

---

[110] DOD Instruction 8510.01, *Risk Management Framework for DOD Information Technology* (Mar. 12, 2014) (Incorporating Change 2, Jul. 28, 2017).

[111] Office of Management and Budget, Circular No. A-130, *Managing Federal Information as a Strategic Resource* (Jul. 28, 2016).

[112] See National Institute of Standards and Technology, *Assessing Security and Privacy Controls in Federal Information Systems and Organizations: Building Effective Assessment Plans*, Special Publication 800-53A, Revision 4 (December 2014); *Security and Privacy Controls for Federal Information Systems and Organizations*, Special Publication 800-53, Revision 4 (April 2013); and *Guide for Applying the Risk Management Framework to Federal Information Systems: A Security Life Cycle Approach*, SP 800-37, Revision 1 (February 2010).

[113] For the purposes of this report, a classified case refers to a case or allegation including classified information.

number and allocation of DODIG and military service IG staff possessing security clearances, and the processes and procedures for storing and accessing classified information within DODIG and the military service IGs against DOD policy related to establishing controls to ensure access to classified information is limited to authorized persons.[114] We assessed the reliability of classified case data by administering questionnaires to cognizant officials, and determined the data were sufficiently reliable for the purpose of reporting the number of classified cases closed in fiscal year 2017.

To determine the extent of substantiated and potential confidentiality violations and retaliatory investigations involving DODIG employees, we obtained and analyzed available fiscal year 2013 through 2018 data on known or perceived violations of confidentiality standards and retaliatory investigations from DODIG and the military service IGs. We selected data covering this period of time because they constituted the most recent and reliable data available, and because DODIG officials told us that data prior to fiscal year 2013 were unreliable. We also reviewed fiscal year 2013–2018 complaint data from the Office of Special Counsel[115] and the CIGIE Integrity Committee in order to identify possible violations of confidentiality standards or retaliatory investigations.[116] We assessed the reliability of DODIG and service IG data by administering questionnaires, interviewing cognizant officials, and reviewing the methods used to query IG case management systems for this information. We determined the data to be sufficiently reliable for the limited purpose of identifying potential confidentiality violations and retaliatory investigations.

To evaluate the extent to which select misconduct and reprisal cases involving civilian DOD Presidential appointee with Senate confirmation (PAS) officials met key documentation and reporting requirements, we

---

[114] DOD Manual 5200.01 Vol.3, *DOD Information Security Program: Protection of Classified Information* (Feb. 24, 2012) (Incorporating change 2, Mar. 19, 2013).

[115] The Office of Special Counsel is an independent agency established under the Whistleblower Protection Act of 1989 to investigate whistleblower reprisal and other federal personnel action complaints.

[116] The CIGIE Integrity Committee receives, reviews, and refers for investigation whistleblower complaints made against inspectors general, designated staff members of an IG, and the Special Counsel and Deputy Special Counsel of the Office of Special Counsel.

reviewed all 125 administrative misconduct and reprisal cases involving Senate-confirmed civilian official subjects that were dismissed by DODIG in fiscal years 2013 through 2017. We chose to review cases from this period because they constituted the most recent and complete data in DODIG's case management system and would therefore most accurately reflect the extent to which the majority of DODIG's cases included required documentation. Also, DODIG officials informed us that information on cases prior to the implementation of the current case management system in fiscal year 2013 were both incomplete and unreliable. During the course of our review, we removed five out-of-scope cases from the original population of 130 cases, reducing the number of cases in our population from 130 to 125. Four cases were removed because the related allegations were investigated, and one case was removed because it was a record used to track an investigation occurring at a military service IG. Table 8 shows the distribution per fiscal year of closed misconduct and reprisal cases involving civilian DOD PAS subjects by the result of the case.

Table 8. Distribution of Dismissed Cases Involving Civilian DOD Presidential Appointees with Senate Confirmation, Fiscal Years 2013-2017

Case Type	Fiscal year 2013	Fiscal year 2014	Fiscal year 2015	Fiscal year 2016	Fiscal year 2017
Misconduct	17	28	17	36	19
Reprisal	0	3	0	2	3
Total	17	31	17	38	22

Source: GAO analysis of Department of Defense Inspector General (DODIG) data. | GAO-19-198.

To conduct the case-file review, we developed and used a data collection instrument to guide our review regarding general case characteristics and the presence of information and documentation required by DOD policies[117] and CIGIE best practices.[118] Core elements of this

[117] Such as Department of Defense Office of Inspector General, *AI Investigations Manual* (Mar. 29, 2016).

instrument were shared with DODIG officials to ensure the instrument aligned with the policies and practices in place when the cases were dismissed. These core elements represented individual documents and data elements. We incorporated DODIG's feedback into our instrument before commencing the file review. Examples of elements in our review that represent key data in DODIG's database or constitute documentation of key steps of the case-handling process include the following:

- case open date,
- case close date,
- protected disclosures,
- personnel actions,
- incoming complaints,
- disposition of the matter at intake,
- dismissal approval,
- required notifications, and
- dismissal rationale.

To validate the data collection instrument and ensure consistency in its application, we developed and followed standard procedures to review a test sample of 11 case files that were selected from each stratum of cases (e.g., misconduct) to ensure that each case type was tested at least once. In reviewing the sample, we adjusted the relevant case file elements for each case based on its type and circumstances and captured responses in our data collection instrument accordingly. To help ensure the accuracy of the information we collected, one analyst reviewed each casefile and coded for the presence of required information using the data collection instrument, and another analyst reviewed the first analyst's work. In the event that disagreement between the two analysts occurred, the analysts discussed and resolved the disagreement by identifying and reviewing supporting database information or documentation, and obtaining the input of a third analyst, if necessary, until a final resolution was made. We reviewed all

[118] CIGIE, *Quality Standards for Investigations* (November 2011).

cases dismissed during this period; for this reason, the results of this analysis do not have a sampling error.

Table 9. Organizations Contacted by GAO

Agency	Agency (child)	Agency (grandchild)
Department of Defense	Department of Defense Office of Inspector General	Administrative Investigations Directorate
	Department of Defense Office of Inspector General	DOD Hotline
	Department of Defense Office of Inspector General	Defense Case Activity Tracking System Program Management Office
	Department of Defense Office of Inspector General	Investigations of Senior Officials Directorate
	Department of Defense Office of Inspector General	Office of the Chief Information Officer
	Department of Defense Office of Inspector General	Office of General Counsel
	Department of Defense Office of Inspector General	Office of the Ombuds
	Department of Defense Office of Inspector General	Office of Professional Responsibility
	Department of Defense Office of Inspector General	Whistleblower Protection Ombudsman
	Department of Defense Office of Inspector General	Whistleblower Reprisal Investigations Directorate
	Office of General Counsel	Standards of Conduct Office
	Air Force Office of Inspector General	Complaints Resolution Directorate
	Air Force Office of Inspector General	Senior Officials Directorate
	Army Office of Inspector General	Assistance Division
	Army Office of Inspector General	Investigations Division
	Marine Corps Office of Inspector General	Assistance & Investigations Division
	Marine Corps Office of Inspector General	Inspections Division
	Naval Office of Inspector General	Information Technology Program Manager
	Naval Office of Inspector General	Military Whistleblower Reprisal Branch
	Naval Office of Inspector General	Special Inquiries Division
Other Organizations	U.S. Office of Special Counsel	n/a
	Council of the Inspectors General on Integrity and Efficiency	Integrity Committee
	Human Rights Watch	n/a
	Government Accountability Project	n/a

Source: GAO | GAO-19-198.

To identify other characteristics of DODIG cases involving civilian DOD PAS officials, we also analyzed fiscal years 2013-2017 case data to determine the number of cases closed by fiscal year, case types, case dispositions, source organizations, and the frequency and type of alleged misconduct. Separately, we also reviewed documentation from DODIG on civilian DOD PAS official allegations and investigation results reported to the Secretary of Defense and Congress since fiscal year 2013.

In addressing our objectives, we met with officials from the organizations identified in Table 9.

We conducted this performance audit from October 2016 to March 2019 in accordance with generally accepted government auditing standards. Those standards require that we plan and perform the audit to obtain sufficient, appropriate evidence to provide a reasonable basis for our findings and conclusions based on our audit objectives. We believe that the evidence obtained provides a reasonable basis for our findings and conclusions based on our audit objectives.

While this audit was initiated in October 2016, work was suspended from December 2016 until September 2017 due to other engagement work.

APPENDIX II: ADDITIONAL EXAMPLES OF DODIG INITIATIVES TO IMPROVE TIMELINESS

This appendix provides additional examples of Department of Defense Office of Inspector General (DODIG) timeliness improvement initiatives. According to DODIG officials, recent steps to improve the timeliness of whistleblower reprisal and senior official misconduct intakes, investigations, and oversight reviews include:

- Transferring the intake of most military reprisal complaints to the DODIG oversight branch for increased consistency.
- Changing the intake metric from 30 to 45 days for non-military reprisal cases to allow for more robust intakes.

- Not requiring a clarification interview when a written reprisal complaint is clear.
- Requesting documents from the employer at the intake stage in contractor reprisal cases.
- Interviewing subjects early in the investigation, when appropriate.
- Conducting investigative travel only when doing so would save time or for other compelling reasons. Otherwise, most interviews are conducted by phone or video teleconference and information is requested in opening letters for investigations to facilitate early receipt of documentary evidence.
- Using summary reports of investigation to facilitate timelier report-writing and review. DODIG issued 24 summary reports in fiscal year 2018, starting in May, for simple, non-substantiated investigations.
- Eliminating the requirement to conduct peer reviews of the reprisal reports of investigation, except at supervisors' discretion.
- Using standardized complaint notification and determination forms across DOD to formalize the processing of complaints received by component and service IGs.
- Implementing a more robust intake process for senior official misconduct investigations, which includes complaint clarifications and more investigative work. According to DODIG officials, most of the complaints reviewed during this new process would have otherwise been investigated by DODIG or the military service IGs, with a negative impact on the overall timeliness of investigations.
- Authorizing the military service IGs to close and simultaneously notify the DODIG reprisal investigations directorate of actions taken for complaints relating to uncooperative complainants, untimely complaints, and withdrawn complaints. This has increased notification rates and decreased processing time, according to DODIG officials.

Appendix III: Characteristics of Closed Misconduct and Reprisal Cases Involving Civilian DOD Presidential Appointees with Senate Confirmation

This appendix provides information on the characteristics of closed and dismissed misconduct and reprisal cases involving civilian DOD Presidential appointee with Senate confirmation (PAS) officials based on our analysis of fiscal year 2013 through fiscal year 2017 case data from the Department of Defense Office of Inspector General (DODIG) case-management system and our review of dismissed cases. DODIG closed 129 cases from October 1, 2012, through September 30, 2017, of which 125 were dismissed. Of the 125 dismissed cases, 117 were misconduct cases and eight were reprisal cases.

Organizational Source of Complaints Dismissed in Fiscal Years 2013-2017

DODIG dismissed 125 civilian DOD PAS official misconduct and reprisal cases. The largest number of cases—40 (32 percent)—were submitted by defense agency employees. Employees from the Navy submitted the next highest number of complaints, with 31 (25 percent), followed by the Army, which accounted for 26 (21 percent) of the complaints. Figure 9 shows the percentage of dismissed cases closed from fiscal years 2013 through 2017, by organizational source.

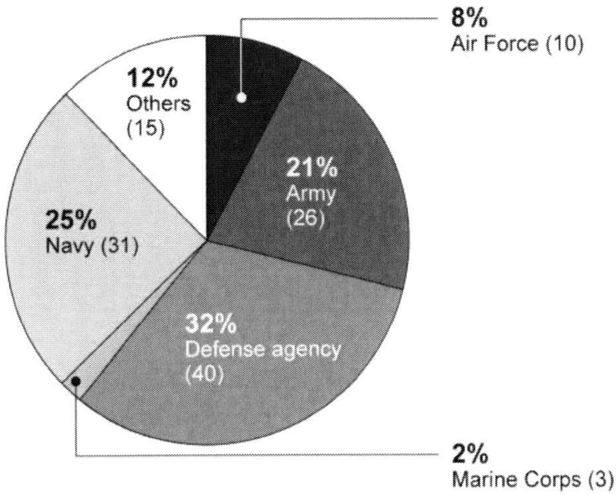

Source: GAO analysis of Department of Defense Office of Inspector General (DODIG) data. | GAO-19-198.

Figure 9. DODIG Dismissed Misconduct and Reprisal Cases Involving Civilian DOD Presidential Appointees with Senate Confirmation, by Organizational Source, Fiscal Years 2013-2017.

DODIG Number of Days to Close Dismissed Cases, Fiscal Years 2013-2017

Our review of the 125 dismissed civilian DOD PAS official cases closed by DODIG from fiscal years 2013 through 2017 showed that the majority of cases were closed in 30 days or less. Specifically, approximately 81 percent of the cases were closed in 30 days or less, and 58 percent of the cases were closed in 10 days or less. Table 10 groups the cases dismissed in each fiscal year from fiscal years 2013 through 2017 by the number of days to close.

Table 10. DODIG Dismissed Misconduct and Reprisal Cases Involving Civilian DOD Presidential Appointees with Senate Confirmation, by Number of Days to Close and Percentage, Fiscal Years 2013-2017

n/a	Case type		
Days to close	Senior officials	Reprisal	Percentage of total
10 or less	71	1	58 percent
30 or less	26	3	23 percent
60 or less	9	2	9 percent
90 or less	5	1	5 percent
Over 90	6	1	6 percent

Source: GAO analysis of Department of Defense Office of Inspector General (DODIG) data. |GAO-19-198.

Notes: Percentages do not equal 100 due to rounding.

DODIG has an internal goal to complete military reprisal intake reviews within 30 days, civilian and contractor reprisal reviews within 45 days, and senior official misconduct intake reviews within 15 days.

DODIG Closed Misconduct Case Allegations, Fiscal Years 2013-2017

We reviewed data on the number and type of allegations made against civilian DOD PAS officials in the 117 closed misconduct cases from fiscal years 2013 through 2017. In total, there were 152 allegations across the 117 closed cases. Allegations are grouped into 13 broad categories and 38 sub-allegation categories. From fiscal years 2013 through 2017, we found that the greatest proportion of allegations, at 47 percent, were personal misconduct and ethical violations. Personnel matters—at 14 percent—and "other"—an indeterminate category at 12 percent—were the next two largest in proportion of allegations. Figure 10 provides the percentages of allegations in closed misconduct cases from fiscal years 2013 through 2017.

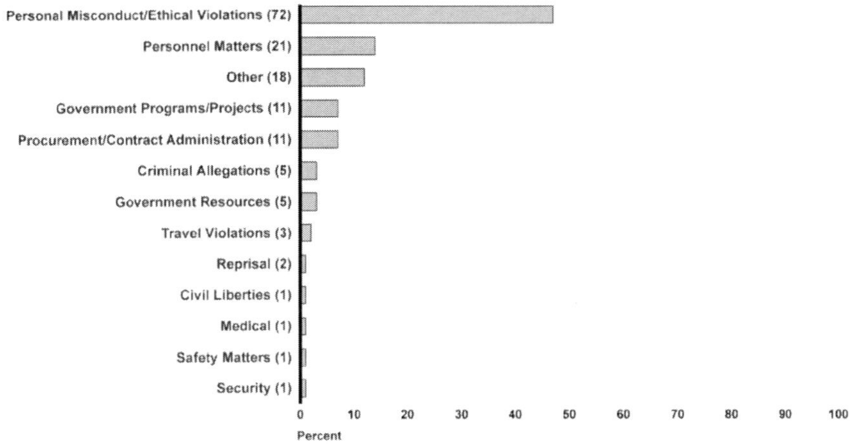

Source: GAO analysis of Department of Defense Office of Inspector General (DODIG) data. |GAO-19-198.

Note: Each allegation includes at least one sub-allegation.

Figure 10. DODIG Closed Misconduct Case Allegations Involving Civilian DOD Presidential Appointees with Senate Confirmation, by Percentage, Fiscal Years 2013-2017.

APPENDIX IV: SURVEY OF SELECT DODIG EMPLOYEES

GAO administered the survey questions shown in this appendix to learn more about DODIG processes related to the access and protection of whistleblower records, and the avenues available to DODIG employees to resolve conflict and report alleged misconduct themselves. The survey was divided into four sections: information access and protection, confidentiality, resolving internal conflict, and reporting misconduct. Survey questions without response options were open-ended. This appendix accurately shows the content of the web-based survey but the format of the questions and responses options have been changed for readability in this chapter. For more information about our methodology for designing and administering the survey, see appendix I.

1) How long have you worked in Administrative Investigations (AI)? Please consider your full tenure across all AI directorates (DOD

Hotline, Investigations of Senior Officials, and Whistleblower Reprisal Investigations) if you have worked in more than one directorate. (Response options provided: radio buttons labeled "Less than 1 year," "1 year or more but less than 5 years," "5 years or more but less than 10 years," and "10 years or more.")

Section I: Information Access and Protection

2) In your current position, are you generally able to access all types of unclassified information necessary to perform the duties required of your position? This could include access to documentary evidence or witnesses, among other information.

□ Yes ⟶ SKIP to Question 3
□ No ⟶ Continue to i

i. Please describe any obstacles that impede your ability to access all types of unclassified information necessary to perform the duties required in your position.

3) Have you been provided guidance that specifies requirements for ensuring that whistleblower records are properly secured, both physically and electronically? For the purposes of this survey, *whistleblower records are not specific to reprisal*, but encompass all contacts, complaints, allegations, cases, and investigations related to possible violations of law, rules, or regulations; mismanagement; gross waste of funds; abuse of authority; reprisal; or substantial and specific danger to public health and safety. Guidance can include but may not be limited to documents, training, emails, or in-person discussions/briefings.

□ Yes ⟶ Continue to i
□ No ⟶ SKIP to iii

1. Have you received any of the following types of guidance that specifies requirements for properly securing whistleblower records? Select one from each row

Category	Yes	No	I don't know	I don't know checked
Formal training (in-person/web-based)				Continue to ii
Informal training (staff meetings/briefings)				Continue to ii
Direction from supervisor				Continue to ii
Written policy/procedure				Continue to ii
Other				Continue to ii
Please describe any other guidance you have received.	n/a	n/a	n/a	Continue to ii

2. Do you believe the guidance identified above is sufficient or insufficient in specifying requirements for properly securing whistleblower records in your directorate? *Select only one*

□ Sufficient ⟶ SKIP to Question 4
□ Insufficient ⟶ Continue to 1 below
□ Not sure ⟶ SKIP to Question 4
□ Why do you believe the guidance is insufficient? ⟶SKIP to Question 4

3. Would guidance that specifies access restrictions and security controls for handling whistleblower records be helpful? (Response options provided: radio button labeled "yes" and "no.")

    1. Please explain why guidance would or would not be helpful.

4) Are you aware of any controls in place to restrict access to D-CATS records to only DODIG employees (either within or outside your directorate) with a need to know? Select only one

□ Yes ⟶ Continue to i
□ No ⟶ SKIP to Question 5
□ I'm not sure ⟶ SKIP to Question 5

i. Please describe the control(s) in place to restrict access to D-CATS records.

5) During your tenure at DODIG, have you or other DODIG employees (either within or outside your directorate) been able to access records in D-CATS without a need to know? This applies to potential access to records, regardless of whether anyone actually accessed records or not.

□ Yes ⟶ Continue to i
□ No ⟶ SKIP to Question 6
□ I don't know ⟶ SKIP to Question 6

i. Which DODIG directorate's records have you or other DODIG employees been able to access without a need to know? (Response options provided: checkboxes labeled "DOD Hotline," "Investigations of Senior Officials," "Whistleblower Reprisal Investigations," and "Office of Professional Responsibility.")

ii. Are you aware of any actions taken to address the ability of DODIG employees to access records without a need to know? Examples of actions taken include a policy or procedure change, additional guidance, or other actions taken.

□ Yes ⟶ Continue to 1 below
□ No ⟶ SKIP to 2 below

1. Please describe the action(s) taken.

2. What improvements, if any, could be made to address the ability of DODIG employees to access records without a need to know?

6) Do you believe protections are sufficient or insufficient to ensure only DODIG employees with a need to know can access records in D-CATS? Select only one

□ Sufficient ⟶ Continue to i
□ Insufficient ⟶ Continue to i
□ Not sure ⟶ SKIP to Question 7

i. Why do you believe the protections are sufficient or insufficient?

7) Are you able to access classified information when needed to perform the duties required of your position? Select only one

□ Yes ⟶ SKIP to Question 8
□ No ⟶ Continue to i
□ I do not require access to classified information to perform the duties of my position ⟶ SKIP to Question 8

i. Please describe any current obstacles to accessing classified information necessary to perform the duties required of your position.

8) Do you believe protections that are in place in your directorate are sufficient or insufficient to ensure that only those people with a need to know handle classified whistleblower records? Select only one

□ Sufficient → Continue to i
□ Insufficient → Continue to i
□ Not sure → SKIP to the next section

i. Why do you believe the protections are sufficient or insufficient?

Section II: Confidentiality

9) Have you been provided guidance that describes how to maintain the confidentiality of all individuals (both known and confidential complainants, witnesses and subjects) involved in the whistleblower records you handle? Guidance can include but may not be limited to documents, training, emails, or in-person discussions/briefings.

□ Yes → Continue to i
□ No → SKIP to iii

i. Have you received any of the following types of guidance that describes how to maintain the confidentiality of all individuals (both known and confidential complainants, witnesses and subjects) involved in the whistleblower records you handle? Select one from each row

Category	Yes	No	I don't know	I don't know checked
Formal training (in-person/web-based)				Continue to ii
Informal training (staff meetings/briefings)				Continue to ii
Direction from supervisor				Continue to ii
Written policy/procedure				Continue to ii
Other				Continue to ii
Please describe any other guidance you have received.	n/a	n/a	n/a	Continue to ii

ii. Do you believe the guidance identified above is sufficient or insufficient in specifying how to maintain the confidentiality of all individuals (both known and confidential complainants, witnesses and subjects) involved in the whistleblower records you handle?

□ Sufficient ⟶ SKIP to Question 10
□ Insufficient ⟶ Continue to 1 below
□ Not sure ⟶ SKIP to Question 10

1. Why do you believe the guidance is insufficient? (After answering, SKIP to Question 10)

iii. Would guidance that describes how to maintain the confidentiality of all individuals (both known and confidential complainants, witnesses and subjects) involved in the whistleblower records you handle be helpful?

□ Yes ⟶ Continue to 1
□ No ⟶ Continue to 1

1. Please explain why guidance would or would not be helpful.

10) To your knowledge, what safeguards, if any, are in place within your directorate to protect the identities of individuals (both known and confidential complainants, witnesses and subjects) involved in whistleblower records? Safeguards may include but are not limited to database restrictions and protocols for sharing information.

11) Have you been provided guidance that specifies how to determine whether disclosing the identity of a complainant or source (e.g., witness) is unavoidable? Guidance can include but may not be limited to documents, training, emails, or in-person discussions/ briefings.

□ Yes ⟶ Continue to i

□ No ⟶ SKIP to iii

i. Have you received any of the following types of guidance that specifies how to determine whether disclosing the identity of a complainant or source (e.g., witness) is unavoidable? *Select one from each row*

Category	**Yes**	**No**	**I don't know**	**I don't know checked**
Formal training (in-person/web-based)				Continue to ii
Informal training (staff meetings/briefings)				Continue to ii
Direction from supervisor				Continue to ii
Written policy/procedure				Continue to ii
Other				Continue to ii
Please describe any other guidance you have received.	n/a	n/a	n/a	Continue to ii

ii. Do you believe the guidance identified above is sufficient or insufficient in specifying how to determine whether disclosing the identity of a complainant or source (e.g., witness) is unavoidable?

□ Sufficient ⟶ SKIP to 2 below

□ Insufficient ⟶ Continue to 1 below

□ Not sure ⟶ SKIP to 2 below

1. Why do you believe the guidance is insufficient?

2. What improvements, if any, do you think could be made to guidance specifying how to determine whether disclosing the identity of a complainant or source (e.g., witness) is unavoidable? (After answering, SKIP to Question 12)

iii. Would guidance that specifies how to determine whether disclosing the identity of a complainant or source (e.g., witness) is unavoidable be helpful?

(Response options provided: radio buttons labeled "yes" and "no.")

1. Please explain why guidance would or would not be helpful.

12) To your knowledge, is there one or more official(s) who is responsible for determining whether disclosing the identity of a complainant or source (e.g., witness) is unavoidable?

□ Yes ⟶ Continue to i
□ No ⟶ SKIP to Question 13
□ I don't know ⟶ SKIP to Question 13

i. Who is responsible for determining whether disclosing the identity of a complainant or source (e.g., witness) is unavoidable?

13) While working in AI, have you ever encountered a situation where disclosing the identity of a complainant or source (e.g., witness) was unavoidable?

□ Yes ⟶ Continue to i
□ No ⟶ SKIP to Question 14

i. Please describe the general circumstance(s) and the steps you took to verify that the circumstance(s) required disclosing the identity of a complainant or source (e.g., witness). Please do not provide individual names related to the actors involved.

14) Between June 1, 2017, and today, are you aware — either by experiencing firsthand or directly observing actions of another person – of an instance where the identity of a complainant or source (e.g., witness) was disclosed by a DODIG employee to an organization or individual without a need to know (i.e., an avoidable disclosure)? Please check only one below.

□ No, I am not aware of any avoidable disclosures → SKIP to Question15
□ Yes, I am aware of one or more avoidable disclosure(s) → Continue to i

i. How many avoidable disclosures are you aware of between June 1, 2017, and today? For example, if the identity of a complainant was revealed to one person who did not have a need to know, please consider that event as one instance. Similarly, if the identity of a source was revealed separately to two different people who did not have a need to know, please consider those events as two instances.

ii. Please describe any actions taken in response to the avoidable disclosure(s) you are aware of between June 1, 2017, and today. Examples of actions taken include but may not be limited to retracting/recalling a referred complaint, a change to policy, procedure or guidance, and notifying the complainant or source, among other actions.

15) What improvements, if any, could be made to prevent avoidable disclosures from happening in the future?

16) Please describe any best practices that you follow to help prevent avoidable disclosures.

Section III: Resolving Internal Conflict

17) Have you ever contacted the DODIG Office of the Ombuds or participated in a DODIG Office of the Ombuds activity in order to address conflict among DODIG employees? Examples of DODIG

Office of the Ombuds activities include but are not limited to providing confidential advice for resolving conflict among peers and supervisors and participating in an Ombuds-led mediation among DODIG employees.

□ Yes ⟶ Continue to i
□ No, but I know about the DODIG Office of the Ombuds ⟶ SKIP to Question 18
□ I do not know about the DODIG Office of the Ombuds ⟶ SKIP to the next section

i. Do you believe the DODIG Office of the Ombuds provided or is providing sufficient or insufficient assistance to address the conflict(s) for which you contacted the Ombuds or participated in an Ombuds activity?

□ Sufficient ⟶ Continue to 1
□ Insufficient ⟶ Continue to 1
□ Too soon to tell ⟶ Continue to 1

1. Please describe, in general terms, your latest experience working with the DODIG Office of the Ombuds. Please do not provide the names of individuals involved with your experience.

18) Have you ever considered reaching out to the DODIG Office of the Ombuds, but ultimately chose not to?

□ Yes ⟶ Continue to i
□ No ⟶ SKIP to the next section

i. How much, if at all, did each of the following contribute to your decision not to utilize DODIG Office of the Ombuds services? *Select one in each row.*

Category	Not at All	Slightly	Somewhat	Very Much	Don't Recall
Resolved the issue through another avenue					
Not sure how to initiate contact with the Ombuds					
Concern about length of process					
Concern about objectivity or conflict of interest within the Office of the Ombuds					
Fear that confidentiality would be compromised					
Fear of retaliation or reprisal from within DODIG					
Other					
Please describe any other factor(s) that contributed to your decision not to utilize DODIG Office of the Ombuds services					

Section IV: Reporting Misconduct

19) As a DODIG employee, have you ever personally reported misconduct against another DODIG employee through DODIG's internal process for investigating alleged misconduct? For the purposes of this survey, "misconduct" refers to (1) a violation of a provision of criminal law, (2) a violation of a recognized standard, such as a federal or DOD regulation, or (3) a matter of concern involving DOD leadership that could reasonably be expected to be of significance to DODIG.

□ Yes ⟶ Continue to i
□ No ⟶ SKIP to iii

i. Did you report misconduct on or before September 30, 2016?

□ Yes ⟶ Continue to 1 below
□ No ⟶ SKIP to ii

i. Do you believe your report(s) of misconduct on or before September 30, 2016 were investigated in a fair and objective manner? (Response options provided: radio buttons labeled “yes” and “no.”)

a. Please describe your general experience(s) in reporting misconduct against a DODIG employee on or before September 30, 2016, including why you do or do not believe your report(s) of misconduct were investigated in a fair and objective manner. Please do not provide the names of individuals related to the misconduct you reported.

ii. Did you report misconduct on or after October 1, 2016?

□ Yes ⟶ Continue to 1 below
□ No ⟶ SKIP to Question 20

1. Do you believe your report(s) of misconduct on or after October 1, 2016 were investigated in a fair and objective manner? (Response options provided: radio buttons labeled “yes,” “no,” and “too early to have an opinion”)

   a. Please describe your general experience(s) in reporting misconduct against a DODIG employee on or after October 1, 2016, including why you do or do not believe your report(s) of misconduct were investigated in a fair and objective manner. Please do not provide the names of individuals related to the misconduct you reported.

iii. Do you know how to report misconduct against another DODIG employee through DODIG’s internal process?

(Response options provided: radio buttons labeled "yes" and "no.")

20) Thinking about the time period on or before September 30, 2016, did you ever consider reporting misconduct against a DODIG employee through DODIG's internal process, but ultimately *choose not to*?

□ Yes ⟶ Continue to i
□ No ⟶ SKIP to Question 21

i. How much, if at all, did each of the following contribute to your decision not to report incident(s) of misconduct on or before September 30, 2016? *Select one in each row.*

Category	**Not at All**	**Slightly**	**Somewhat**	**Very Much**	**Don't Recall**
Resolved the issue through another avenue					
Not sure how to report misconduct					
Concern about length of process					
Concern about objectivity or conflict of interest within DODIG's internal process to report misconduct					
Fear that confidentiality would be compromised					
Fear of retaliation or reprisal from within DODIG					
Other					
Please describe any other factor(s) that contributed to your decision not to report incidents of misconduct on or before September 30, 2016.	n/a	n/a	n/a	n/a	n/a

21) Thinking about the time period on or after October 1, 2016, did you ever consider reporting misconduct against a DODIG employee through DODIG's internal process, but ultimately choose not to?

□ Yes ⟶ Continue to i below
□ No ⟶ SKIP to Question 22

i. How much, if at all, did each of the following contribute to your decision not to report incident(s) of misconduct on or after October 1, 2016? Select one in each row.

Category	**Not at All**	**Slightly**	**Somewhat**	**Very Much**	**Don't Recall**
Resolved the issue through another avenue					
Not sure how to report misconduct					
Concern about length of process					
Concern about objectivity or conflict of interest within DODIG's internal process to report misconduct					
Fear that confidentiality would be compromised					
Fear of retaliation or reprisal from within DODIG					
Other					
Please describe any other factor(s) that contributed to your decision not to report incidents of misconduct on or after October 1, 2016.	n/a	n/a	n/a	n/a	n/a

22) How well, if at all, do you believe DODIG's internal process for reporting misconduct protects the confidentiality of DODIG employees? (Response options provided: radio buttons labeled "Not at all," "Slightly," "Somewhat," "Very well," and "I don't know.")
23) What improvements, if any, do you think could be made to DODIG's internal process for reporting misconduct to protect the confidentiality of DODIG employees?
24) How well, if at all, do you believe DODIG's internal process handles misconduct allegations against DODIG employees? This includes activities associated with both assessing incoming complaints and subsequently investigating them, as appropriate. (Response options provided: radio buttons labeled "Not at all," "Slightly," "Somewhat," "Very well," and "I don't know.")
25) What factors contribute to your opinion about DODIG's internal process for handling misconduct allegations against DODIG employees?

26) What improvements, if any, do you think could be made to DODIG's internal process to improve the handling of misconduct allegations?
27) If you would like to comment on any of the topics covered by this survey, or anything else that you feel might be relevant to our review on the DOD whistleblower program, please do so below.

APPENDIX V: COMMENTS FROM THE DEPARTMENT OF DEFENSE

This letter relates to GAO-19-198.

INSPECTOR GENERAL
DEPARTMENT OF DEFENSE
4800 MARK CENTER DRIVE
ALEXANDRIA, VIRGINIA 22350-1500

FEB 19 2019

Ms. Cathleen A. Berrick, Managing Director
Defense Capabilities and Management
U.S. Government Accountability Office
441 G. Street, N.W.
Washington, DC 20548

Dear Ms. Berrick,

This is the DoD Office of Inspector General's (DoD OIG) response to the GAO's report, "Whistleblower Protection: Analysis of DoD's Actions to Improve Case Timeliness and Safeguard Confidentiality (GAO 19-128)."

We appreciate the GAO's careful review of the Department of Defense's whistleblower protection program and its professional communications with the DoD OIG and the offices of the military service Inspectors General (IGs).

We value the GAO's oversight, and we believe that this report, and its recommendations, will help further improve whistleblower reprisal investigations by the DoD OIG and the military service IGs. As noted below, we concur with the report's recommendations and will seek to implement them. Additionally, the military service IGs concur with the report's recommendations. We have enclosed their responses as exhibits to this letter.

We also appreciate this report's recognition of the many improvements that we have been making in the timeliness of intake reviews, investigations, and oversights, as well as the safeguarding of whistleblower information and confidentiality. For example, the report noted that the DoD OIG met its timeliness goals for civilian and contractor case intakes and for senior official misconduct oversight reviews, despite the 98 percent increase in whistleblower reprisal complaints over the past 5 years. (See page 13 of the GAO report.)

Further, the report noted that that the DoD OIG completed a record number of 60 reprisal investigations in fiscal year 2018, compared to 37 investigations in fiscal year 2017. We have reduced the average case age of open and closed whistleblower reprisal investigations, and the average age of open investigations on December 1, 2018, was 284 days, compared to 370 days in November 2018. In addition, the average age of the DoD OIG's reprisal investigations has continued to improve since the GAO's draft report was issued. On January 31, 2019, the average age of open investigations was 215 days. We will continue to focus on this issue and expect that the average age of open cases will continue to decline.

The report noted that the DoD OIG and the military service IGs met quality goals related to the thoroughness and completeness of senior official and whistleblower reprisal investigations. (See page 17 of the GAO report.) The report further noted that the DoD Hotline met quality goals for thoroughness of complaint referrals in 97 percent of the assessment criteria evaluated

by the GAO, and 100 percent of the DoD OIG's reprisal investigations complied with quality goals for thoroughness and documentation. (See pages 18-19 of the GAO report.)

The report also noted that the DoD OIG case files for dismissed misconduct and reprisal cases contained key documentation and data to demonstrate compliance with significant aspects of the case handling process. (See page 45 of the GAO report.)

The report acknowledged the important initiatives that the DoD OIG and Military Service IGs have implemented to improve timeliness. (See page 23 of the GAO report.) For example, the DoD OIG increased its staff to address the significant increase in DoD Hotline, senior official misconduct, and reprisal cases. Specifically, we increased from 114 in fiscal year 2016 to 147 full-time equivalents in fiscal year 2018, and are further increasing the staff assigned to these matters. Similarly, the Marine Corps IG hired an additional investigator, and the Army IG reassigned staff to improve its efforts in addressing the reprisal caseload.

The report also noted the DoD OIG's implementation of an alternative dispute resolution (ADR) process to mediate reprisal complaints. This program seeks to resolve many complaints with the voluntary agreement of the parties, avoiding lengthy investigations and providing relief for complainants quickly. In fact, the DoD OIG's ADR program was recently praised in the Project on Government Oversight's July 9, 2018, report, "THE WATCHDOGS AFTER FORTY YEARS: Recommendations for Our Nation's Federal Inspectors General." That report stated, "It can take years to resolve whistleblower reprisal claims, and, in the meantime, the whistleblower is often forced to wait with their life on hold. To increase efficiency, CIGIE [the Council of Inspectors General on Integrity and Efficiency] should assess the DoD IG's recent alternative dispute resolution initiative as a potential model for larger OIGs."[1]

The GAO report noted that the DoD OIG has established policies and procedures to protect whistleblower confidentiality, including obtaining express whistleblower consent to disclose their identity outside the DoD Hotline on a need-to-know basis, and documenting the whistleblower's consent decision in the case record. The GAO also found that 80 percent of DoD OIG respondents to a GAO survey said guidance they receive on protecting confidentiality is sufficient to maintain confidentiality of individuals involved in OIG investigations. (See page 26 of the GAO report.)

We also appreciate the recognition of other DoD OIG ongoing initiatives in these and other areas. We believe that the initiatives referenced in GAO Table 3 (on page 23) and Appendix II of the report will further improve the timeliness of intakes, investigations, and oversights, while enhancing the quality of IG reports. Several of the more significant initiatives noted by the GAO include:

- Using summary reports of investigation for simple, non-substantiated investigations, to facilitate more timely investigations and issuance of reports.
- Implementing a more robust intake process for senior official misconduct investigations, including complaint clarification interviews, which has had a positive impact on the overall timeliness of investigations.

[1] https://docs.pogo.org/report/2018/2018-07-09_POGO_The_Watchdogs_After_40_Years_IG_Report.pdf?_ga=2.261802829.1385200566.1541546549-334568156.1508359103)

- Establishing standardized complaint notification and determination forms across the DoD to formalize and make more efficient the processing of complaints received by component and military service IGs.
- Centralizing intake functions to shorten complaint review processes and enhance the consistency of intake evaluations.

However, we recognize, and agree with the GAO, that more improvements can and should be made, and we will seek to implement the recommendations to continue the improvement process.

Finally, we believe it is important to note some areas in the report where the GAO's findings and statements warrant further context. We describe a few of these areas below.

Timeliness Issues

The report's findings concerning the DoD OIG's fiscal year 2018 timeliness goals present data in a manner that understates the DoD OIG's improvements in timeliness. For example, the report states that the DoD OIG did not meet timeliness goals related to average days of senior official and military reprisal intakes, and average days for reprisal oversight reviews. However, the statistics in Figure 2 show that the DoD OIG met its timeliness goals in more than 60 percent of all senior official and reprisal intake cases, including in 87 percent of senior official oversight review cases. Further, while the DoD OIG's average number of days for completing senior official intakes was 17 days – against a goal of 15 days – the DoD OIG met the 15-day goal in more than 70 percent of the 631 senior official intakes it concluded during the fiscal year.

We also appreciate the report's mention of the burgeoning whistleblower reprisal caseload. The GAO report states, on page 13, that the number of whistleblower reprisal cases increased from 1,013 to 2,002 over the past 5 years, and that in fiscal year 2018, the DoD Hotline received 12,470 complaints from potential whistleblowers. (See page 2 of the GAO report.) To better illustrate this point, the following chart shows the increase in reprisal and restriction complaints received since fiscal year 2013:

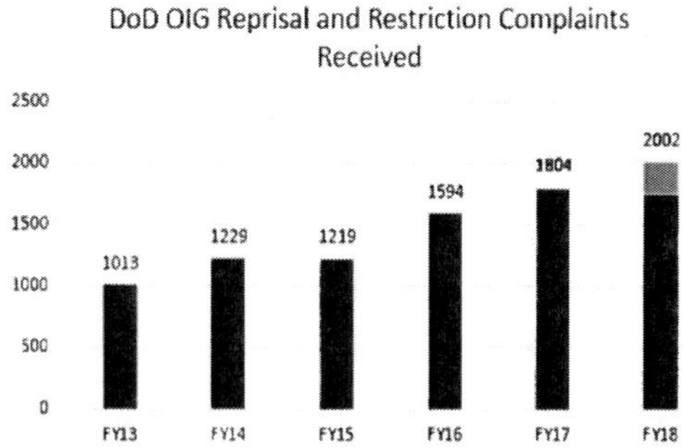

Confidentiality and Accessibility Issues

The report made several findings and recommendations concerning the existence and effectiveness of policy guidance for protecting the confidentiality of whistleblowers. We generally concur with those findings and recommendations. However, the report presented some information in a manner that could create an incomplete impression of the DoD OIG's commitment to protecting whistleblower confidentiality.

For example, the report presented survey data on some DoD OIG employees' concerns about the DoD OIG's internal processes to protect whistleblowers in complaints involving other DoD OIG employees and leaders. The GAO's presentation of the data may leave a misleading impression, because of the focus on the small number of respondents who had negative impressions of the internal processes. In fact, the survey results show that more than 80 percent of respondents either believed that the DoD OIG's internal processes protected whistleblower confidentiality somewhat or very well, or did not know whether they did so. Only 14 percent of respondents expressed a belief that internal processes did not protect confidentiality or did so only slightly.

We also believe the portions of the report addressing restrictions on DoD OIG employee access to sensitive whistleblower information needs further context. The report referred to a lack of cross-directorate access controls within the DoD OIG's Administrative Investigations (AI) Directorate – including the DoD Hotline, the Investigations of Senior Officials unit, and Whistleblower Reprisal Investigations unit. However, it is important to note that while some records, for a period of time, may have been accessible to DoD OIG employees within those AI units who were not working on the particular matter, and the DoD Office of General Counsel and Office of Professional Responsibility, there is no evidence that any person without a need to know actually accessed any records containing sensitive whistleblower information. To be clear, no one outside the DoD OIG – or even outside AI, the DoD Office of General Counsel, or the DoD OIG Office of Professional Responsibility – had access to any of those records.

Further, it is important to note that all the instances of potential accessibility noted by GAO were first identified by DoD OIG employees, and that when the DoD OIG became aware of such issues it took corrective action to resolve the potential access issue. In one instance, for example, an error in the management of system permissions for SharePoint, which created an accessibility issue, was resolved approximately 48 hours after an AI leader first brought the error to systems administrators' attention. When system administrators corrected the error, they also locked all users out of the SharePoint to avoid unintentional access within the OIG to any protected records.

Most important, as noted above, there is no evidence that anyone without a need to know ever accessed any of these records. The GAO's report – and particularly the report's Highlights – do not make this point as clearly as it could.

DoD OIG Response to GAO Recommendations

Finally, as noted above, we concur with the GAO's recommendations and will seek to implement them in a timely manner. We believe they will help us to continue our substantial improvements to the whistleblower protection program and our handling of whistleblower complaints.

If you have any questions, please contact me or David A. Core, Associate General Counsel.

Sincerely,

Glenn A. Fine
Principal Deputy Inspector General
Performing the Duties of Inspector General

DEPARTMENT OF THE ARMY
OFFICE OF THE INSPECTOR GENERAL
1700 ARMY PENTAGON
WASHINGTON, DC 20310-1700

SAIG-AC

14 January 2019

MEMORANDUM FOR Department of Defense Office of Inspector General, ATTN: David A. Core, Associate General Counsel, 4800 Mark Center Drive, Alexandria, VA 22350-1500

SUBJECT: U.S. Army Inspector General Response to the Government Accountability Office Draft Report, "Whistleblower Protection", dated January 2019

1. We reviewed the draft report and concur with the findings presented. However, we would like to provide additional background regarding two areas of interest.

2. The Government Accountability Office (GAO) noted timeliness of complaint resolution is a challenge across the Department of Defense. We agree. Over the last five years, the United States Army Inspector General Agency (USAIGA) invested significant resources to achieve improvements in case throughput and timeliness of case resolution. We reduced the whistleblower reprisal (WBR) case load by over 40% from 472 non-senior WBR cases in August 2016 to 278 cases as of 10 January 2019. While the draft report noted some actions to address timeliness of complaint notifications to the Department of Defense Inspector General (DoDIG), we are also working on several additional initiatives to include education, training, doctrinal refinements, escalation strategies, and increased leader emphasis. Additionally, we collaboratively made specific recommendations pending implementation in the DoDIG led High Level Working Group.

3. The second area of interest concerns access to IG records within the Army Inspector General database of record, IGARS. While the draft report indicates individuals could have access to sensitive information pertaining to cases where they may not have a need-to-know or involving complaints pertaining to inspectors general (IGs), the report did not identify the existing policy and procedural safeguards in place within the Army to minimize inappropriate access to such information. For example, most IGs are only granted access to IGARS after being centrally trained and credentialed. Moreover, access is only granted through an IG leader driven process ultimately approved at the USAIGA level. Our policies and procedures achieve the appropriate balance between limiting access and enhancing case processing efficiency. Most unit level IG offices are not robustly manned; most have less than ten personnel and some are as small as two personnel. Because each IG team member may be required to assist with any case within an office, we authorize IGs access to cases within their office. At higher levels, such as this headquarters level, IGs have greater access but only in accordance with established guidelines, appropriate authorization, and that which is necessary to perform assigned duties. In the event of an allegation against an IG, the IG's Directing Authority (Commander) and several USAIGA senior leaders, to include The Inspector General, are involved in the decision making process that reviews the circumstances and decides whether to suspend or remove that individual's access to IG records. While it is possible that an IG could inappropriately access information, the processes in place provide judicious access and control necessary to achieve an appropriate balance between efficient operations and minimizing risk.

Leslie C. Smith

LESLIE C. SMITH
Lieutenant General, USA
The Inspector General

DEPARTMENT OF THE AIR FORCE
WASHINGTON DC

Office of the Secretary

January 23, 2019

MEMORANDUM FOR DEPARTMENT OF DEFENSE INSPECTOR GENERAL

FROM: SAF/IG

SUBJECT: GAO Draft Report, GAO-19-198

Attached is our response to the GAO Draft Report GAO-19-198, 'WHISTLEBLOWER PROTECTION: Analysis of DoD's Actions to Improved Case Timeliness and Safeguard Confidentiality,' dated December 21, 2019 (GAO Code 101192)."

SAMI D. SAID
Major General, USAF
Deputy Inspector General

GAO DRAFT REPORT DATED DECEMBER 19, 2018
GAO-19-198 (GAO CODE 101192)

"WHISTLEBLOWER PROTECTION: ANALYIS OF DOD'S ACTIONS TO IMPROVE CASE TIMELINESS AND SAFEGUARD CONFIDENTIALITY"

DEPARTMENT OF DEFENSE COMMENTS TO THE GAO RECOMMENDATION

RECOMMENDATION: The Air Force Inspector General should establish procedures to fully reflect and implement DOD policy on the protection of whistleblower confidentiality.

DoD RESPONSE: Air Force Instruction (AFI) 90-301, *Inspector General Complaints Resolution*, 28 Dec 18, Chapter 3 paragraph 3.2.1. states that "At the time the IG receives a complaint, he or she will advise the complainant:

3.2.1.1.2 The Inspector General shall not, after receipt of a complaint or information from an employee, disclose the identity of the employee without the consent of the employee, unless the Inspector General determines such disclosure is unavoidable during the course of the investigation and/or complaint analysis. (T-0).

The language is essentially the same as 5 United States Code Appendix § 7. The "T-0" indicates that no official in the Air Force, at any level, can waive the requirement to inform the complainant of the non-disclosure requirement.

RECOMMENDATION: The Air Force Inspector General should consider interim actions as the whistleblower enterprise case management system is being developed to help ensure that access for users of existing applications is limited to information that is necessary to accomplish assigned tasks in accordance with organizational missions and business functions.

DoD RESPONSE: As noted in the recommendation, the Air Force plans to transition from its case management system to an enterprise case management system being developed by the DoD IG, and therefore no longer funds development its system. Nevertheless, the Air Force IG is exploring the ability of the Air Force Administrative Assistant, Enterprise Business Solutions (the office the maintains the Air Force case management system) to modify the system to more fully limit user access to data.

DEPARTMENT OF THE NAVY
HEADQUARTERS, UNITED STATES MARINE CORPS
3000 MARINE CORPS PENTAGON
WASHINGTON, DC 20350-3000

IN REPLY REFER TO
7510
DMCS-A
15 Jan 19

From: Head, Audit Coordination, Office of the Director, Marine Corps Staff
To: Primary Action Officer, Office of the Inspector General, U.S. Department of Defense

Subj: GAO DRAFT REPORT GAO-19-198, "WHISTLEBLOWER PROTECTION: ANALYSIS OF DOD'S ACTIONS TO IMPROVE CASE TIMELINESS AND SAFEGUARD CONFIDENTIALITY," DATED DECEMBER 21, 2018 (GAO CODE 101192)

Ref: (a) DoDI 7650.02 w/Ch 1, GAO Reviews and Reports
(b) DoD WHS-ESD (GAO Affairs) Memo to DODIG dtd 2 JAN 19

Encl: (1) U.S. Marine Corps Responses

1. Reference (a) requires timely responses to GAO reviews and reports. Reference (b) provided guidance on responding to draft report GAO-19-198.

2. Enclosure (1) provides our comments to the subject draft report for OSD Primary Action Office consideration in its response to GAO.

CHARLES K. DOVE

GAO DRAFT REPORT DATED 21 DECEMBER 2018
GAO-19-198 (101192)

"WHISTLEBLOWER PROTECTION: ANALYSIS OF DOD'S ACTIONS TO IMPROVE CASE TIMELINESS AND SAFEGUARD CONFIDENTIALITY"

U.S. MARINE CORPS COMMENTS
TO GAO RECOMMENDATIONS

GAO is making a total of 12 recommendations to the Department of Defense (DOD). The 2 recommendations directed to the Marine Corps are:

RECOMMENDATION 4: The Marine Corps Inspector General should establish procedures to fully reflect and implement DOD policy on the protection of whistleblower confidentiality.

USMC RESPONSE: Inspector General of the Marine Corps (IGMC) concurs. DoD OIG's policy concerning protection of Complainant confidentiality, found in DoD Instruction (DoDI) 7050.01, "DoD Hotline Program," and which applies to all Military Departments, derives from the Inspector General (IG) Act of 1978, Section 7(b):

> The Inspector General shall not, after receipt of a complaint or information from an employee, disclose the identity of the employee without the consent of the employee, unless the Inspector General determines such disclosure is unavoidable during the course of the investigation.

DoD OIG's Office for Administrative Investigations (AI) manual for investigations, dated 29 March 2016, elaborates for cases of whistleblower reprisal:

> Investigators should inform witnesses that the DoD IG is committed to protecting their confidentiality to the maximum extent possible within the law; however, there may be some circumstances when the IG determines that releasing their identity or testimony is necessary or unavoidable. For example, in whistleblower reprisal cases it will be necessary to disclose the name of the whistleblower who is claiming reprisal in order to conduct the investigation.

IGMC's policy follows DoD OIG's guidance. During the complaint intake process and the initial clarification interview with a Complainant, IGMC personnel explain that IGMC never can guarantee confidentiality and that whistleblower reprisal investigations require disclosure of whistleblowers' names in order to conduct the investigation. Unlike other services, IGMC does not task military whistleblower reprisal investigations to personnel in other offices or organizations. Only IGMC investigators conduct military whistleblower reprisal investigations within the Marine Corps (for the rare circumstance when IGMC is conflicted and cannot conduct a certain investigation, a service level Naval IG or DoD OIG investigator do so on IGMC's behalf).

Marine Corps Order (MCO) 5370.8A, "Marine Corps Hotline Program," which is currently under revision, requires IGMC and its lower echelon Command Inspectors General (CIG) to comply with DoDI 7050.01 and DoD Directive (DoDD) 7060.01, "Military Whistleblower Reprisal." IGMC's own written guidance does not specifically address the requirement to protect Complainant confidentiality because DoD publications, which require compliance from all Marine Corps IGs, already articulate the requirement.

IGMC concurs with GAO that technical flaws in IGMC's Case Management System (CMS), which sometimes cause IGMC's protection of whistleblower confidentiality to fail, should never occur, that IGMC must correct the problem, and that IGMC's solution must reflect DoD OIG policy. IGMC will soon be able to implement reliable procedures to restrict access to whistleblower information when IGMC's new database, Case Action Manager (CAM), which is currently in production, becomes active. IGMC previously identified the flaw GAO references in recommendation 11, and included strict information access controls in CAM's functions. IGMC estimates transitioning to CAM during September 2019.

To improve IGMC's compliance with all investigative standards, in December 2018, IGMC hired a GS-15 Director of Investigations, with supervisory authority for all matters related to Marine Corps IG investigations.

RECOMMENDATION 11: The Marine Corps Inspector General should develop a plan to ensure that its redesigned whistleblower management application restricts user access information based on what is needed to accomplish assigned tasks in accordance with organizational missions and business functions.

USMC RESPONSE: IGMC concurs. IGMC's new, custom case management system, CAM, which is currently in production, will restrict user access information based on what is needed to accomplish assigned tasks in accordance with organizational missions and business functions. IGMC estimates transitioning to CAM during September 2019.

C. E. SHELTON
Deputy
Inspector General of the Marine Corps

Appendix VI: Accessible Data

Data Tables

Accessible Data for Figure 2: Timeliness of Fiscal Year 2018 DODIG Senior Official Misconduct Cases Resolved During Intake, Reprisal Intakes, and Oversight Reviews

Category	Days
Senior official intake	17
Military reprisal intake	84
Civilian and contractor reprisal intake	37
Senior official oversight review	18
Reprisal oversight review	12

Accessible Data for Figure 3: Timeliness of Fiscal Year 2018 DODIG Senior Official Misconduct and Reprisal Investigations

Category	Days
Senior official investigations	250
Military/contractor reprisal investigations	541
Civilian reprisal investigations	596

Accessible Data for Figure 4: Timeliness of Fiscal Year 2018 DOD Hotline Referrals and Oversight of Completion Reports

Category	Days
Priority 1 referrals	1
Priority 2 referrals	3
Priority 3 referrals	6
Completion reports	9

Accessible Data for Figure 5: Timeliness of Fiscal Year 2018 Military Service IG Senior Official Misconduct Notifications, Reprisal Notifications, and Reprisal Intake Reviews

Category	Military branch	Average days
Senior official notifications	Air Force	45
Senior official notifications	Army	31
Senior official notifications	Navy	26
Senior official notifications	Marine Corps	8
Reprisal notifications	Air Force	54
Reprisal notifications	Army	84
Reprisal notifications	Navy	17
Reprisal notifications	Marine Corps	23
Reprisal intake reviews	Air Force	280
Reprisal intake reviews	Army	407
Reprisal intake reviews	Navy	208
Reprisal intake reviews	Marine Corps	86

Accessible Data for Figure 6: Timeliness of Military Service IG Senior Official Misconduct and Reprisal Investigations

Category	Military branch	Average days
Senior official investigations	Air Force	247
Senior official investigations	Army	287
Senior official investigations	Navy	318
Senior official investigations	Marine Corps	136
Reprisal investigations	Air Force	476
Reprisal investigations	Army	537
Reprisal investigations	Navy	481
Reprisal investigations	Marine Corps	408

Accessible Data for Figure 8: Disposition of DODIG Closed Misconduct and Reprisal Cases Involving Civilian DOD Presidential Appointees with Senate Confirmation, Fiscal Years 2013–2017

Fiscal year	Dismissed	Investigated -substantiated	Investigated -notsubstantiated
2013	17	0	2
2014	31	2	0
2015	17	0	0
2016	38	0	0
2017	22	0	0

Accessible Data for Figure 9: DODIG Dismissed Misconduct and Reprisal Cases Involving Civilian DOD Presidential Appointees with Senate Confirmation, by Organizational Source, Fiscal Years 2013-2017

Air Force	Army	Defense agency	Marine Corps	Navy	Others
8	21	32	2	25	12

Accessible Data for Figure 10: DODIG Closed Misconduct Case Allegations Involving Civilian DOD Presidential Appointees with Senate Confirmation, by Percentage, Fiscal Years 2013-2017

Category	Percent
Personal Misconduct/Ethical Violations	47
Personnel Matters	14
Other	12
Government Programs/Projects	7
Procurement/Contract Administration	7
Criminal Allegations	3
Government Resources	3
Travel Violations	2
Reprisal	1
Civil Liberties	1
Medical	1
Safety Matters	1
Security	1

In: Whistleblowers
Editor: Isabelle Guertin
ISBN: 978-1-53616-310-0

Chapter 2

INTELLIGENCE COMMUNITY WHISTLEBLOWER PROTECTIONS: IN BRIEF*

Michael E. DeVine

ABSTRACT

Whistleblowing is "the act of reporting waste, fraud, abuse and corruption in a lawful manner to those who can correct the wrongdoing." Intelligence community (IC) whistleblowers are those employees or contractors working in any of the 17 elements of the IC who reasonably believe there has been a violation of law, rule, or regulation; gross mismanagement; waste of resources; abuse of authority; or a substantial danger to public health and safety. The IC has publicly recognized the importance of whistleblowing, and supports protections for whistleblowers who conform to guidelines to protect classified information. The Director of National Intelligence (DNI) whistleblowing policy and guidance is publicly available and specifically addresses the process for making protected disclosures and whistleblower protections for IC contractors, members of the Armed Forces, and federal employees. There are differing opinions, however, on whether the IC's internal

* This is an edited, reformatted and augmented version of Congressional Research Service, Publication No. R45345, dated January 18, 2019.

processes have the transparency necessary to ensure adequate protections against reprisal, and whether protections for IC contractors are sufficient.

IC whistleblower protections have evolved in response to perceptions of gaps that many believed left whistleblowers vulnerable to reprisal. The first whistleblower legislation specific to the IC was limited to specifying a process for IC whistleblowers to make a complaint but offered no specific protections. Subsequent legislation included only general provisions for protecting IC whistleblowers with no additional guidance on standards for implementation. Presidential Policy Directive (PPD)-19, signed in 2012, provided the first specific protections against reprisal actions for making a complaint. The Intelligence Authorization Act for Fiscal Year 2014 codified these provisions, which were further supported with IC implementation policy. Separate legislation under Title 10 of the U.S. Code, along with DOD implementing guidance, provides protections for members of the Armed Forces, including those assigned to elements of the IC. In early 2018, Congress passed legislation to address perceived gaps in protections for IC contractors.

INTRODUCTION

Whistleblowing is "the act of reporting waste, fraud, abuse and corruption in a lawful manner to those who can correct the wrongdoing."[1] Intelligence Community (IC) whistleblowers are those employees or contractors working in any of the 17 elements of the IC who reasonably believe there has been a violation of law, rule, or regulation; gross mismanagement; waste of resources; abuse of authority; or a substantial danger to public health and safety. The essential distinction between whistleblowers generally and those in the IC (or those who otherwise have security clearances) is the concern for protecting classified information that may be involved in an IC-related incident or complaint. The IC has recognized that whistleblowing can save taxpayers' dollars, help ensure an ethical and safe working environment, and enable timely responses for corrective action.

Whistleblowing protections for employees and contractors in the IC are extended only to those who make a lawful disclosure. They do not

[1] Daniel Coats, Director of National Intelligence, "IC Leadership Support," *Introducing IC Whistleblowing*, at https://www.dni.gov/ICIG-Whistleblower/.

cover disclosures that do not conform to statutes and directives prescribing reporting procedures intended to protect classified information, such as leaking to the media or a foreign government. The whistleblower protections do not apply to a difference of opinion over policy, strategy, analysis, or priorities for intelligence funding or collection unless there is a reasonable concern over legality or constitutionality. Whistleblowing protections also do not protect against legitimate adverse personnel or security clearance eligibility decisions if the agency can demonstrate that it would have taken the same action in the absence of a protected disclosure.

Congress and the executive branch have defined in statute and directives procedures for IC whistleblowers to make protected disclosures that also provide for the security of classified information. The Director of National Intelligence (DNI) whistleblowing policy and guidance is publicly available and specifically addresses whistleblower process and protections for IC contractors, members of the Armed Forces, and federal employees.[2] There are differing opinions, however, on whether the IC's internal processes have the transparency necessary to ensure adequate protections against reprisal, and whether protections for IC contractors are sufficient.

IC whistleblower protections have evolved in response to perceptions of gaps that many believed left whistleblowers vulnerable to reprisal. The first whistleblower legislation specific to the IC was the Intelligence Community Whistleblower Protection Act (ICWPA) of 1998. It was limited to specifying a process for an IC whistleblower to make a complaint but offered no specific protections. The Intelligence Authorization Act for Fiscal Year 2010 included provisions for protecting IC whistleblowers, though these were general and subject to different standards of implementation. Presidential Policy Directive (PPD)-19, signed in 2012, provided the first specific protections in response to perceptions that IC whistleblowers remained vulnerable to reprisal actions for making a complaint. The Intelligence Authorization Act for Fiscal Year 2014 codified the PPD-19 provisions and Intelligence Community

---

[2] https://www.dni.gov/ICIG-Whistleblower/process-how.html.

Directive (ICD)-120 established a PPD-19 implementation policy. For members of the Armed Forces assigned to elements of the IC, 10 U.S.C. §1034 provides whistleblower protections. Department of Defense (DOD) implementing guidance for Section 1034 can be found in DOD Directive 7050.06, *Military Whistleblower Protection.* In January 2018, Congress passed P.L. 115-118. Section 110 amended the National Security Act of 1947 and the Intelligence Reform and Terrorism Prevention Act of 2004 to include provisions to address perceived gaps in protections for IC contractors.

INTELLIGENCE COMMUNITY WHISTLEBLOWER PROTECTION ACT (ICWPA) OF 1998

The Intelligence Community Whistleblower Protection Act of 1998 (ICWPA)[3] was intended to assist whistleblowers in the IC who are specifically excluded from the Whistleblower Protection Act of 1989. It should be noted that the ICWPA makes no explicit mention of members of the Armed Forces assigned to an IC element.[4] It amended previous acts of Congress—the Central Intelligence Agency Act of 1949 and the Inspector General Act of 1978—to enable an IC government employee or contractor "who intends to report to Congress a complaint or information with respect to an urgent concern" to report to the Inspector General (IG) of the employee's or contractor's IC agency.[5] Congress noted that the absence of this provision in law previously "may have impaired the flow of information needed by the intelligence committees to carry out oversight

[3] Title VII of the Intelligence Authorization Act for Fiscal Year 1999, P.L. 105-272 §§701-702.

[4] See below in this report. 10 *U.S.C.* §1034 provides whistleblower protections for members of the Armed Forces, including those who may be assigned to an element of the IC.

[5] The ICWPA defines an "urgent concern" as (1) a serious or flagrant problem, abuse, violation of law or executive order, or deficiency relating to the funding, administration, or operations of an intelligence activity involving classified information; (2) a false statement to the Congress on, or willful withholding from the Congress of, an issue of material fact relating to the funding, administration, or operation of an intelligence activity; or (3) an action constituting reprisal in response to an employee's reporting of an urgent concern. See P.L. 105-272, §702(a).

responsibilities."[6] Consequently, the ICWPA defines formal processes for submitting complaints that ensure the protection of classified information that may be involved:

- It requires the IG to report within 14 days all credible complaints to the Director of the CIA or to the head of the establishment who, in turn, is required to report the complaint to the congressional intelligence committees within 7 days.
- In the event the IG does not report the complaint or reports it inaccurately, the employee or contractor has the right to submit the complaint to Congress directly. This may be done (1) after the employee has provided notice to the IG, and (2) after the employee has obtained from the IG procedures for protecting classified information when contacting the congressional intelligence committees.

Although the ICWPA provides a process for IC whistleblowers—employees and contractors—to securely report complaints to Congress via the relevant IC agency IG, it offers no specific provisions for protecting whistleblowers from reprisal or punishment.[7]

INTELLIGENCE AUTHORIZATION ACT (IAA) FOR FISCAL YEAR 2010

The IAA for FY2010 (P.L. 111-259) included the first general provisions for protection of whistleblowers as part of legislation that established the Office of the Inspector General of the Intelligence Community (OIGIC), headed by the Inspector General of the Intelligence

[6] P.L. 105-272, §701.

[7] Subsequent legislation that specifically prohibits actions taken in reprisal for an IC employee making a lawful disclosure (a disclosure that adheres to the 1998 ICWPA process for making a complaint while protecting classified information) underscores the perception that the ICWPA process alone did not constitute a protection for a whistleblower against adverse personnel action.

Community (IGIC). Section 405(a)(1) of the IAA for FY2010 added a new Section 103H to the National Security Act of 1947. Section 103H(g) permitted lawful disclosures to the IGIC, but lacked the specificity of later whistleblower protection legislation and directives:

> (3) The Inspector General [of the Intelligence Community] is authorized to receive and investigate, pursuant to subsection (h), complaints or information from any person concerning the existence of an activity within the authorities and responsibilities of the Director of National Intelligence constituting a violation of laws, rules, or regulations, or mismanagement, gross waste of funds, abuse of authority, or a substantial and specific danger to the public health and safety. Once such complaint or information has been received from an employee of the intelligence community—
>
> (A) the Inspector General shall not disclose the identity of the employee without the consent of the employee, unless the Inspector General determines that such disclosure is unavoidable during the course of the investigation or the disclosure is made to an official of the Department of Justice responsible for determining whether a prosecution should be undertaken; and
>
> (B) no action constituting a reprisal, or threat of reprisal, for making such complaint or disclosing such information to the Inspector General may be taken by any employee in a position to take such actions, unless the complaint was made or the information was disclosed with the knowledge that it was false or with willful disregard for its truth or falsity.[8]

Section 405 does cover contractors in addition to federal employees of IC elements:

> The Inspector General [of the IC] shall have access to any employee, or any employee of a contractor, of any element of the intelligence community needed for the performance of the duties of the Inspector General."[9]

---

[8] 50 *U.S.C.* §3033(g).

[9] 50 *U.S.C.* §3033(g)(2)(B).

> An employee of an element of the intelligence community, an employee assigned or detailed to an element of the intelligence community, or an employee of a contractor to the intelligence community who intends to report to Congress a complaint or information with respect to an urgent concern may report such complaint or information to the Inspector General.[10]

Section 425(d) of the IAA for FY2010 also amended the Central Intelligence Agency Act of 1949 clarifying existing protections against reprisals against CIA employees who make lawful disclosures to the CIA Inspector General.[11]

PRESIDENTIAL POLICY DIRECTIVE (PPD)-19

PPD-19, *Protecting Whistleblowers with Access to Classified Information*, signed by President Obama on October 10, 2012, provided the first executive branch protections for IC whistleblowers. PPD-19 specifically protects some employees in the IC (it specifically excludes members of the Armed Forces)[12] with access to classified information, from personnel actions taken in reprisal for making a lawful disclosure.[13]

PPD-19 defines a protected disclosure in part as follows:

---

[10] 50 *U.S.C.* §3033(k)(5)(A).

[11] P.L. 111-259 §425(d). The provisions for prohibiting reprisal actions for lawful whistleblower disclosures to the CIA Inspector General can be found in 50 U.S.C. §3517(e)(3)(A)-(B).

[12] In addition to excluding members of the Armed Forces, PPD-19 otherwise does not define *employee*, and does not include any reference to IC contractors. To some this is an important omission. The following year, 2013, Edward Snowden, a Booz Allen Hamilton contractor working at the National Security Agency, leaked classified documents to the media claiming there were no protections for someone with his status as a contactor to submit a whistleblowing complaint. The ICWPA of 1998, which provides for a process for submitting a whistleblowing complaint (but does not specify protections against prohibited reprisals), applies to contractors as well as federal IC employees. See Joe Davidson, "No Whistleblower Protections for Intelligence Contractors," *The Washington Post,* June 19, 2013, at https://www.washingtonpost.com/politics/federal_government/no-whistleblower-protections-for-intelligencecontractors/2013/06/19/dc3e1798-d8fa-11e2-a9f2-42ee3912ae0e_story.html?utm_term=.3319c1b46f47.

[13] The Directive pertains to all elements of the IC with the specific exception of the Federal Bureau of Investigation (FBI).

a disclosure of information by the employee to a supervisor in the employee's direct chain of command up to and including the head of the employing agency, to the Inspector General of the employing agency or Intelligence Community Element, to the Director of National Intelligence, to the Inspector General of the Intelligence Community, or to an employee designated by any of the above officials for the purpose of receiving such disclosures, that the employee reasonably believes evidences (i) a violation of any law, rule, or regulation; or (ii) gross mismanagement, a gross waste of funds, an abuse of authority, or a substantial and specific danger to public health or safety.

- PPD-19 prohibits reprisals (1) that could affect a whistleblower's eligibility for access to classified information; or (2) involve a personnel action against the IC employee making a protected disclosure.[14]
- PPD-19 requires IC elements to certify to the DNI a process for IC employees to seek a review of personnel actions the employee believes are in reprisal for making a lawful disclosure. The review process also must provide for the security of classified information involved in a disclosure.
- As part of the review process, PPD-19 requires the IC element Inspector General to determine whether a personnel action was in reprisal for a lawful disclosure. The IG makes recommendations for corrective action in the event of a determination that a violation took place.
- The agency head "shall carefully consider the findings of and actions recommended by the agency Inspector General."[15] The agency head does not have to accept an IG's recommendation for corrective action.
- IC agencies also have to certify to the DNI that the agency has a review process that permits employees to appeal actions involving eligibility for access to classified information that are

---

[14] Adverse personnel actions might include demotion, transfer, termination, suspension, lower performance evaluation or punitive changes in duties and responsibilities.

[15] Presidential Policy Directive (PPD)-19, *Protecting Whistleblowers with Access to Classified Information*, The White House, October 10, 2012, at https://www.va.gov/ABOUT_VA/docs/President-Policy-Directive-PPD-19.pdf.

alleged to be in violation of prohibitions against retaliation for making lawful disclosures.

- PPD-19 allows for a whistleblower to request an external review by an IG panel chaired by the IGIC if the employee has exhausted the agency review process. In the event the panel decides in the employee's favor, the agency must consider but does not have to accept the panel's recommendation for corrective action.
- It requires the IGIC to report annually to the congressional intelligence committees the IG determinations and recommendations and IC element head responses to the determinations and recommendations.
- PDD-19 requires the executive branch to provide training to employees with access to classified information (not including contractors or members of the Armed Forces) regarding protections for whistleblowers.

TITLE VI OF THE INTELLIGENCE AUTHORIZATION ACT (IAA) FOR FISCAL YEAR 2014

Title VI of the FY2014 IAA (P.L. 113-126) codified provisions of PPD-19 and provided the first expansive statutory protections for IC whistleblowers against personnel or security clearance actions made in reprisal for protected disclosures.[16]

- Section 601 of Title VI protected IC whistleblowers from any personnel action made in retaliation for a lawful disclosure.[17] This

[16] The provisions under this legislation cover all IC elements *except* the Intelligence Branch of the Federal Bureau of Investigation (FBI/IB). See 50 *U.S.C.* §3234(a)(2)(B).

[17] The scope of personnel actions covered by the legislation includes an appointment, promotion, disciplinary or corrective action, detail, transfer, reassignment, demotion, suspension, termination, reinstatement or restoration, a performance evaluation, a decision concerning pay, benefits or awards, a decision concerning education or training if such education or training may reasonably be expected to lead to an appointment, promotion, or performance evaluation, or any other significant change in duties, responsibilities or working conditions. See 50 *U.S.C.* §3234(a)(3).

includes a lawful disclosure to the Director of National Intelligence (or any employees designated by the DNI for such purpose), the Inspector General of the Intelligence Community, the head of the employing agency (or an employee designated by the head of that agency for such purpose), the appropriate inspector general of the employing agency, and a congressional intelligence committee, or a member of a congressional intelligence committee.

- Section 601 of Title VI made no specific mention of protections for contractors, however.
- A lawful disclosure is defined in the legislation as a disclosure that an IC employee whistleblower reasonably believes is a violation of "Federal law, rule or regulation ... or mismanagement, a gross waste of funds, an abuse of authority, or substantial and specific danger to public health and safety."
- Section 602 of Title VI provided protections against retaliatory revocation of the security clearance of a covered government employee whistleblower for making a lawful disclosure.[18]
- Section 602 also requires the development of *appeal* policies and procedures for any decision affecting a whistleblower's security clearance that the whistleblower alleges is in reprisal for having made a protected disclosure. This provision also enabled the whistleblower to retain his/her current employment status in the government, pending the outcome of the appeal.[19]
- Section 602 of Title VI did not permit judicial review, nor does it permit a private right of action.[20]
- Section 602 of Title VI does not make any mention of contractors.

[18] 50 *U.S.C.* §3341(j). Coverage for this legislation on protections against retaliatory revocation of security clearances includes all elements of the IC—including the FBI/IB—in addition to other Executive Branch departments and agencies. It makes no mention of members of the Armed Forces who might be assigned to an IC element.

[19] 50 *U.S.C.* §3341(b)(7).

[20] A private right of action would permit an individual to bring a lawsuit.

INTELLIGENCE COMMUNITY DIRECTIVE (ICD)-120

First signed in 2014, and updated on April 29, 2016, ICD-120, *Intelligence Community Whistleblower Protection*, provides IC implementing guidance for PPD-19. ICD-120 provisions include the following:

- Protections against reprisal involving a personnel action against the IC employee making a protected disclosure.[21] ICD-120 excludes members of the Armed Forces, and makes no reference to contractors.[22]
- Protections from reprisal for a protected disclosure that could affect an IC whistleblower's eligibility for access to classified information.[23] This provision includes contractors and members of the Armed Forces.
- A requirement for each IC element to have a review process to permit appeals for any decision involving a security clearance allegedly in retribution for making a lawful disclosure. The provision allows the whistleblower to maintain his/her employment status while a decision is pending.
- Provision for an employee alleging a reprisal who has exhausted the internal agency review process to request an External Review Panel chaired by the IGIC.
- A requirement for IC-wide communications and training on whistleblower protections.

---

[21] The ICD-120 provision protecting against personnel actions made in retaliation for a lawful disclosure covers all elements of the IC with the specific exception of the FBI. See ICD-120(E)(1)(d), at https://www.dni.gov/files/documents/ICD/ICD%20120%20-%20IC%20Whistleblower%20Protection%20(29%20Apr%202016).pdf.

[22] See ICD-120(E)(1)(b)(4). Protections for members of the Armed Forces against personnel actions made in reprisal for a lawful disclosure are covered by 10 U.S.C. §1034. See below, Whistleblower Protections for Members of the Armed Forces Assigned to the IC.

[23] "Employee" is defined to include a person "employed by, detailed or assigned to" an IC element including members of the Armed Forces, an expert or consultant to an agency, a contractor, licensee, certificate holder or grantee of an agency, or personal services contractor, or "any other category of person who acts for or on behalf of an agency as determined by the appropriate agency head." See ICD-120(F)(1)(b)(1).

Whistleblower Protections for Members of the Armed Forces Assigned to the IC

Section 1034 of Title 10 *U. S. Code* provides protections against personnel actions taken in retaliation for protected communications by members of the Armed Forces.[24] The Office of the DNI cites this statute as applicable to members of the Armed Forces assigned to the IC elements.[25] Section 1034—unlike the ICWPA, which makes no mention of applicability to the Armed Forces—does not provide a process for making a protected communication that also protects classified information. Section 1034

- allows members of the Armed Forces to communicate with a Member or Members of Congress; an Inspector General; a member of the DOD audit, inspection, investigation, or law enforcement organization; any person or organization in the chain of command; a court-martial proceeding; or any other organization designated pursuant to regulations or other established administrative procedures for such communications; or testimony, or otherwise participating in or assisting in an investigation or proceeding involving Congress or an Inspector General;
- specifies prohibited personnel actions in reprisal for a member of the Armed Forces making a protected communication;[26]

---

[24] This statute uses the term *communication* instead of *disclosure*.

[25] See Office of the Director of National Intelligence, "What Are My Protections?" at https://www.dni.gov/ICIGWhistleblower/protected.html. See also DOD Directive 7050.06, *Military Whistleblower Protection*, April 17, 2015.

[26] 10 *U.S.C.* §1034(b)(2)(A) states the following: The actions considered for purposes of this section to be a personnel action prohibited by this subsection shall include any action prohibited by paragraph (1), including any of the following: (i) The threat to take any unfavorable action. (ii) The withholding, or threat to withhold, any favorable action. (iii) The making of, or threat to make, a significant change in the duties or responsibilities of a member of the armed forces not commensurate with the member's grade. (iv) The failure of a superior to respond to any retaliatory action or harassment (of which the superior had actual knowledge) taken by one or more subordinates against a member. (v) The conducting of a retaliatory investigation of a member.

- enables the DOD to take action to mitigate hardship for an Armed Forces member following a preliminary finding concerning an alleged reprisal for a protected communication;[27]
- requires the inspector general conducting an investigation into a protected communication to provide periodic updates to Congress, the whistleblower, the Secretary of Defense, and the relevant service;[28] and
- requires the DOD Inspector General to prescribe uniform standards for (1) investigations of allegations of prohibited personnel actions, and (2) training for staffs of Inspectors General on the conduct of such investigations.[29]

LEGISLATION TO ADDRESS PERCEIVED GAPS IN PROTECTIONS FOR IC CONTRACTORS

Coverage of contractors in existing IC whistleblower protection legislation is inconsistent. The ICWPA of 1998, which provides for a process for reporting a whistleblower complaint, does cover contractors, as do protections in Section 405 of the IAA for FY2010, and Title VI of the IAA of 2014. However, PPD-19 and ICD-120 do not mention contractors. There have been three subsequent efforts in Congress to address the gap in perceived coverage, culminating on January 19, 2018, when Congress passed P.L. 115-118, an amendment to the Foreign Intelligence

---

[27] 10 *U.S.C.* §1034(c)(4)(E).

[28] 10 *U.S.C.* §1034(e)(3)(A).

[29] 10 *U.S.C.* §1034, note ("Uniform Standards for Inspector General Investigations of Prohibited Personnel Actions and Other Matters"). The National Defense Authorization Act (NDAA) for Fiscal Year 2017 also required the Comptroller General of the United States to review the integrity of the DOD whistleblower protection program and report to the Senate and House Armed Services Committees no later than 18 months after the date of enactment of the NDAA on whether the program satisfies Executive Branch whistleblower protection policy. See P.L. 114-328 §536(a)-(b). Department of Defense (DOD) implementing guidance for 10 *U.S.C.* §1034 can be found in DOD Directive 7050.06, *Military Whistleblower Protection.*

Surveillance Act of 1978, which included Section 110 provisions to address perceived gaps in protections for IC contractors.

S. 2002, 115th Congress, Ensuring Protections for IC Contractor Whistleblowers Act of 2017

Senator McCaskill introduced S. 2002 on October 24, 2017. It was referred to the Senate Select Committee on Intelligence (SSCI) and no further action was taken. S. 2002 would have provided protections for IC employees—to include applicants, former employees, contractors, personal services contractors, and subcontractors—from being "discharged, demoted, or otherwise discriminated against" as a consequence of making a protected disclosure. It also included provisions for a process for making a complaint.

S. 794, 114th Congress, a Bill to Extend Whistleblower Protections for Defense Contractor Employees of Contractors of the Elements of the IC

On March 18, 2015, Senator McCaskill introduced S. 794. It was referred to the SSCI and no further action was taken. The bill would have amended Section 2409 of Title 10 *U.S. Code* by extending protections for contractor employees on a contract with DOD or other federal agencies to contractor employees on a contract with an IC element who comply with an existing lawful process for making a whistleblower complaint, to include protection of classified information that is part of a court action.[30]

---

[30] 10 *U.S.C.* §2409(e)(1) currently excludes contractor employees of IC elements. See Joe Davidson, "No Whistleblower Protections for Intelligence Contractors," *The Washington Post*, June, 19, 2013, at https://www.washingtonpost.com/politics/federal_government/no-whistleblower-protections-for-intelligencecontractors/2013/06/19/dc3e1798-d8fa-11e2-a9f2-42ee3912ae0e_story.html?utm_term=.3319c1b46f47.

Section 110 of P.L. 115-118, Whistleblower Protections for Contractors of the Intelligence Community

On January 19, 2018, Congress passed P.L. 115-118, an amendment to the Federal Intelligence Surveillance Act of 1978. Section 110 amended Section 1104 of the National Security Act of 1947 by providing protections for IC contractor whistleblowers.[31] Section 110 amended existing whistleblower protections to enable IC *contractors* to make lawful disclosures to the head of the contracting agency (or an employee designated by the head of that agency for such purpose), or to the appropriate inspector general of the contracting agency, as well as to the DNI, IGIC, and the congressional intelligence committees (or members of the committees). These protections are similar to those for IC employees under Title VI of the IAA for FY2014 (P.L. 113-126). That legislation, however, included no provisions for contractors.

Section 110 provides unambiguous protections for IC contractors making a lawful complaint against any retaliatory personnel action involving an appointment, promotion/demotion, disciplinary or corrective action, detail, transfer or reassignment, suspension, termination, reinstatement, performance evaluation, decisions concerning pay, benefits, awards, education, or training. The protections extend to lawful complaints involving,

> a violation of any Federal law, rule or regulation (including with respect to evidence of another employee or contractor employee accessing or sharing classified information without authorization); or gross mismanagement, a gross waste of funds, an abuse of authority, or a substantial and specific danger to public health or safety.[32]

---

[31] P.L. 115-118, §110.

[32] 50 U.S.C. §3234(c)(1)(A)-(B). The previous paragraph of §3234 governing lawful disclosures by IC agency employees differs from that for the paragraph for contractor employees only in one word: Contractor employees may disclose "*gross* mismanagement" while agency employees may disclose "mismanagement."

These protections extend to contractors of the FBI—including contractors of the IC element of FBI, the Intelligence Branch—similar to the protections for IC employees and contractors under the Section 3234 of Title 50, *U.S. Code,* as amended.[33]

Section 110 also amended Section 3341(j) of Title 50, *U.S. Code,* to include protections for IC contractors who make lawful whistleblower disclosures against retaliatory revocation of their security clearances.

Resources to Enhance Whistleblower Investigations

H. Amdt. 894, 113th Congress, to the DOD Appropriations Act for Fiscal Year 2015 (H.R. 4870), was agreed by a voice vote on June 18, 2014, redirecting $2 million dollars to fund the IC Whistleblower and Source Protection Directorate. This directorate exists within the OIGIC. The funds, which augmented the Intelligence Community Management Account, were to support the hiring of investigators and support staff to provide the IGIC greater ability to investigate fraud, waste, and abuse. Although it does not provide protections for whistleblowers per se, the measure addressed an underfunded capability in order to enable responsive follow-up on whistleblower complaints.[34]

---

[33] See §110(b)(1)-(5) of P.L. 115-118.

[34] See Department of Defense Appropriations Act for Fiscal Year 2015 (H.R. 4870, 113th Cong.), Title VII, Amendment Offered by Mr. Holt, pp. H5466-H5467.

In: Whistleblowers
Editor: Isabelle Guertin
ISBN: 978-1-53616-310-0

Chapter 3

SUPREME COURT INTERPRETS DODD-FRANK WHISTLEBLOWER PROTECTIONS: IMPLICATIONS FOR SECURITIES LAW AND BEYOND*

Nicole Vanatko

On February 21, 2018, the Supreme Court decided in *Digital Realty Trust, Inc. v. Somers* that the anti-retaliation protections in the Dodd-Frank Wall Street Reform and Consumer Protection Act of 2010 (Dodd-Frank) apply only to whistleblowers who report suspected securities law violations to the Securities and Exchange Commission (SEC or Commission). In so doing, the Court rejected a more expansive reading of Dodd-Frank that would have extended its whistleblower protections to those who report securities violations internally within their organization and suffer retaliation, even if they did not take the additional step of reporting to the SEC. The ruling not only has potentially important

* This is an edited, reformatted and augmented version of Congressional Research Service Publication No. LSB10093, dated March 8, 2018.

implications for the nature and quantity of potential whistleblower actions brought under federal securities law, but *Digital Realty* also provides broader insights into the Supreme Court's current approach toward statutory interpretation.

The details of the *Digital Realty* case and the circuit court split leading up to the Court's review are discussed in a prior Sidebar. In short, the respondent Somers argued that Dodd-Frank whistleblower protections applied to his reports of suspected securities law violations to upper management at Digital Realty, even though he only reported internally and not to the SEC. While the Sarbanes-Oxley Act of 2002 (SOX) already affords employees certain anti-retaliation protections for internal reporting, Dodd-Frank provides more generous protections for "whistleblowers," including the ability to file suit directly in federal district court without first exhausting an administrative process, a longer statute of limitations, and recovery of double back-pay with interest. *Digital Realty* hinged on whether Dodd-Frank protects a narrower class of individuals than SOX based on Dodd-Frank's definition of the term "whistleblower." The relevant section of Dodd-Frank defines a "whistleblower" as "any individual who provides . . . information relating to a violation of the securities laws *to the Commission*." However, setting up the parties' dispute, Dodd-Frank's anti-retaliation provision also prohibits an employer from discriminating against a "whistleblower" who, among other things, makes "disclosures that are required or protected under" SOX. Because SOX, in turn, protects internal reporting, Somers argued that the Dodd-Frank provision encompassed internal reporters as well.

The Supreme Court unanimously held that the definition of "whistleblower" provided "an unequivocal answer" that resolved the case, affirming the principle that "[w]hen a statute includes an explicit definition, we must follow that definition." The Court distinguished the case from prior instances in which it did not hold a statutory definition to control because, unlike those cases, the results here would not be incongruous with Congress's regulatory scheme. Namely, the Court emphasized several times throughout its opinion that the purpose of the enhanced whistleblower provision was "to motivate people who know of securities law violations *to tell the SEC*," quoting a Senate Report regarding Dodd-Frank. Moreover, the Court rejected Somers's arguments that requiring reporting to the SEC to qualify as a "whistleblower" would lead to results incompatible with Congress's intent. For example, the Court reasoned that the Dodd-Frank anti-retaliation provision's reference to SOX would still be meaningful under the narrower definition because it would protect those who report *both* internally and to the SEC, but incur retaliation for the internal report. The Court observed that such a scenario may in fact be commonplace because, as data from the SEC presented to the Court showed, approximately 80% of those receiving SEC whistleblower awards in 2016 had indeed reported internally before making their complaints to the SEC.

The ultimate impact of *Digital Realty's* more narrow scope for Dodd-Frank's whistleblower provisions is unclear. In supporting the petitioner's arguments in *Digital Realty*, notable *amici* like the U.S. Chamber of Commerce favored the narrower whistleblower definition because, in their view, an expansive definition encompassing internal reporters would have allowed for a greater quantity of costly whistleblower suits to be filed against companies in federal court, while spurning internal and administrative processes set up by SOX. However, commentators have also noted that the Court's ruling may have the practical effect of incentivizing whistleblowers to report complaints directly to the SEC instead of attempting resolutions to complaints internally, potentially leading to increased regulatory action and greater costs for companies.

Digital Realty also provides several statutory interpretation takeaways. In addition to affirming the importance of a statute's definitions section, as noted above, the *Digital Realty* decision also presented an opportunity for the Supreme Court to revisit—and differ on—the propriety of considering legislative history when interpreting statutory language. While concurring that the "whistleblower" definition controlled the outcome of the case, Justice Thomas, joined by Justices Alito and Gorsuch, wrote separately regarding their disagreement with the Court opinion's reliance on the Senate Report in interpreting the definition of whistleblower. Rather, they "join[ed] the Court's opinion only to the extent it relies on the text of

Dodd-Frank," elaborating that the language of a statute enacted by Congress should ultimately control, rather than potentially unreliable documents explaining congressional intent. Justice Sotomayor, on the other hand, authored another concurring opinion, joined by Justice Breyer, in which she stressed that it is appropriate to look to legislative history as an interpretive aid, "even when, as here, a statute's meaning can clearly be discerned from its text," in order to confirm and enhance the Court's understanding of the language. In these respects, the *Digital Realty* case has potentially broad import for Congress in considering how courts may view statutory definitions and legislative history.

In: Whistleblowers
Editor: Isabelle Guertin
ISBN: 978-1-53616-310-0

Chapter 4

WHISTLEBLOWERS: KEY PRACTICES FOR CONGRESS TO CONSIDER WHEN RECEIVING AND REFERRING INFORMATION*

United States Government Accountability Office

ABBREVIATIONS

CIGIE	Council of the Inspectors General on Integrity and Efficiency
IG	Inspectors General
OSC	Office of Special Counsel
MSPB	Merit Systems Protection Board

* This is an edited, reformatted and augmented version of United States Government Accountability Office; Report to Congressional Requesters, Publication No. GAO-19-432, dated May 2019.

WHY GAO DID THIS STUDY

Federal whistleblowers—employees who report violations of law, agency mismanagement or ethical violations—help to safeguard the federal government against waste, fraud, and abuse. Whistleblowers can report to various entities, including the Congress. While these reports are a key source of information for federal oversight, whistleblowers can risk reprisal. Therefore, it is important to appropriately handle whistleblowers' information and identity.

The House Committee on Appropriations Report 115-696 included a provision for GAO to identify congressional avenues, resources, and best practices for working with whistleblowers. This chapter describes (1) how the Congress receives whistleblower information, (2) the policies and training currently available to congressional staff, and (3) key practices that the Congress could consider for receiving and referring information from whistleblowers. GAO interviewed congressional staff, officials from the Office of Special Counsel (OSC) and the Council of the Inspectors General on Integrity and Efficiency (CIGIE), and selected advocacy groups that have experience working with whistleblowers. GAO analyzed congressional websites and queried congressional staff regarding policies and training on whistleblowers for congressional staff. To develop key practices, GAO reviewed literature, existing procedures, and standards.

GAO is not making recommendations, but is available to assist the Congress with practices for working with whistleblowers. OSC and CIGIE provided technical comments that were incorporated as appropriate.

WHAT GAO FOUND

The Congress receives whistleblower information in multiple ways. Congressional staff and advocacy groups said whistleblowers who contact the Congress typically reach out to oversight committees, the offices of their own representatives or senators, or authorizing committees. Congressional staff said some whistleblowers contact and work with multiple congressional offices simultaneously. Congressional office websites GAO reviewed included contact information to provide whistleblowers with multiple options for reporting suspected wrongdoing, including email links, hotlines, and web-based forms.

Congressional staff can access resources for guidance on working with whistleblowers including congressional advice and internal training on oversight, committee-specific training related to handling whistleblower cases, and training from external advocacy groups on techniques for working with whistleblowers. Staff from several committees said direct experience is important for building skills to effectively work with whistleblowers.

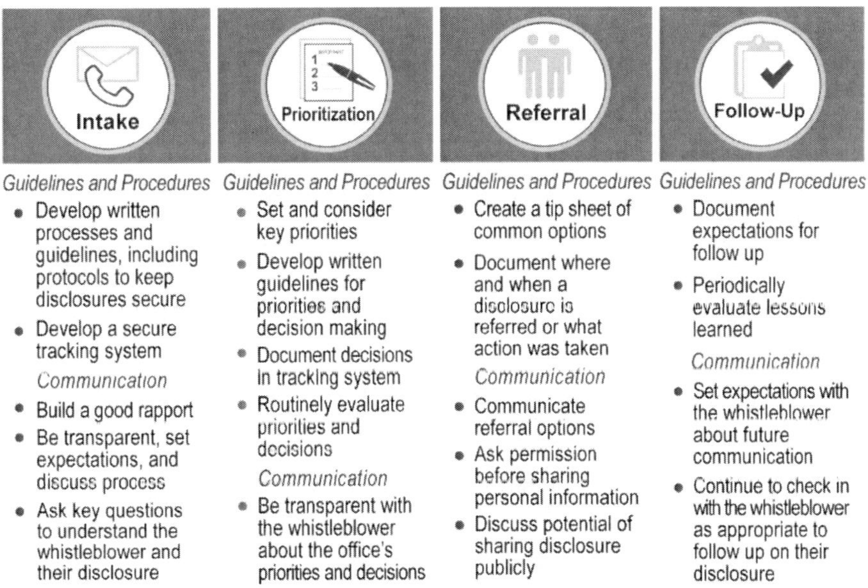

Source: GAO analysis of academic literature, applicable internal controls, and existing procedures and standards. | GAO-19-432

Key Practices for Congressional Staff to Consider When Working with Federal Whistleblowers.

GAO identified key practices the Congress could consider when receiving and referring whistleblower information to other committees and federal agencies. These practices can serve as a resource for congressional offices and staff to intake, prioritize, refer, and follow-up with whistleblowers who contact their office or committee. For each step, GAO identified practices to help offices develop guidelines and procedures as well as for communication, including key questions staff can ask the whistleblower.

May 7, 2019

The Honorable Tim Ryan
Chairman

The Honorable Jaime Herrera Beutler
Ranking Member
Subcommittee on the Legislative Branch
Committee on Appropriations
House of Representatives

Federal whistleblowers—employees who report violations of law, or agency mismanagement or ethical violations—help to safeguard the federal government against waste, fraud, and abuse. Whistleblowers can report this type of information—called a disclosure—to various entities. These disclosures are a key source of information for the Congress in its oversight of the federal government. Whistleblowers' willingness to come forward holds the potential to improve government operations, but these individuals can risk reprisals, such as demotion, reassignment, or termination as a result of their disclosures. To ensure these valuable disclosures continue, it is important to appropriately handle whistleblowers' information and identity.

Federal laws protect current and former federal employees and applicants for federal employment from adverse personnel actions related to whistleblowing. Federal employees may become whistleblowers by disclosing information to the Congress or multiple federal and non-governmental entities including Inspectors General (IG), the Office of

Special Counsel (OSC), and the press. Federal law also provides certain whistleblower protections to contractors and grantees.

House Report 115-696 included a provision for us to identify congressional avenues, resources, and best practices for the Congress in working with whistleblowers.[1] This chapter describes (1) the ways in which whistleblowers can report information to the Congress, (2) the policies and training currently available to congressional staff on working with whistleblowers, and (3) key practices that the Congress could consider for receiving and referring information from whistleblowers.

Our work for all objectives focused on civilian federal employees (current employees, former employees, and applicants for federal employment), contractors, subcontractors and grantees. Our findings do not apply to servicemembers or employees who are part of the intelligence community as their options for disclosing, available protections, and recourse options differ.[2] Our work applies to congressional staff working with employees making any type of protected disclosure, whether or not they have made this disclosure elsewhere or if any related actions, including reprisals, have occurred.

For all objectives, we interviewed congressional staff, executive officials, and advocacy groups. Consistent with the government-wide scope of our engagement, we interviewed staff from three congressional oversight committee offices about their experiences working with whistleblowers across the government. We also interviewed staff from the office of a member of the House Whistleblower Protection Caucus, OSC, and the Council of the Inspectors General on Integrity and Efficiency (CIGIE) on their procedures for and experiences with working with whistleblowers. We interviewed representatives of the Project on Government Oversight, the Government Accountability Project, and the

---

[1] H.R. Rep No. 115-696 (2018).

[2] Military servicemembers are protected by the Military Whistleblower Protection Act, 10 U.S.C. § 1034. Intelligence community officials are protected by the Intelligence Community Whistleblower Protection Act of 1998, Pub. L. 105-272 (1998). See GAO, *Whistleblower Protection: Opportunities Exist for DOD to Improve the Timeliness and Quality of Civilian and Contractor Reprisal Investigations*, GAO-17-506 (Washington, D.C.: September 29, 2017); and *Whistleblower Protection, DOD Needs to Enhance Oversight of Military Whistleblower Reprisal Investigations,* GAO-15-477 (Washington, D.C.: May 7, 2015).

National Whistleblower Center on their experiences working with whistleblowers. We selected these advocacy organizations based on the suggestions of staff from executive agencies and congressional committees that work with whistleblowers, as well as organizations consulted in our past work on whistleblowing.

To describe the ways in which whistleblowers might report information to the Congress, we used a web-scraping program to identify congressional websites with terms related to whistleblowing (e.g., "whistleblower," "whistle blow," "blow the whistle," "whistleblower hotline," and "whistleblower tipline"), reviewed the content of the identified websites to verify relevance, and analyzed the results to determine methods available for potential whistleblowers to report information.[3] To supplement this analysis, we performed similarly structured searches using online search engines to identify congressional websites with whistleblower terms. To identify any additional ways in which whistleblowers may report information to the Congress, we also queried selected congressional staff on the ways in which whistleblowers contact their offices.

To describe the policies and training available to congressional staff on working with whistleblowers, we asked the staff for congressional committees that also provide support for congressional staff—the House Committee on Rules, Committee on House Administration, Senate Committee on Rules and Administration, House Committee on Ethics and Senate Select Committee on Ethics, and House and Senate Counsel—for any information on training they provide to congressional staff on working with whistleblowers. To identify the resources currently provided to congressional staff on interacting with whistleblowers, we interviewed the House Office of General Counsel, the Senate Select Committee on Ethics, the Congressional Research Service, the Project on Government Oversight and the Government Accountability Project about training they provide to congressional staff.

---

[3] "Web-scraping" refers to the automated process of discovering web pages and copying them for subsequent analysis.

To develop key practices for congressional staff working with whistleblowers, we reviewed IG and OSC procedures, our prior work, and our interviews with advocacy groups and congressional staff. We conducted a literature review to ensure that our key practices incorporated applicable academic and government research and findings. Our literature review included searches of several academic, literature, and government sources, such as ProQuest, Scopus, and DIALOG, for articles or studies published from January 1, 2008, to August 2018.[4] We supplemented these searches with a web search.[5] One analyst reviewed the results to identify relevant articles and a second analyst reviewed these determinations. To analyze and summarize the results of the literature search, one analyst used a data collection instrument to review each relevant article, document information relevant to our objectives, and identify key themes to inform our key practices. A second reviewer then reviewed this analysis.

Using these multiple sources, we identified key practices[6] that align with internal controls and could inform congressional office policies and guidelines.[7] For each step that we identified, we considered relevant internal controls, such as clear and transparent internal and external communication, implementation of policies, and evaluation of existing policies and procedures to identify risks and assess their effect on achieving the defined objectives of the office. To ensure the applicability of our draft key practices, we requested that current and former

---

[4] The search focused on articles using several combinations of relevant key words such as variants of "whistleblow," "disclose," and "report" with terms such as "government," "department," "agency," "official," or "federal." We conducted a second search on potential best practices or policies in whistleblowing management in the public sector. Whistleblowing and related terms were searched, as well as terms such as "best," "leading," and "practices." This search included the databases above, as well as the Harvard Kennedy School Think Tank Search tool, Lexis CQ hearing transcripts and ProQuest Congressional, and internet searches of government websites. We retrieved 25 academic and 79 grey literature results from the second search. Grey literature comprises documents produced by government, academia, business, and industry in print and electronic formats that are protected by intellectual property rights, but not controlled by commercial publishers.

[5] This search included ".org" sites using "whistleblower" and "best practices" or "leading practices."

[6] We did not assess existing policies and guidelines to determine the extent to which they applied these practices.

[7] GAO, *Standards for Internal Control in the Federal Government*, GAO-14-704G (Washington: D.C.: September 2014).

congressional staff and executive officials review the identified practices and provide feedback on their validity and potential usefulness. These officials included those that we had previously interviewed or were referred to by those we interviewed due to their experience working with whistleblowers.

We conducted our work from July 2018 to May 2019 in accordance with all sections of GAO's Quality Assurance Framework that are relevant to our objectives. The framework requires that we plan and perform the engagement to obtain sufficient and appropriate evidence to meet our stated objectives and to discuss any limitations in our work. We believe that the information and data obtained, and the analysis conducted, provide a reasonable basis for any findings and conclusions in this product.

BACKGROUND

How is the Term "Whistleblower" Defined?

In this chapter, we use the term whistleblower more broadly than it is defined by the Whistleblower Protection Act.[8] Our definition of whistleblower includes any federal employee, contractor, or grantee who discloses suspected wrongdoing—regardless of reprisal status or nature of their disclosure. To trigger whistleblower protections under the Whistleblower Protection Act, the disclosure must be a contributing factor to an adverse personnel action, commonly called a reprisal. The act, which covers certain federal employees, defines personnel actions to include effects on performance evaluations or significant changes in working conditions.[9]

---

[8] 5 U.S.C. § 2302(c).

[9] Employees exempted from competitive service because of their policy-making character are not protected by the Whistleblower Protection Act. Additionally, employees at the U.S. Postal Service, GAO, and intelligence agencies are not protected by the act. Federal law designates 12 personnel actions. See 5 U.S.C. 2302 § (a)(2)(A)(i)-(xii).

Table 1. Whistleblower Protections for Different Types of Federal Employees, Contractors, and Grantees

Type of employee	Is communication with the Congress protected?	What types of disclosures are protected?	What types of protections are given?	What is the legal basis?
Civilian Federal Employees, Retirees, and Applicants	Yes	Any disclosure an employee reasonably believes evidences a violation of law, rule, or regulation, or evidences gross mismanagement, gross waste of funds, abuse of authority, or a substantial and specific danger to public health.	Protects against prohibited personnel practices including retaliation	Lloyd-LaFollette Act of 1912 5 U.S.C. § 7211, Whistleblower Protection Act, Whistleblower Protection Enhancement Act, CivilService Reform Act of 19785 U.S.C. § 2302
Military Service-members	Yes	Making or preparing to make a lawful communication to a Member of Congress, Inspector General, a member of a Department of Defenseaudit organization, etc., regarding what the servicemember reasonably believes to be evidence of (1) a violation of law or regulation, (2) gross mismanagement, (3) a gross waste of funds, (4) an abuse of authority, or a substantial and specific danger to public health or safety, or a threat by another servicemember or civilian employee or damage to military, federal, or civilian property.	Unfavorable personnel action, including actions such as performance evaluations or disciplinary or other corrective actions	Lloyd-LaFollette Act of 1912 5 U.S.C. § 7211, Military Whistleblower Protection Act of 1988 10. U.S.C. § 1034

Type of employee	Is communication with the Congress protected?	What types of disclosures are protected?	What types of protections are given?	What is the legal basis?
Intelligence Community (employees and contractors)	Yes	Complaints and information to congressional intelligence committees with respect to an "urgent concern," such as a serious or flagrant problem, abuse, violation of law or executive order or deficiency relating to the funding, administration, or operations of an intelligence activity involving classified information, a false statement to or willful withholding from Congress.	Protects against prohibited personnel practices including retaliation when employees report to congressional intelligence committees a complaint or information with respect to an "urgent concern"	Lloyd-LaFollette Act of 1912 5 U.S.C. § 7211 (for federal employees), Intelligence Community Whistleblower Protection Act of 1998, Pub. L. 105-272 Presidential Policy Directive PPD-19 (October 10, 2012) 50 U.S.C. § 3234 5 U.S.C. § 2302(a)(2)(A)
Civilian, Department of Defense, and National Aeronautics and Space Administration Federal Contractors, Subcontractors, and Grantees	Yes	Information that the employee believes is evidence of (1) gross mismanagement of a federal contract or grant, a gross waste of federal funds, an abuse of authority relating to a federal contract or grant, (2) a substantial and specific danger to public health or safety, and (3) a violation of law, rule, or regulation related to a federal contract (including the competition for or negotiation of a contract) or grant.	Provides protection against such actions as demotion and discharge	The National Defense Authorization Act for Fiscal Year 2013 (made permanent in P.L. 114-261 and codified in 41 U.S.C. § 4712 (civilian) and 10 U.S.C. § 2409 (Department of Defense and National Aeronautics and Space Administration))

Source: GAO analysis of applicable legal protections.| GAO-19-432

The act further defines a protected disclosure as any disclosure that an employee reasonably believes evidences "a violation of any law, rule, or regulation" or "gross mismanagement, a gross waste of funds, an abuse of authority, or a substantial and specific danger to public health or safety." Federal laws protecting other types of employees generally have similar definitions for personnel actions and protected disclosures.

What are the Protections for Federal Whistleblowers?

The Civil Service Reform Act of 1978 provided the first whistleblower protections for disclosures of violations of laws, mismanagement, or gross waste of funds for federal employees, former employees, and applicants for employment, among other things.[10] To strengthen protections for those who claim whistleblower retaliation, the Congress passed the Whistleblower Protection Act of 1989. In 2012, the Whistleblower Protection Enhancement Act clarified the scope of protected whistleblowing under the Whistleblower Protection Act and mandated broader outreach to inform certain federal employees of their whistleblower rights, among other things.[11] The No Fear Act requires agencies to notify and train employees, former employees, and applicants of their rights under antidiscrimination and whistleblower protection laws and requires the Office of Personnel Management to report annually on certain topics regarding antidiscrimination and whistleblower protection laws, including disciplinary actions taken for conduct that is inconsistent with these laws.[12] Further, the Dr. Chris Kirkpatrick Whistleblower Act of 2017 enhanced disciplinary penalties for supervisors who engage in whistleblower retaliation.[13] For a summary of protections provided to different types of federal employees, contractors, and grantees, see Table 1.

---

[10] 5 U.S.C. § 2302(b)(8).
[11] Pub. L. No. 112-199, 126 Stat. 1465 (Nov. 27, 2012).
[12] Notification and Federal Employee Antidiscrimination and Retaliation Act of 2002, Pub. L. 107-174 (2002).
[13] Dr. Chris Kirkpatrick Whistleblower Protection Act of 2017. Pub. L. 115-73 (2017).

How Does the Congress Use Information from Whistleblowers As Part of Its Oversight Activities?

Congressional offices conduct oversight of the federal government through congressional hearings, informal contacts with executive officials, staff reports on investigations, and oversight letters to agencies asking for information or urging them to take certain actions. As part of their oversight activities, the Congress also uses studies prepared by others, such as statutory commissions, Inspectors General, and us.

Members of Congress may initiate oversight action using information from a whistleblower that they receive through constituent services. These activities include case work and fielding public comments related to federal policies, programs, and services, including responding to disclosures of suspected wrongdoing from federal employees, contractors, and grantees. Individual congressional offices manage and prioritize their own casework activities, subject to House or Senate rules and relevant laws.

Where Else Can a Federal Whistleblower Turn?

In addition to the Congress, a civilian federal employee, contractor, or grantee can report wrongdoing to other entities. Congressional staff and executive officials told us that whistleblowers often reach out to multiple entities concurrently. Entities that work with whistleblowers have different roles and potential remedies.

- Agency management: Employees can make disclosures to supervisors or management, who may have the ability to take action to address the concern. These disclosures are protected against reprisal, but whistleblowers may fear that they could be demoted, reassigned, or fired as a result of their disclosure.
- Inspectors General (IG): IGs are independent units within agencies that investigate potential fraud, waste, abuse, and mismanagement

in their agency's programs and operations.[14] IGs are to report to both the agency head and the Congress about deficiencies in agency programs and operations, and progress in correcting those deficiencies. The agency IG may make recommendations to the agency head, but cannot require action to be taken. Many IGs are required to designate a Whistleblower Coordinator. The Whistleblower Coordinator is required to educate agency employees about prohibitions on retaliation for protected disclosures and inform employees who have made, or are contemplating making, a protected disclosure of their rights and remedies against retaliation for protected disclosures.[15] IGs are also required to prepare semiannual reports summarizing the activities of the office. Such reports include, among other things, a detailed description of any instance of whistleblower retaliation, including information about the official found to have engaged in retaliation.[16]

- U.S. Office of Special Counsel (OSC): As an independent federal investigative and prosecutorial agency, OSC reviews disclosures from current federal employees, former employees, and applicants for federal employment.[17] If OSC's review determines that there is a substantial likelihood that the types of wrongdoing described above may have occurred, it will refer the allegation to the head of the subject agency for investigation. The subject agency must then report back to OSC on its findings and actions it plans to take as a result of the investigation. OSC then reviews the report to determine if the agency's findings are reasonable and shares it with the whistleblower for comment. OSC then shares the agency

[14] As of 2014, CIGIE reported that there are 72 statutory IG offices across the federal government. Inspector General Act of 1978, Pub. L. 85-452 (1978).

[15] §3(d)(C)(i)-(iii) of the Inspector General Act of 1978, Pub. L. 95-452 (1978), as amended by the Whistleblower Protection Coordination Act, Pub. L. 115-192 (2018).

[16] §5(a)(20) of the Inspector General Act of 1978, Pub. L. 95-452 (1978), as amended by the Whistleblower Protection Coordination Act, Pub. L. 115-192 (2018).

[17] GAO, *Office of Special Counsel: Actions Needed to Improve Processing of Prohibited Personnel Practice and Whistleblower Disclosure Cases*, GAO-18-400 (Washington, D.C.: June 14, 2018).

report, OSC comments or recommendations, and the whistleblower comments with the Executive Office of the President and the chairmen and ranking members of the congressional committees with oversight responsibilities for the agency. OSC also sends the agency and the whistleblower a closure letter and posts the case information on OSC's public website.[18] If a reprisal has occurred, an employee can make an allegation that a prohibited personnel practice has occurred. OSC then investigates and can seek a stay, corrective actions, or disciplinary actions.

- Merit Systems Protection Board (MSPB): An independent federal agency, MSPB considers certain allegations from federal employees who believe they have experienced retaliatory personnel actions in response to making a protected disclosure.[19] When an employee is subject to a personnel action, such as a reassignment with no reduction in pay or grade, and claims that the action was taken because of whistleblowing or other covered protected activity, the employee can appeal to MSPB only after filing a complaint with OSC and if OSC does not seek corrective action on the individual's behalf. Certain personnel actions—such as a removal, demotion, or suspension of more than 14 days due to claims of whistleblowing are directly appealable to MSPB, rather than first exhausting the OSC process. If MSPB determines the appeal is under its jurisdiction, an administrative judge will review both the appealable matter and the claim of reprisal. The employee may appeal the administrative judge's decision to the three-Member board of MPSB or to the U.S. Court of Appeals.[20]
- GAO's FraudNet: FraudNet is a component of our investigative unit that serves as a government-wide clearinghouse for reports of

---

[18] https://osc.gov/Pages/Resources-PublicFiles.aspx (last accessed March 19, 2019).

[19] GAO, *Whistleblower Protection: Additional Actions Would Improve Recording and Reporting of Appeals Data*, GAO-17-110 (Washington, D.C.: Nov. 28, 2016).

[20] As of April 23, 2019, the MSPB board had not had a quorum since January 2017. Two nominees for the board had been reported favorably out of committee but the Senate had not yet voted on their nominations.

potential fraud, waste, abuse, and mismanagement in federal programs. FraudNet may refer an allegation of wrongdoing to the appropriate IG or federal, state, and local law-enforcement agencies.

See Figure 1 below.

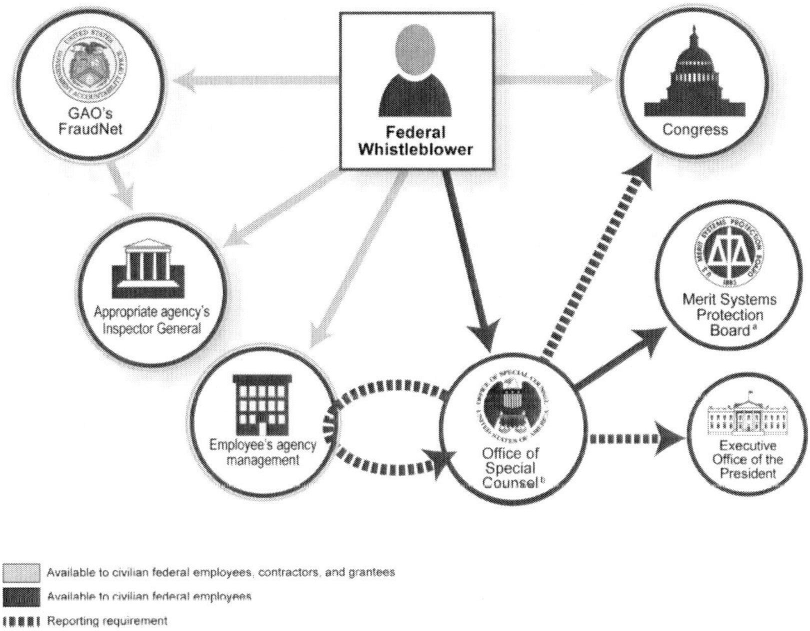

Source: GAO analysis of applicable laws and procedures. | GAO-19-432.

Note: Federal whistleblowers may also go to law enforcement officials with their disclosures.

[a] Certain personnel actions—such as a removal, demotion, or suspension of more than 14 days—due to claims of whistleblowing are directly appealable to the Merit Systems Protection Board, rather than first exhausting the Office of Special Counsel (OSC) process.

[b] OSC will refer the allegation to the head of the subject agency for investigation. The subject agency must then report back to OSC on its findings and action it plans to take as a result of the investigation.

Figure 1. Federal Whistleblower Options Available to Federal Civilian Employees, Contractors, and Grantees.

Congress Receives Whistleblower Information in Multiple Ways

Whistleblowers Typically Contact Oversight Committees, Their Congressional Representatives, or Select Authorizing Committees

The congressional offices and advocacy groups we spoke with told us that whistleblowers who contact the Congress typically reach out to oversight committees, the offices of their own representatives or senators, or select authorizing committees. Congressional oversight committees—the House Committee on Oversight and Reform and the Senate Committee on Homeland Security and Governmental Affairs—have jurisdiction over federal operations in executive branch agencies and regularly work with whistleblowers who are current and former federal employees, contractors, and grantees.

Whistleblowers often contact and work with multiple congressional offices simultaneously, according to congressional staff and advocacy groups we spoke with for this review. Congressional offices regularly exchange whistleblower referrals—with whistleblowers' consent—and, in some instances, collaborate on whistleblower disclosures based on the jurisdiction and relevant expertise of each office. For example, Senate oversight committee staff told us that they worked on a whistleblower disclosure with their counterparts in an authorizing committee because the authorizing committee had jurisdiction over the agency involved in the whistleblower disclosure. House oversight committee staff told us that they were often consulted by Members' congressional staff regarding whistleblower disclosures from their constituents because of the committee's experience in working with whistleblowers.

While data are not available on the number of whistleblower disclosures across Congress, a staff member at one congressional office said the office can receive hundreds of whistleblower disclosures each year. Oversight committee staff told us that the volume of whistleblowers their offices receive tends to increase when congressional oversight issues are prominent in the news media. They said that congressional oversight actions—such as letters to agency officials—can signal congressional interest to agency employees and influence whistleblower disclosures to Congress.

Congress Provides Multiple Ways for Whistleblowers to Disclose Information

Congressional offices include contact information on their websites that provide the public with multiple options for submitting information to representatives' and senators' offices and to congressional committees. Of the congressional websites we reviewed, we found that oversight committees, some authorizing committees, and some Members of Congress have specific contact information on their websites for whistleblowers to use for disclosing suspected wrongdoing. We found the following examples of ways congressional committee and individual Member's websites provide whistleblowers with options for disclosing information:

- Email: Email addresses are highlighted for whistleblowers to use for disclosing suspected wrongdoing to a congressional office.
- Hotlines: Hotlines allow whistleblowers to call to disclose suspected wrongdoing to a congressional office and, in some instances, include information for relevant federal agency IG hotlines and GAO's FraudNet as additional options.
- Web-based forms: Web-based forms allow whistleblowers to submit comments and other information online in a consistent format that can facilitate intake. While the format of these web-based forms varies, most include fields for whistleblowers to (1) identify the agency in which the suspected wrongdoing occurred, (2) describe the suspected wrongdoing, and (3) disclose contact information should the congressional office require additional

information. Congressional web intake forms we reviewed either allow for anonymous submission or include disclaimer statements assuring the confidentiality of whistleblower information.

While congressional offices provide whistleblowers with the above options for disclosing information, all congressional staff we spoke with noted the importance of interacting with whistleblowers by phone or in person. For example, oversight committee staff told us whistleblower interactions by phone can help them determine the credibility of the whistleblower's information, the seriousness of the issue being disclosed, and what congressional action, if any, can address the matter.

Congressional Staff Can Request Training on Working with Whistleblowers

There are a range of resources and training available to congressional staff on working with whistleblowers. Internal resources include oversight training and legal advice on specific inquiries related to whistleblowing when requested. Committees or staff may also create training on whistleblowers and provide on-the-job training to their staff. Lastly, external organizations provide training to congressional staff on congressional oversight and working with whistleblowers.

- General training and advice on congressional oversight: Both the House Office of General Counsel and Senate Office of Legal Counsel said they provide advice on working with whistleblowers when requested. House Office of General Counsel staff told us they provide training to House Members and staff upon request, including training focused on whistleblower topics, such as legal protections and risks as well as advice for working with whistleblowers. House Office of General Counsel staff also told us they frequently address working with whistleblowers when providing general training on congressional oversight and legal advice to Members and staff. Senate Office of Legal Counsel staff told us they give occasional verbal advice to Members and staff on working with whistleblowers in response to specific inquiries.

The Congressional Research Service provides congressional staff with training on constituent services and oversight, but does not provide training specifically focused on working with whistleblowers. Congressional Research Service training provides concepts and materials for congressional offices to adapt to their own use and needs.

- Committee-specific training related to whistleblowing: Staff from the House Committee on Oversight and Reform stated that they have created internal training for their staff on working with whistleblowers. During these training sessions, they distribute committee guidelines and policies for handling whistleblower cases, such as what information to ask for and how to prioritize among whistleblower claims. These training sessions also include discussion of skills such as building rapport and managing the whistleblower's expectations.

  Oversight staff we spoke with told us that direct experience working with whistleblowers is important. Staff at one committee told us that they identify opportunities for new staff to directly observe more experienced staff members as they work with whistleblowers to build these skills.
- External training: Oversight committee staff told us they leveraged outside training on congressional oversight from external advocacy groups. Staff stated that these training sessions are tailored to congressional staff and focus on how to manage calls and varying techniques for working with whistleblowers. Selected advocacy groups also told us that they provide training for congressional staff on working with whistleblowers.

The congressional committees we queried that support congressional staff—including the House Committee on Rules, Committee on House Administration, Senate Committee on Rules and Administration, House Committee on Ethics and Senate Select Committee on Ethics, and House and Senate Counsel—told us that they do not provide training or policies to all congressional staff on working with whistleblowers.[21]

KEY PRACTICES FOR CONGRESSIONAL CONSIDERATION WHEN RECEIVING AND REFERRING INFORMATION FROM WHISTLEBLOWERS

While the Congress provides different ways for whistleblowers to disclose information, congressional staff and executive officials we spoke with told us that it is important that this information and the whistleblowers' identity are effectively handled once it is received. We identified key practices to help guide congressional staff receiving information from whistleblowers and to help inform future training based on our review of IG and OSC practices, academic research, current congressional practices, and internal controls.

Our review found four basic steps to follow when receiving and referring information from whistleblowers. We identified intake as the first step in the process. Intake is the initial communication with the whistleblower where key information is collected and a relationship is established. The office can then consider its priorities as a second step, before deciding what action to take with the whistleblower disclosure. This decision process can lead to an oversight action or a referral. The third step we identified is referral of the whistleblower, which includes considering different options such as internal referrals to different congressional committees or personal offices, or Executive Branch referral options such as OSC, IGs, or MSPB. At the fourth and final step, the office can consider its follow-up strategy to provide the whistleblower with updates on the status of their disclosure and determine whether delayed reprisal occurred.

---

[21] In January 2019, the House of Representatives established an Office of Whistleblower Ombudsman and directed the Ombudsman to develop best practices for whistleblower intake for House offices and provide training to House offices on how to safely receive information from whistleblowers. Adopting the Rules of the House of Representatives for the One Hundred Sixteenth Congress, and for other purposes, H.Res. 6, 116th Cong. (2019).

Table 2. Key Practices for Congressional Staff to Consider When Working with Federal Whistleblowers (Potential Investigation to Be Done At the Discretion of Each Office)

Key Steps	Key Practices

Intake of whistleblower disclosures	*Internal guidelines and procedures:*
	• Develop written processes and guidelines for congressional staff, such as:
	  • Key steps in the offices' process for intake of whistleblowers and key considerations
	  • Protocols to keep disclosures secure and protected, while appropriately limiting access to information on a need-to-know basis
	    • Ensure personally identifiable information (PII) is handled appropriately[a]
	    • Ensure sensitive or classified information is handled appropriately
	• Develop a secure tracking system to document the process for status updates, trends, referrals, etc.:
	  • Document contacts and attempted contacts with the whistleblower, such as in a form or tracking sheet
	  • After initial receipt, create a case file that contains key information that can be updated as necessary
	  • Allow for staff to evaluate and identify trends and risks within the federal government
	• Routinely evaluate the office's processes and guidelines for intake to ensure the process is relevant, clear, and actionable
	External communication with the whistleblower:
	• Build a good rapport and trusting relationship with the whistleblower by communicating respectfully, practicing active listening, and responding in a timely manner
	• Share key information with the whistleblower:
	  • Explain the entire process to make it as transparent as possible
	  • Set clear expectations for the process:
	    • How the office determines whether or not it will take on a disclosure, information the office can or cannot receive, how the information might be used, and abilities of the office to assist the whistleblower, ensuring not to overpromise
	    • Timelines, potential outcomes, and available avenues to file complaints or disclose information while not providing legal advice given the nature of congressional staff's role, which is distinct from the role of legal counsel for the whistleblower
	  • Discuss the extent to which whistleblowers are willing to have their information and identity shared, and receive their permission before releasing information or discussing the details of their disclosure with another government entity[b]
	  • Be transparent about the level of anonymity and confidentiality that can be guaranteed

Table 2. (Continued)

Key Steps	Key Practices

Intake of whistleblower disclosures	• Ask the whistleblower key questions at this stage, such as:
	• Are you a current, former, or prospective federal employee or federal grant recipient? If not, are you an employee of a contractor for the federal government?
	  • If so, what federal agency?
	• Are you in immediate danger or does this disclosure pertain to an immediate threat?
	• Have you filed this disclosure with your agency inspector general or any investigative entity? If so, do you know the status or outcome of this investigation?
	• Have you filed this disclosure or shared this information elsewhere?
	  • If with another Member of Congress, do we have permission to communicate with that office?
	• Do you have legal representation? If so, do you prefer that we communicate through them?
	• Where (and how) did you obtain this information?
	• Do you have any documentation to submit?
	• Do you have any colleagues that can corroborate your disclosure?
	• Does this disclosure have implications for federal policy or require oversight or legislative action?
	• Has the agency taken, failed to take, or threatened to take a personnel action against you?
	• Are you a constituent of this Member?

Prioritization of whistleblower disclosures	*Internal guidelines and procedures:*
	• Set key priorities or standards that will be considered for each disclosure, such as does the disclosure pertain to:
	  • Urgent issues/ Dangers to public health or safety
	  • Oversight of the executive branch
	  • Government-wide issues
	  • Issues related to leadership's priorities
	• Develop written guidelines to explain your office's priorities, and how to decide if a whistleblower disclosure will be handled in the office or referred elsewhere
	• Document the outcome of prioritization in the office's tracking system
	• Evaluate the priorities that the office set to determine whether the office's priorities and objectives are addressing identified risks and trends within the federal government
	• Routinely discuss priorities with office leadership
	External communication with the whistleblower:

Key Steps	Key Practices
Prioritization of whistleblower disclosures	• Be transparent to the whistleblower about the type of disclosures the office will take on for further action, understanding that they cannot take on every disclosure

Referral of whistleblower disclosures	*Internal guidelines and procedures:*
	• Create a document that provides easily available information—such as a tip sheet—for staff that includes the options for whistleblowers and advantages, implications, and appropriateness of each option
	  • Common options include the Office for Special Counsel, Inspectors General, Merit Systems Protection Board, relevant committees, and appropriate Members
	• The office's tracking system should document where and when a disclosure was referred or action was taken
	External communication with the whistleblower:
	• Consider the following additional questions at this stage:
	  • Has this person been reprised against?
	  • Is this person a constituent?
	  • Is this person's disclosure within my office's jurisdiction?
	  • Does this person's disclosure satisfy my office's key standards/priorities?
	• Clearly communicate referral options to the whistleblower
	• Ask whistleblowers for permission before sending their disclosure outside of your office
	• Give the whistleblower the opportunity to discuss or review potential communications as appropriate to ensure the information is accurate and appropriately protects their identity to their desired extent
	• Communicate with the whistleblower about the potential of their disclosure being shared publicly and ensure that the whistleblower approves sharing their information with others
	  • For those whistleblowers who do not want to share their identity, ask if they have colleagues who would be comfortable speaking to the issue, and help identify if the issue is widespread.

Follow-up on whistleblower disclosures	*Internal guidelines and procedures:* • Document expectations for follow-up practices, including timelines for follow-up, in internal written policies • Periodically evaluate lessons learned and the identification of risks to achieving the office's objectives *External communication with the whistleblower:* • Communicate when the whistleblower should expect to hear final follow-up from the office and ensure that this communication occurs, even if the office chooses not to act on the disclosure

Table 2. (Continued)

Key Steps	Key Practices
Follow-up on whistleblower disclosures	• Was the disclosure referred? • Was the issue resolved at the agency? • Was there a hearing? Continue to check in with the whistleblower as appropriate to determine if he or she has experienced delayed harassment or reprisal or has new information to share

Source: GAO analysis of academic literature, applicable internal controls, and existing procedures and standards. | GAO-19-432

[a] PII is any information that can be used to distinguish or trace an individual's identity, such as name, date, and place of birth, Social Security number, or other types of personal information that can be linked to an individual, such as medical, educational, financial, and employment information.

[b] Offices may have policies for requesting permission from the whistleblower to allow executive branch agencies to share information with the office. See 5 U.S.C. §552a and Congressional Research Service, *Casework in a Congressional Office: Background, Rules, Laws, and Resources*, accessed September 17, 2018, https://www.crs.gov/reports/pdf/RL33209.

For each step, we identified practices to help offices develop office guidelines and procedures to keep the whistleblowers' information and identity secured and ensure all staff know the office's process and priorities. We also identified practices for communication, including key questions that staff can ask the whistleblower to help gather the necessary information to assess the disclosure. In addition, we intend appendix I to be a one-page resource for congressional staff with the practices for communication with the whistleblower as well as referral options.

Recognizing the value of the information that whistleblowers provide the Congress, the following key practices for working with whistleblowers in Table 2 can supplement existing guidance and training available within the Congress, including direct experience working with whistleblowers. Not all considerations are applicable in every instance. We recognize that congressional offices have discretion when determining their processes and procedures for working with whistleblowers, subject to House or Senate rules and relevant laws. Further, each office must consider resource trade offs inherent in dedicating staff to these efforts and instituting procedures such as ensuring the security of information provided by whistleblowers. These key practices can be used to inform the policies and procedures within individual congressional offices. They can also be helpful as the Congress develops any routine training and resources for staff on interacting with and referring whistleblowers. We are available to further assist the Congress in these efforts to work with whistleblowers.

AGENCY COMMENTS

We provided a draft of this chapter to the Special Counsel and the Chair of the Council of the Inspectors General on Integrity and Efficiency for comment. The Office of Special Counsel and the Council of the Inspectors General on Integrity and Efficiency provided technical comments that were incorporated as appropriate.

We are sending copies of this chapter to the appropriate congressional committees, the Special Counsel, the Chair of the Council of the Inspectors General on Integrity and Efficiency, and other interested parties.

Sincerely yours,

Michelle Sager
Director
Strategic Issues

APPENDIX I: KEY PRACTICES AND REFERRAL OPTIONS FOR FEDERAL WHISTLEBLOWERS

CONSIDERATIONS FOR

CONGRESSIONAL COMMUNICATION WITH WHISTLEBLOWERS

Communicate respectfully | Practice active listening | Respond in a timely manner

Make process as transparent as possible | Set clear expectations: do not over promise

Discuss the extent to which whistleblowers are willing to have their information or identity shared

INTAKE

Ask the whistleblower:

- Are you a federal employee, contractor, or grant recipient?
- Are you in immediate danger?
- Have you filed this disclosure or shared this information with your Inspector General or anywhere else?
- Do you have legal representation?
- Where (and how) did you obtain this information?
- Do you have any documentation to submit?
- Do you have any colleagues that can corroborate your disclosure?
- Does this disclosure have implications for federal policy or require oversight or legislative action?
- Has the agency taken, failed to take, or threatened to take a personnel action against you?
- Are you a constituent of this Member?

PRIORITIZATION

- Be transparent about the type of complaints you will take on and which you will refer elsewhere

REFERRAL

- Clearly communicate referral options to the whistleblower

APPROPRIATE OFFICE OF INSPECTOR GENERAL

MERIT SYSTEMS PROTECTION BOARD

U.S. OFFICE OF SPECIAL COUNSEL

GAO'S FRAUDNET

- Ask permission before sending disclosure outside your office
- Give the whistleblower the opportunity to discuss or review potential communications, as appropriate, to ensure accuracy and appropriate protection of identity
- Communicate the potential of their disclosure being shared publicly and ensure whistleblower approves of sharing their information with others

FOLLOW-UP

- Communicate when the whistleblower should expect to hear final follow-up
- Let them know if the complaint was referred, if the issue was resolved at the agency, if there was a hearing, etc.
- Continue to check in with the whistleblower as appropriate, to determine whether he or she has experienced delayed harassment or reprisal or has new information to share

In: Whistleblowers
Editor: Isabelle Guertin
ISBN: 978-1-53616-310-0

Chapter 5

NASA CONTRACTOR WHISTLEBLOWERS: STEPS TAKEN TO IMPLEMENT PROGRAM BUT IMPROVEMENTS TO TIMELINESS AND GUIDANCE NEEDED*

United States Government Accountability Office

ABBREVIATIONS

FAR	Federal Acquisition Regulation
FPDS-NG	Federal Procurement Data System - Next Generation
JSC	Johnson Space Center
NASA	National Aeronautics and Space Administration
NSSC	NASA Shared Services Center

* This is an edited, reformatted and augmented version of United States Government Accountability Office; Report to the Ranking Member, Committee on Homeland Security and Governmental Affairs, U.S. Senate; Accessible Version, Publication No. GAO-18-262, dated March 2018.

NFS	NASA FAR Supplement
NFS clause	NFS 1852.203-71
OIG	Office of Inspector General

WHY GAO DID THIS STUDY

NASA obligated over $18 billion in contracts and more than $1 billion in grants in fiscal year 2016, and it relies on a significant number of contractor and grantee employees to accomplish its work. These employees are legally protected from reprisal—such as demotion or firing—for whistleblowing.

GAO was asked to review NASA's whistleblower reprisal protections for contractor and grantee employees. This chapter addresses, among other things, the extent to which (1) NASA's Inspector General investigated contractor and grantee whistleblower reprisal complaints; (2) NASA's Administrator reviewed reprisal complaints in a timely manner; and (3) NASA communicated the applicable whistleblower reprisal protections to contractors. GAO reviewed NASA and its Inspector General's policies and guidance; reviewed a generalizable sample of 100 contracts from all NASA centers with contracts in fiscal year 2016; and interviewed relevant officials and contractors, grantees, and advocacy groups.

WHAT GAO RECOMMENDS

GAO is making three recommendations to NASA, including evaluating the process for reviewing reprisal complaints to ensure it is meeting the required timeframe and clarifying guidance on when protections apply to contractor employees. NASA agreed with the recommendations and plans to develop a documented process to ensure it reviews reprisal complaints in a timely manner and clarify guidance as appropriate, among other things.

WHAT GAO FOUND

From 2008 through June 2017, National Aeronautics and Space Administration (NASA) contractor and grantee employees submitted 48 reprisal complaints such as alleged firing or demotion for reporting fraud, waste, or abuse within the government. NASA's Inspector General addressed all 48 complaints, completed investigations for 6 of those complaints, and forwarded investigation reports to the NASA Administrator, who is responsible for making a final determination of whether reprisal occurred. The Administrator determined that none of the complaints qualified for protection under the law.

Further, in 5 of the 6 cases forwarded by the OIG, the Administrator was required by statute to make a final determination of reprisal within 30 days. GAO found that the Administrator did not meet this required time frame for all 5 cases and had no documented response for one of them (see figure for all 5 cases). According to officials from NASA's Office of General Counsel, each case must be handled on a case by case basis to ensure due process and 30 days is insufficient time to issue an order of final determination of reprisal. However, in order to ensure that whistleblower reprisal complaints are handled within required timeframes, NASA would have to monitor and evaluate its processes for making final determinations of reprisal, but it has not yet taken this step. Consequently, NASA does not know what changes may be needed to ensure that it is meeting the statutory 30-day requirement.

NASA communicates whistleblower protections to contractors through inclusion of a required contract clause. For example, GAO found that almost all—98 percent—of contracts would be expected to include a whistleblower clause as required by statute. However, certain elements of NASA whistleblower protection guidance have contributed to a different understanding of reprisal protections among officials at headquarters, a NASA center, and the Inspector General. For example, a July 2014 procurement notice and contract clause language resulted in different interpretations about when the protections apply. Federal internal control standards require that an entity should communicate necessary quality information internally to meet the objectives of its mission. Without additional clarity in its guidance on when the protections apply, NASA centers and procurement officials will be at risk of inconsistent implementation of the law.

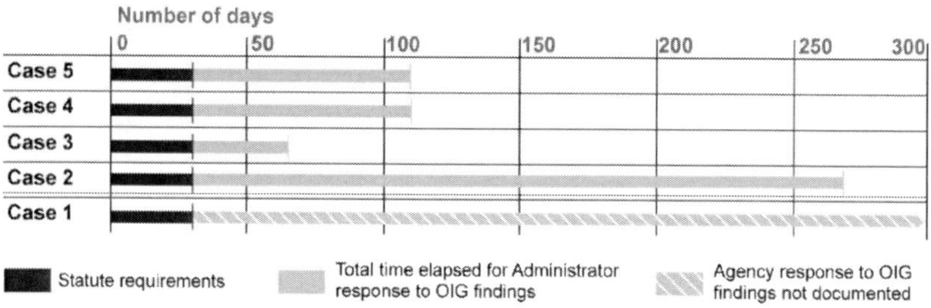

Source; GAO analysis of documents provided by National Aeronautics and Space Administration Office of Inspector General (OIG) and Administrator. | GAO-18-262.

Figure. Timeline for NASA Administrator's Response for 5 Investigated Reprisal Cases Subject to Statutory 30-Day Final Determination from 2008 through June 2017.

441 G St. N.W.
Washington, DC 20548

March 8, 2018

The Honorable Claire McCaskill
Ranking Member
Committee on Homeland Security and Governmental Affairs
United States Senate

Dear Senator McCaskill:

When contractor and grantee employees report fraud, waste, abuse, and mismanagement, agencies should ensure they are prepared to fully investigate reprisal complaints—such as demotion or firing—for whistleblowing. Agencies also need to make a formal determination on whether reprisal occurred. Employees of contractors and grantees conduct a significant amount of work for the National Aeronautics and Space

Administration (NASA). Given the sometimes enormous safety risks involved in space exploration, having an established process in place to investigate reprisal claims helps ensure NASA is able to act quickly whenever a whistleblower reports experiencing reprisal. In fiscal year 2016, NASA obligated over $18 billion in contracts to support acquisitions such as satellites and the construction of a solar plant; and more than $1 billion in grants for things such as science, technology, engineering, and math education initiatives and a student stipend for space-related research.

Although some protections for contractor employee whistleblowers have existed for years, section 2409 of Title 10, U.S. code (the statute), was amended in 2008, 2013, and 2014 to give contractor and grantee employee whistleblowers at NASA enhanced protection from reprisal. The statute establishes that an employee of a contractor, subcontractor, grantee, subgrantee, or personal services contractor may not be subject to reprisal for disclosing certain whistleblower complaints to certain authorities.[1]

You asked us to evaluate NASA's implementation of whistleblower reprisal protections. This chapter addresses the extent to which (1) NASA's Inspector General has investigated contractor and grantee whistleblower reprisal complaints, including meeting statutory timeliness requirements, and developed guidance for the investigations; (2) NASA's Administrator meets statutory timeliness requirements to review reprisal complaints; (3) NASA communicated externally and internally about the applicable contractor whistleblower reprisal protections; and (4) NASA communicated with grantees the applicable whistleblower reprisal protections.

To assess the extent to which NASA's Office of Inspector General (OIG) investigated reprisal complaints and developed guidance for the investigations, and the NASA Administrator met timeliness requirements, we obtained NASA guidance and relevant documentation. We conducted interviews with agency officials, including officials from the OIG and the Office of General Counsel on behalf of the Administrator about their processes and practices to conduct duties outlined in the statute. We

---

[1] In this report, we use the term "contractors and grantee employees" to also include both subcontractors and subgrantees.

reviewed data provided by the NASA OIG on the total number of whistleblower allegations of fraud, waste, abuse, misconduct, or mismanagement and reprisal complaints; the number of contractor and grantee employee whistleblower allegations and reprisal complaints; and the outcomes or decisions reached by the OIG of a reprisal complaint from fiscal years 2008, the year the enhanced protections were put in place, through 2017.[2] We assessed the reliability of these data by asking the NASA OIG to describe the source(s) of information used and steps taken to identify the numbers provided, and limitations and caveats that would affect our use of these data—such as the data being self-reported by the OIG and Administrator. Based on these steps, we determined the data to be sufficient for our purposes of determining the extent to which the complaints were addressed.

To assess the extent to which NASA communicates whistleblower protections externally, to contractors and grantees, we identified new fiscal year 2016 contract awards over $300,000 as reported in the Federal Procurement Data System-Next Generation (FPDS-NG). We selected contracts that were not only over the simplified acquisition threshold (generally $150,000), but were over $300,000 to account for possible exceptions and to ensure that we were sampling contracts that would be required to include a whistleblower reprisal clause. To determine whether the required NASA Federal Acquisition Regulation (FAR) Supplement clause 1852.203-71 (NFS clause) or other potentially applicable clauses were included in NASA contracts, we selected for review a generalizable random sample of 100 contracts from a total of 270 contracts.[3] The sample is projectable to NASA fiscal year 2016 contracts; however, making a legal determination of compliance would require a case by case review, which we did not do for contracts not in our sample. The 100 contracts consist of a random selection of 10 contracts from each NASA center that awarded

---

[2] While OIG officials track whistleblower reprisal complaints, they do not specifically track disclosures as a separate category. The numbers are based on a search of their database using key terms such as "disclosure" or "contractor employee" in the complaint field. Officials pointed out that complaints made through the OIG hotline may qualify for whistleblower protections, but the complainant may not identify him or herself as a whistleblower or even want to be considered a whistleblower.

[3] FAR clauses 52.203-15, 52.203-17, and 52.212-4.

new contracts in fiscal year 2016; for those centers that did not have 10 contracts, we selected all contracts.[4] The remaining contracts were pulled from NASA Shared Services Center (NSSC), because that center does the most contracting. We estimated the percent of NASA contracts expected to include whistleblower clause(s) as the weighted average of results from the 10 contracting centers. Additionally, we selected a non-generalizable random sample of 10 grants awarded by NASA in fiscal year 2016 for review to determine whether NASA grants included a mechanism notifying grantee employees of their whistleblower rights and reprisal protections.[5] For both the sample of contracts and grants, we conducted data reliability checks by comparing the data to the documentation and concluded the data were sufficiently reliable for our purposes to determine if relevant whistleblower reprisal protections information was communicated externally.

To assess internal communication about whistleblower protections, we reviewed relevant documentation, including guidance, and conducted interviews with procurement officials, NASA Headquarters, NASA's Office of General Counsel, and Chief Counsels at Johnson Space Center (JSC), NSSC, and Marshall Space Flight Center. We also conducted interviews with contractors, grantees, and whistleblower advocacy groups. For additional information on our scope and methodology, see appendix I.

We conducted this performance audit from March 2017 to March 2018 in accordance with generally accepted government auditing standards. Those standards require that we plan and perform the audit to obtain sufficient, appropriate evidence to provide a reasonable basis for our findings and conclusions based on our audit objectives. We believe that the evidence obtained provides a reasonable basis for our findings and conclusions based on our audit objectives.

---

[4] NASA is comprised of 12 centers and 7 facilities located throughout the United States.

[5] We selected 10 random grants from 2016 with positive dollar values to avoid grants captured in FPDS-NG as negative numbers due to deobligations.

BACKGROUND

For contractor and grantee employees at NASA, whistleblower protections have changed over time. For example, by statute, in 2007, NASA contractor employees were protected against reprisal if they disclosed information relating to a substantial violation of law related to a contract. However, in 2008, amendments to the whistleblower statute provided protections only to those contractor employees at NASA who reported “a substantial and specific danger to public health or safety.” In 2013, the statute was amended again to include disclosures of gross mismanagement of a NASA contract or grant, a gross waste of Administration funds, and abuse of authority relating to a NASA contract or grant, or a violation of law, rule, or regulation related to a NASA contract or grant. In 2014, the statute was further amended with the only significant change to protect grantee and subgrantee employees. See Table 1 for detailed description of the 2008, 2013, and 2014 amendments of the statute.

Disclosure: An allegation to certain bodies and individuals made by an employee who believes he or she has witnessed certain wrongdoing, such as gross mismanagement or gross waste.

Source: GAO analysis based on 10 U.S.C. § 2409(a) | GAO-18-262.

Reprisal Complaint: Following a disclosure, a complaint that an employee has experienced reprisal as a result of the disclosure, such as demotion or discharge.

Source: GAO analysis based on 10 U.S.C. § 2409(b) | GAO-18-262.

Table 1. Selected Summary of Amendments to the Whistleblower Reprisal Protections for NASA Contractor and Grantee Employees

10 U.S.C. § 2409	After fiscal year 2008 National Defense Authorization Act (NDAA) amendments[a]	After fiscal year 2013 NDAA amendments[b]	After fiscal year 2014 NDAA amendments[c]	Summary of selected changes
Employees covered	Contractor employees, same as previous.	Contractor and subcontractor employees.	Contractor, subcontractor, grantee, and subgrantee employees.	Expanded protections to subcontractor, grantee, and subgrantee employees.
Protected whistleblower disclosures	A substantial and specific danger to public health or safety.	Same as 2008, plus gross mismanagement of NASA contract or grant, a gross waste of Administration funds, an abuse of authority relating to an Administration contract or grant, or a violation of law, rule, or regulation related to an Administration contract (including the competition for or negotiation of a contract) or grant.	Same as previous	Extended protected disclosures to include gross mismanagement, waste, or abuse of funds,among other things for NASA contractor and grantee employees.[d]
Length of investigation	180 days/no limit Office of Inspector General (OIG) and complainant may agree to additional time to investigate.	180 days/360 maximum OIG may request up to an additional 180 days, with complainant approval.	Same as previous	Limited OIG to an extension up to 180 daysin addition to the initial 180 day investigative time frame.
Agency head review	30 days	Same as previous	Same as previous	No change

Table 1. (Continued)

10 U.S.C. § 2409	After fiscal year 2008 National Defense Authorization Act (NDAA) amendments[a]	After fiscal year 2013 NDAA amendments[b]	After fiscal year 2014 NDAA amendments[c]	Summary of selected changes
Employee notification	No requirement for contractors to communicate whistleblower protections to their employees.	NASA must ensure that its contractors and subcontractors inform their employees in writing of the rights and remedies provided by the statute in the predominant language of the workplace.[e]	Same as previous Although grantees protections were added, no requirement to ensure grantees inform employees of rights and remedies provided by statute.	NASA now includes a NASA Federal Acquisition Regulation Supplement clause in contracts requiring that its contractors and subcontractors inform their employees of whistleblower protections.

Source: GAO analysis of amendments to 10 U.S.C. § 2409 | GAO-18-262.

[a]Pub. L. No. 110-181, § 846 (enacted January 28, 2008). 10 U.S.C. § 2409 also applies to the Department of Defense and Coast Guard. For purposes of this table, we selected information specific to NASA.

[b]Pub. L. No. 112-239, § 827 (enacted January 2, 2013; amendments effective 180 days after enactment).

[c]Pub. L. No. 113-291, § 856(a) (enacted December 19, 2014).

[d]Prior to the 2008 amendments, NASA contractor employees were protected for disclosing information relating to a substantial violation of law related to a contract (including the competition for or negotiation of a contract). 10 U.S.C. § 2409 (2007).

[e]The statute does not include a requirement to inform grantee and subgrantee employees of their whistleblower reprisal protections.

Requirements under the Current Statute

Under the current statute, the NASA Office of Inspector General and Administrator have different responsibilities. Since the 2014 amendments, contractor, subcontractor, grantee, and subgrantee employees are protected from reprisal if they disclose to certain persons or bodies information they reasonably believe is evidence of gross mismanagement of a federal contract or grant, a gross waste of federal funds, an abuse of authority relating to a federal contract or grant, a substantial and specific danger to public health or safety, or a violation of law, rule, or regulation related to a federal contract or grant. Additionally, contractor employees may make whistleblower disclosures to several entities, including a management official at the contractor. Figure 1 depicts the disclosure process and the complaint process.

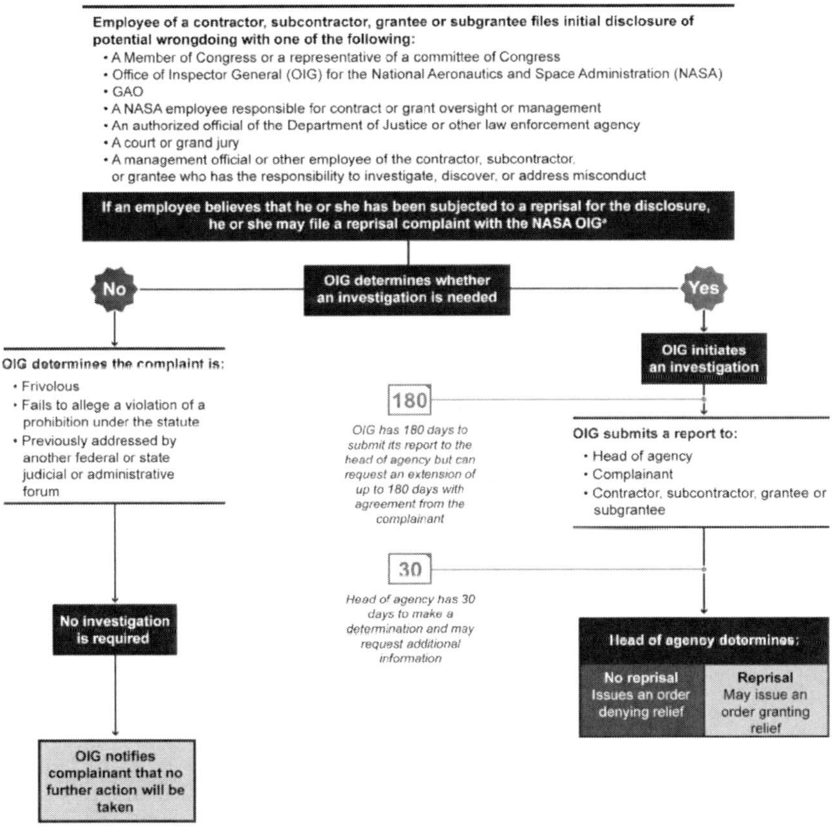

Source: GAO analysis of 10 U.S.C. § 2409. | GAO-18-262.

[a]An employee has three years from when the alleged reprisal took place to file a complaint.

Figure 1. Disclosure and Reprisal Complaint Investigation and Review Processes for NASA Contractor and Grantee Employees.

NASA OIG Role

Upon receiving a reprisal complaint, the OIG must evaluate whether a reprisal complaint is covered under the statute. In addition to the steps described in Figure 1 for investigating complaints, there are instances when the OIG does not investigate. The OIG might not investigate for a variety of reasons, such as in cases where the complaint is already under investigation by another authority such as another OIG, or otherwise does not allege a violation of the law, such as if whistleblower disclosure does not constitute gross fraud, waste, abuse or mismanagement. If the OIG determines the case is not covered under the statute, it may then notify the complainant that no further action will be taken on the reprisal complaint.

Administrator Role

Upon receipt of the NASA OIG investigation report, the NASA Administrator (the head of agency) has 30 days to determine whether the contractor made a prohibited reprisal and issue an order denying or granting relief. According to NASA officials, during the 30-day period after the agency head receives the OIG report, the agency practice has been to ask the OIG for any additional investigative work and also afford the complainant and the contractor an opportunity to submit a written response to the OIG report. Any person adversely affected or aggrieved by the administrator's order may, within 60 days of issuance, obtain a limited review by the U.S. circuit court of appeals.

Agency Procurement Official Role

Under the NFS regulations, NASA contracting officers are also responsible for inserting an NFS whistleblower clause into applicable contracts that requires contractors communicate to their employees their rights under the statute.[6] The NFS whistleblower clause lays out the responsibility of contractors to communicate to their employees their rights under the statute, in writing and in their predominant native language. All contracts over the simplified acquisition threshold awarded on or after July 29, 2014, require a whistleblower clause. The statute also requires NASA

[6] NFS 1852.203-71.

to make best efforts to include a clause providing for the applicability of the 2013 amendments in contracts awarded before July 1, 2013—the effective date of the 2013 amendments—that have undergone major contract modifications. The terms "best efforts" and "major modifications" are not defined in the statute.[7] Unlike provisions affecting contractors, the statute does not require NASA to ensure that grantees or subgrantees notify employees in writing of their rights under the statute.

NASA OIG Investigated Reprisal Complaints within Required Time Frames and Recently Updated Incomplete Guidance

From 2008 to June 2017, NASA OIG addressed whistleblower reprisal complaints within required time frames, according to OIG officials. At the time we initiated this review, the OIG's guidance for handling reprisal complaints had been updated to reflect most statutory changes; however, it did not include guidance regarding subgrantees. During the course of our review, the OIG updated the investigation guidance in October 2017 to include subgrantee employees.

NASA OIG Handled Reprisal Complaint Investigations ithin Required Time Frames

NASA OIG completed 6 reprisal investigations within required time frames.[8] The OIG received 277 whistleblower disclosures leading to 48

---

[7] Several different whistleblower protections exist in the FAR and agency supplements, with each applicable depending on considerations such as the agency in question, acquisition procedures, and source of funding. For some contracts, the FAR clause 52.203-17 is applicable. For all commercial item acquisitions, contracting officers must insert the FAR clause 52.212-4 that requires the contractor to comply with 10 U.S.C. § 2409. Contracts that obligate American Recovery and Reinvestment Act of 2009 funds require whistleblower protections unique to the Act found in FAR clause 52.203-15.

[8] For those reprisal complaints covered under the 2013 amendments, the investigations must be completed within the time frame of 180 days, and an allowable, mutually agreed upon, one-time extension of 180 days for a total of up to 360 days.

reprisal complaints from 2008 through June 2017, and handled those complaints within required time frames, according OIG officials.[9]

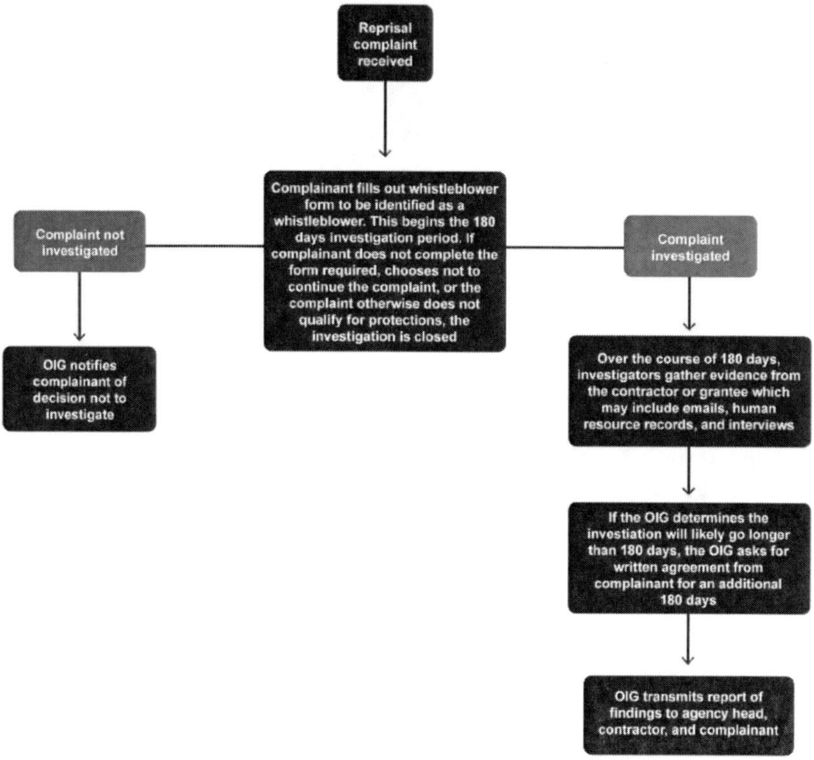

Source: GAO analysis of information and documentation received from National Aeronautics and Space Administration Office of Inspector General (OIG). | GAO-18-262.

Figure 2. NASA Office of Inspector General (OIG) Process for Investigating Reprisal Complaints.

For the 6 of those reprisal complaints that were investigated, the OIG used extensions. OIG officials said that extensions may be necessary for a number of reasons, including that the complaint may be highly technical in nature, requiring the OIG to find subject matter expertise to better

---

[9] Reprisal complaints included instances of firing and demotion for reporting fraud, waste, or abuse.

understand the nature of the whistleblower complaint and whether it constitutes gross fraud, waste, abuse, or mismanagement.

When the OIG receives a reprisal complaint, complainants are asked to fill out a whistleblower complaint form and an investigation is initiated. See Figure 2 below for the process by which the OIG conducts its investigations.

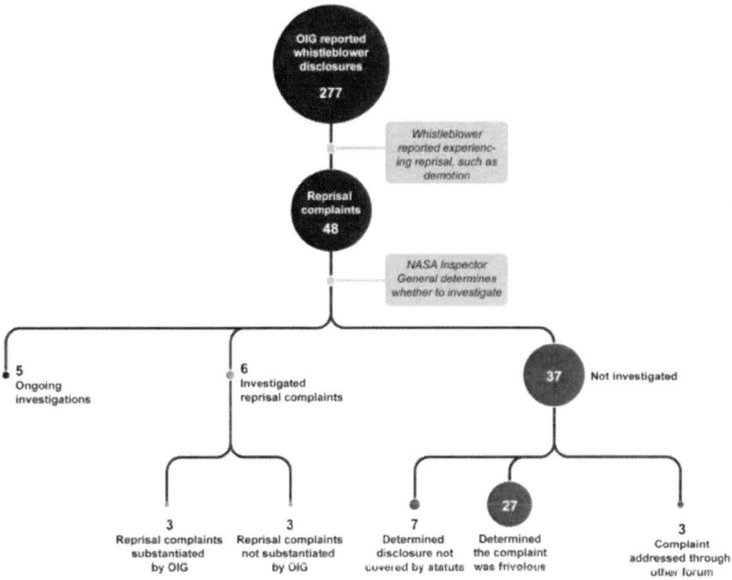

Source: GAO analysis of National Aeronautics and Space Administration's (NASA) Office of Inspector General (OIG) data. | GAO-18-262.

Note: Of the 48 reprisal complaints received by the OIG, one was made by the employee of a grantee; the rest were made by employees of contractors.

Figure 3. Disposition of Reprisal Complaints Received by NASA's Office of Inspector General (OIG) from 2008 through June 2017.

In addition, there were 5 complaints currently under investigation and 37 complaints during this time frame that the NASA OIG did not investigate because the OIG deemed them to be frivolous, determined they were not covered under the statute, or the complaint was handled in another forum, such as the court system or by another OIG.[10] Complaints were deemed frivolous for several reasons, including if the complainant did not want to disclose his or her identity and proceed with the claim, or the whistleblower disclosure happened after the reprisal. OIG officials told us that when cases are disposed of without an investigation, the OIG notifies the complainant of the decision in writing. Figure 3 shows the disposition of the 48 reprisal complaints received from 2008 through June 2017.

The OIG Updated Investigation Guidance

The OIG has developed guidance for conducting investigations, which includes a chapter on contractor and grantee whistleblower reprisal complaints. Although most changes to the statute (such as to whom reprisal may be reported) had been incorporated into the investigation guidance, the initial guidance provided to us by the OIG did not include a 2014 statutory requirement to extend protections to subgrantees. During the course of our review, in October 2017, the OIG updated its guidance for investigating reprisal complaints to include subgrantee employees. Because subgrantees are now protected by statute, including them in the investigation policy will help ensure they are consistently extended protections through OIG investigations.

In addition to its guidance, OIG officials said they have developed training specific to whistleblower investigations for new investigators, conducted internal training for investigators, and external training for contractor employees. Additionally, the OIG Investigators' Central Field Office conducts periodic training for investigators that includes any updates to whistleblower protections.[11] With regard to external training, the OIG officials said that investigators at some of the NASA centers—with

[10] OIG officials said that all 37 complaints not investigated were closed before the 180 day time frame requirement for investigations.

[11] The OIG Investigators' Central Field Office includes JSC, Marshall Space Flight Center, Kennedy Space Center, and Stennis Space Center.

the largest contract activity—have conducted on-site training for some contractors. This training is conducted as part of general fraud awareness training.

NASA Administrator Did Not Meet the Required Time Frames for Reprisal Complaint Review

The Administrator failed to meet the required review time frame and issue an order of final determination of reprisal for 5 completed investigations received from the OIG from 2008 through June 2017.[12] In all 5 cases, the Administrator took longer than the 30 days to issue an order. In one of those 5 complaints, an official from the Office of General Counsel was unable to provide us with the issued order and said he did not believe one was completed, and could not provide an explanation as to why an order was not completed.

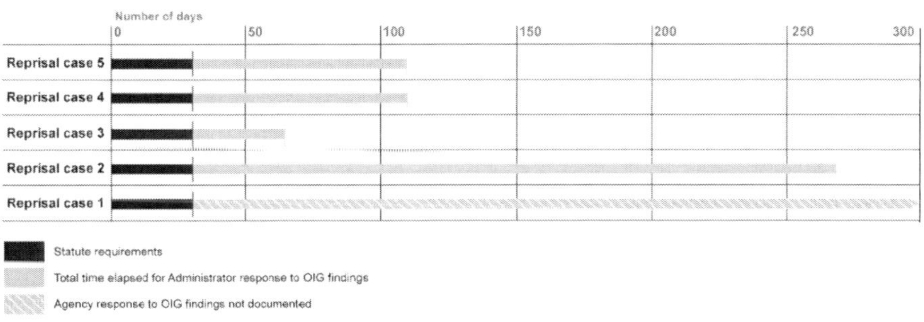

Source: GAO analysis of documents provided by National Aeronautics and Space Administration Office of Inspector General (OIG) and Administrator. | GAO-18-262.

Figure 4. Timeline for NASA Administrator's Response for 5 Investigated Reprisal Cases Subject to Statutory 30-Day Final Determination from 2008 through June 2017.

---

[12] During this time period, the Administrator received 6 reports; however, only 5 were subject to the requirement that the Administrator make final determination of reprisal within 30 days. The sixth report of findings was based on a complaint made before the 2008 amendment to the statute was in effect; therefore, the 30-day requirement was not applicable.

For the 5 reprisal complaints, Figure 4 shows the number of days from when the Administrator received an OIG report of findings to the time when an order of final determination was documented.

In addition to the 5 complaints mentioned above, there was another OIG investigation of a reprisal complaint that did not require response from the administrator within 30 days, but was finalized within our review time frame, for a total of 6 completed OIG investigations of reprisal complaints. For 3 of the 6 complaints, the OIG found that reprisal had occurred and reported those findings to the administrator for final determination of reprisal. The Administrator determined that none of these 3 complaints qualified for protection under the law. For 2 of these complaints, the Administrator found that they did not qualify for protections because they fell under the 2008 version of the statute and failed to allege a violation specific to public health and safety.[13] In 2017, a court affirmed the Administrator's position.[14] For the third complaint, the Administrator determined reprisal could not be substantiated due to the complainant not meeting the standards of evidence under the statute.[15]

Further, we found that NASA does not have a standard process in place for the Administrator to review cases that qualify for protections under the statute and issue an order of final determination. According to an official from the Office of General Counsel, the agency has no standard process to ensure the contractors are afforded due process, among other things. The official from Office of General Counsel said the Administrator may need to conduct an additional investigation in some cases.[16] He said

[13] After the 2008 amendments, 10 U.S.C. § 2409 provided protections to those contractor employees at NASA who disclosed "a substantial and specific danger to public health or safety." Whistleblower complaints made about general fraud, waste, abuse, and mismanagement alone, but not related to a substantial and specific danger to public health or safety, were not protected disclosures under the statue at that time.

[14] *Javery v. Bolden*, No. 16-60221, 2017 WL 2703790 (5th Cir. June 21, 2017).

[15] The Administrator determined the OIG report of findings and subsequent responses did not contain sufficient grounds to clearly support a finding that the complainant had been reprised against.

[16] NASA General Counsel explained that in its view there is not a one-size-fits-all answer to what process is due, because it is necessarily a fact-driven question. NASA General Counsel said its concerns stem from the Eighth Circuit's decision in *Business Communications, Inc. v. U.S. Dept. of Ed.*, 739 F.3d 374 (8th Cir. 2013). In that case, the Department of Education determined that a contractor had retaliated against a whistleblower in violation of section

that each case is different and would have to be handled on a case by case basis. In addition, the official said the Administrator may need to conduct hearings, independent of the OIG. Moreover, the official from Office of General Counsel highlighted concern that the Administrator's office does not have the resources to conduct additional investigative work, which he said is a key contributor for the office's inability to meet the 30-day timeline to issue an order of final determination. Despite acknowledging these challenges, the Administrator does not have a formal process or criteria to monitor and evaluate the way the office handles issuing an order of final determination of reprisal to ensure that it meets the statutory time requirements.

Because the Administrator took longer than 30 days to respond to all reprisal complaints, including one where the Office of General Counsel failed to provide evidence that the Administrator responded at all, there may be the unintended consequence of disincentivizing future whistleblowers from making disclosures who fear their complaint will not be handled timely. Internal controls require that management should establish and operate monitoring activities to monitor the internal control system, evaluate the results, and take appropriate action to address issues on a timely basis.[17] Without monitoring, evaluating, and taking appropriate corrective action based on the way the Administrator or his or her designee makes a final determination of reprisal, there is no assurance that whistleblower reprisal complaints will be handled within required time frames in the future.

1553 of the American Recovery and Reinvestment Act of 2009, which provides substantively similar whistleblower protections to the NASA Whistleblower statute. The contractor appealed. The court held that before the department could order relief for the whistleblower, it had to provide the contractor due process, including a hearing and the opportunity for the contractor organization to confront and cross examine adverse witnesses.

[17] GAO, *Standards for Internal Control in the Federal Government*, GAO 14 704G (Washington, D.C.: September 2014).

NASA Almost Always Communicates Whistleblower Protections to Contractors, but Internal Guidance Is Unclear

In almost all of the contracts we reviewed, NASA had met its obligation to ensure its contractors are communicating whistleblower protections to their employees through a whistleblower contract clause. We also found that NASA has put in place guidance to its contracting workforce on the protections, and guidance on when to include the whistleblower clause in contracts. However, we found that some NASA officials have interpreted this guidance differently. Further, NASA's guidance does not reflect an agency-wide policy on when to include the whistleblower clause when modifying a contract.

Whistleblower Clause Included in Almost All Contracts, but a Few Were Missing the Required Clause

In most cases, NASA included a clause regarding whistleblower reprisal protections in applicable contracts to ensure contractors communicate rights to its employees. But we found that the clause was not included in all relevant contracts in our review. Based on our review of a generalizable sample of contracts, we estimate that 98 percent of contracts would be expected to include a whistleblower clause at the time new contracts were awarded in applicable contracts in 2016, and 2 percent would not.[18] Within our sample, 4 contracts did not have a whistleblower reprisal clause.[19] After we shared our contract file review findings with

[18] To assess legal compliance we would have to make a determination on case by case basis, which we did not do.

[19] Our review of a generalizable sample of 100 contracts found that 96 contracts in the sample included whistleblower language while 4 did not. The weighted estimate of the percentage of NASA contracts that would be expected to include whistleblower language is 97.7 percent, with a 95 percent confidence interval of 92.5 to 99.6 percent. The weighted estimate of the percentage of NASA contracts that would not be expected to include whistleblower language is 2.3 percent, with a 95 percent confidence interval of 0.4 to 7.5

NASA officials, they modified 3 of the 4 contracts to include the missing required whistleblower clause. For the remaining contract, the contractor performance was complete, the contract had been closed, and no further action will be taken.

According to NASA procurement officials, human error, combined with its former contract writing system, could explain why the contracts in our sample did not have the required clause. They explained that the former contracting writing system relied on templates and did not automatically include the NFS clause into all contracts. Under this system, contracting officers used templates that included a list of all potential or applicable NFS and FAR clauses, which are incorporated through a manual process. Officials said that if a clause were included in the templates, it is unlikely that it would be removed because doing so would require supervisory approval.

NASA procurement officials told us that the agency launched a new contract writing system in June 2017. They said that under the new contract writing system, contracting officers use a logic system that prepopulates each contract with required clauses. They said that the new automated system will likely lead to fewer human errors because inserting the clause will not be a manual process. Because the new system is still being implemented, we were unable to evaluate whether the risk of human error has been reduced or eliminated to ensure applicable contract awards have the clause.

Under the previous and current systems, NASA contracts are to undergo various levels of review prior to award—including attorney review—at the centers or headquarters based on risk level and dollar thresholds. For example, contracts awarded by JSC valued at over $50 million are to be reviewed by headquarters. NASA procurement officials stated that they conduct procurement management reviews, and centers conduct annual self-assessments; however, at one center, officials pointed out that these reviews have not previously included whether a

percent. See Appendix I for more information on sampling error. Of the 96 contracts with a whistleblower clause, 84 had the NFS clause and 12 had an alternative whistleblower clause.

whistleblower clause is included in new contracts or major modifications. They said this is because reviews typically focus on known issues or program risk, and inclusion of the whistleblower clause has not been previously identified as an issue or risk. Contractors we spoke with were generally aware of their responsibilities to communicate reprisal protections to their employees because their contracts with NASA included the required NFS whistleblower clause. In response to our review, NASA procurement officials said they plan to include a review of the inclusion of NFS whistleblower clause in future compliance reviews as an area of emphasis and will instruct centers to include whether the clause is included in applicable contracts as part of the centers' self-assessment process.

NASA's Guidance Contributes to Different Understanding of Reprisal Protections

Three elements of NASA's whistleblower reprisal protection guidance—its procurement notice, NFS clause, and definition of major modification— contribute to potential confusion or inconsistent application of whistleblower reprisal protections.

First, in July 2014, NASA notified its contracting officials of the changes to the NFS required by the 2013 amendments to section 2409 Title 10 of the U.S. code through a procurement notice 04-80, but this notice has been interpreted differently by officials in NASA Headquarters, a NASA center, and the OIG. Procurement notices are drafted by NASA Headquarters, reviewed and approved by NASA general counsel and NASA's Office of Procurement. The NASA centers, acting through their procurement offices and, as needed their legal counsel, review and implement the notices.

After the procurement notice was issued, some NASA officials interpreted it differently. For example, in one instance, a NASA center Chief Counsel's office attorney advised a center procurement official that reprisal protections found in the 2013 amendments extend to contractors' employees working on contracts awarded before the effective date of the amendments. This is true, he said, regardless of whether the contract contains any clause explicitly making the 2013 amendments applicable. However, both the OIG and the Administrator's counsel have expressed a different understanding of the statute conveyed in the notice, stating that a clause making the 2013 amendments applicable must be in a contract in order for the complainant to be protected under the statute. Later, the attorney from the center Chief Counsel's office revised his understanding of the statute and concluded the procurement notice was not accurate as written.

Second, NASA personnel have different understandings about whether the NFS clause is sufficient for contractor employees to be covered by the statute. The NFS clause instructs contractors to inform their employees in writing of contractor whistleblower employee rights; but, unlike the FAR clause that is used to implement similar legislation for other agencies, the NFS clause does not state that employees working on the contract are subject to the whistleblower rights and remedies. The attorney from a NASA center said that the NFS clause is enough to ensure contractor employees are given rights under the statute. However, OIG officials have said that without including that element of the clause, employees working under NASA contracts awarded prior to the effective date of the 2013 amendments may not be covered by those amendments. See Table 2 for description of the clauses and their differences.

Third, the lack of agency-wide guidance for when to include the clause in major modifications leads to different implementation of the requirement. The 2013 amendments require that NASA makes best efforts to include a whistleblower clause in contracts undergoing a major modification. NASA's July 2014 procurement notice also encourages contracting officers to include the NFS whistleblower clause when issuing major modifications to contracts awarded before July 29, 2014. However, it does not specify what a major modification is under this statute, and the statute itself does not define "major." According to NASA procurement officials at headquarters and at two NASA centers, it is at the discretion of the NASA Centers' offices of procurement and contracting officers to decide if a clause is inserted into modifications, and whether they are considered major.

Table 2. Description of Two Whistleblower Reprisal Protection Clauses

Federal Acquisition Regulation (FAR) Clause 52.203-17	NASA FAR Supplement Clause 1852.203-71	Difference
Contractor Employee Whistleblower Rights and Requirement to Inform Employees of Whistleblower Rights (Apr. 2014) (a) This contract and employees working on this contract will be subject to the whistleblower rights and remedies in the pilot program on Contractor employee whistleblower protections established at 41 U.S.C. 4712 by section 828 of the National Defense Authorization Act for Fiscal Year 2013 (Pub. L. 112- 239) and FAR 3.908. (b) The Contractor shall inform its employees in writing, in the predominant language of the workforce, of employee whistleblower rights and protections under 41 U.S.C. 4712, as described in section 3.908 of the Federal Acquisition Regulation. (c) The Contractor shall insert the substance of this clause, including this paragraph (c), in all subcontracts over the simplified acquisition threshold.	Requirement To Inform Employees Of Whistleblower Rights (Aug. 2014) (a) The Contractor shall inform its employees in writing, in the predominant native language of the workforce, of contractor employee whistleblower rights and protections under 10 U.S.C. 2409, as described in subpart 1803.9 of the NASA FAR Supplement. (b) The Contractor shall include the substance of this clause, including this paragraph (b), in all subcontracts.	The NASA clause does not explicitly state that contractor employees will be subject to whistleblower remedies.

Source: GAO analysis of Federal Acquisition Regulation and National Aeronautics and Space Administration (NASA) FAR Supplement whistleblower protection clauses. | GAO-18-262.

Procurement officials and the contracting officers we spoke with told us that there is no definition of major modifications in the law, regulation, or NASA Headquarters or Center policies or guidance. NASA procurement officials said this is because it could be different for each contract and the contracting officer makes the determination based upon the facts related to the situation. Nevertheless, without communicating the factors to consider when determining whether a modification is major and whether that contract should or should not include the clause, NASA and the Centers' procurement officials are at risk of potential inconsistent incorporation of the clause among applicable contracts.

One attorney in NASA's General Counsel's Office said there may be costs associated with asking a contractor to insert new clauses—such as the whistleblower clause—into an existing contract during a major modification because it would require a bilateral negotiation between the contractor and the agency. However, one contractor we spoke with said that there would be no cost to adding the clause and that doing so would not be an issue because the whistleblower clause is consistent with the internal whistleblower policies and practices of the institution. Further, he said that the institution he represents would be hesitant to argue against inclusion of the NFS clause in its contracts with NASA.

Internal control standards require that an entity should internally communicate necessary quality information in order to meet requirements of the mission. These 3 areas of potential confusion related to NASA's current guidance could result in different application of the law, unless they are clarified.

NASA Has Not Established a Mechanism to Communicate Whistleblower Protections to Grantees

Although whistleblower protections are now extended to grantee employees by statute, NASA does not have a mechanism in place to communicate the protections to grantees or subgrantee employees. Unlike the requirement for NASA to ensure contractors communicate whistleblower reprisal rights to their employees in writing and in the employees' predominant language, the statute does not prescribe a similar requirement for NASA to ensure that grantees communicate whistleblower reprisal rights to their employees. During the grant application process, NASA requires grantees to attest that they will not require grantee employees to sign confidentiality agreements that would prohibit them from reporting fraud, waste, and abuse.

NASA officials said that grant awards do not include a mechanism, such as a term or condition, to encourage NASA grantees to notify their employees of their whistleblower reprisal protections. In the 10 NASA grants from fiscal year 2016 that we reviewed, there was no requirement included for grantees to communicate these protections to employees. However, we found that all 10 grants included a statement that each award was subject to all applicable laws and regulations of the United States in effect on the date of award, including the Uniform Guidance. For federal grants in general, the Uniform Guidance provides a government-wide framework for grants management.[20] Within this guidance, there is a reference to the whistleblower protections in the statute; however, it does not explicitly describe the statute's requirements.[21]

The grant advocacy group and representatives of three NASA grantees we spoke with were aware that some protections exist and noted that many grantees have their own whistleblower policies, but were not aware of the specific protections provided by the statute, which indicates that opportunities exist for improving communications between NASA and its grantees about these protections. Further, representatives of the grant advocacy group noted that the whistleblower protections for grantee employees were not specifically mentioned at recent annual meetings where grantees and federal officials discuss issues that affect grantees. Internal controls require that management externally communicate the necessary quality information to achieve the entity's objectives. Without additional communication about the protections provided by the statute, grantees may not fully understand or appreciate the significance of the rights afforded to their employees, and grantee employees may not be aware of their whistleblower reprisal protections, which could hinder their willingness to report instances of fraud, waste, and abuse.

---

[20] Office of Management and Budget produces the *Uniform Administrative Requirements, Cost Principles, and Audit Requirements for Federal Awards* also referred to as "Uniform Guidance."

[21] 2 CFR § 200.300(b).

CONCLUSION

Because contractor and grantee employee whistleblowers risk reprisal after disclosing potential fraud, waste, abuse and mismanagement, ensuring they are protected from retaliation or adverse consequences is critical. Without monitoring and evaluating the timeliness of reviewing and responding to reprisal complaints, the Administrator may not be prepared to determine reprisal on future cases within the statutorily required 30 days.

Additionally, although NASA has developed guidance related to contractor protections, this guidance has led to inconsistent interpretation of the law and could potentially lead to inconsistent application of how contractor protections for employees are conveyed. More clear guidance would help contracting officers determine when to incorporate the NFS clause into major modifications to ensure consistency throughout the agency.

Finally, because unlike contracts, there is no similar clause for grants, NASA is in the position to help ensure grantees know their employees' rights against reprisal if they observe and disclose fraud, waste, abuse or mismanagement. However, NASA has not effectively communicated to grantees information about these provisions and as a result grantees and their employees may not be fully aware of these protections. Consequently, if they witness fraud, waste, abuse or mismanagement, they may not be willing to disclose those for fear of reprisal.

RECOMMENDATIONS FOR EXECUTIVE ACTION

We are making three recommendations to NASA:

The Administrator should monitor, evaluate, and make appropriate corrective actions, such as a documented process, to ensure it reviews reprisal complaints in a timely manner. (Recommendation 1)

The Administrator should review NASA's guidance or develop other guidance, including defining major modification, to clarify when whistleblower protections are conveyed. (Recommendation 2)

The Administrator should communicate whistleblower protections to grantees and subgrantees and their employees. (Recommendation 3)

AGENCY COMMENTS AND OUR EVALUATION

We provided a draft of this product to NASA for review and comment. NASA provided written comments on a draft of this chapter. In its written comments, reprinted in appendix II, NASA concurred with all three recommendations. In its response to our recommendations NASA agreed to develop and document a process to ensure it reviews reprisal complaints in a timely manner to ensure all parties' due process rights are protected, review existing procurement policy and clarify guidance as appropriate, and update NASA grant guidance to communicate whistleblower protections to grantees, sub-grantees and their employees. As agreed with your office, unless you publicly announce the contents of this chapter earlier, we plan no further distribution until 30 days from the report date. At that time, we will send copies to the appropriate congressional committees and members.

Sincerely yours,

Shelby S. Oakley
Director, Contracting and National Security Acquisitions

APPENDIX I: OBJECTIVES, SCOPE, AND METHODOLOGY

To assess the extent to which National Aeronautics and Space Administration's (NASA) Office of Inspector General (OIG) has investigated contractor and grantee whistleblower reprisal complaints and developed guidance for the investigations, we reviewed data provided by the NASA OIG on the total number of whistleblower allegations of fraud, waste, abuse, misconduct, or mismanagement and reprisal claims. We also reviewed the number of contractor and grantee employee whistleblower allegations and reprisal complaints provided by the OIG and the outcomes or decisions reached by the OIG of a reprisal complaint from fiscal years 2008 through 2017.[22] We assessed the reliability of these data by asking the NASA OIG to describe the source(s) of information used and steps taken to identify the numbers provided, and limitations and caveats that would affect GAO's use of the data—such as the data being self-reported by the OIG and Office of General Counsel. Based on these steps, we determined the data to be sufficient for our purposes of determining how the complaints were addressed. Additionally, we reviewed relevant documentation to assess the extent to which the NASA OIG was conducting investigations and communicating findings to the NASA Administrator within required time frames. To determine the extent NASA OIG developed guidance, we interviewed or obtained written answers from OIG officials about their processes and practices for investigating whistleblower reprisal complaints. We reviewed the guidance and training and other materials that NASA OIG uses to implement whistleblower protection investigations. We also visited Johnson Space Center (JSC)—selected because it had the highest number of reprisal cases from 2008 through 2017—to discuss policies and procedures specific to that center with OIG investigators and the OIG program manager for whistleblower protections. Because they are also a part of the Investigators' Central Field Office, we also spoke with investigators at Marshall Space Flight Center and Kennedy Space Center.

To assess the extent to which NASA's Administrator meets the statutory timeliness requirements to review reprisal complaints, we

---

[22] While OIG officials track whistleblower reprisal complaints, they do not specifically track disclosures as a separate category. The numbers are based on a search of their database using key terms such as "disclosure" or "contractor employee" in the complaint field. Officials pointed out that complaints made through the OIG's hotline may quality for whistleblower protections, but the complainant may not identify him or herself as a whistleblower or even want to be considered a whistleblower.

reviewed the timeliness of the Administrator's final determination to ensure that NASA was meeting statutory requirements. Specifically, we reviewed relevant documentation to assess the extent to which the Administrator was making final determination of reprisal in 30 days—the required review period specified by statute. We reviewed the Administrator's documentation on the final disposition of reprisal investigations and compared the date of the Administrator's final decision to the date of receipt of the reprisal investigations from the NASA OIG. We also conducted interviews with the Office of General Counsel, who spoke on behalf of the Administrator.

To assess the extent to which NASA communicated the applicable whistleblower reprisal protections externally with contractors, we reviewed a generalizable sample of NASA contracts to determine the extent a required whistleblower clause was included. We used the Federal Procurement Data System-Next Generation (FPDS-NG) to generate a sample of contract actions over $300,000 that were awarded by NASA in fiscal year 2016. We selected contracts that were not only over the simplified acquisition threshold (generally $150,000), but were over $300,000 to account for possible exceptions and to ensure that we were sampling contracts that would be required to include a whistleblower reprisal clause. From the 270 contracts identified, for purposes of examining the inclusion of NASA Federal Acquisition Regulation Supplement (NFS) clause 1852.203-71 (or other potentially applicable clauses) in NASA contracts, a legal requirement, we selected a generalizable random sample of 100 contracts. The sample is projectable to NASA fiscal year 2016 contracts; however, we did not make a case by case legal determination for contracts not in our sample. We randomly selected 10 contracts from each center that awarded new contracts in 2016, and for those centers that did not have 10 contracts, we selected all contracts.[23] The remaining contracts were then pulled from the NASA Shared Services Center (NSSC) because that center does a majority of NASA's contracting. We asked for contracts awarded in fiscal year 2016 to ensure we were

---

[23] NASA is comprised of 12 centers and 7 facilities located throughout the United States.

sampling contracts that are required to have the clause and would be reasonably accessible by NASA. We excluded interagency contracts and task or delivery orders awarded using blanket purchase agreements to ensure we sampled base contracts awarded by NASA, not other agencies.

We estimated the percentage of NASA contracts expected to include whistleblower clause(s) as the weighted average of results from the 10 contracting centers. Because we followed a probability procedure based on random selections, our sample is only one of a large number of samples that could have been drawn. Because each sample could have provided different estimates, we express the uncertainty associated with any particular estimate as a 95 percent confidence interval. This is the interval that, with repeated sampling, would be expected to contain the actual population value for 95 percent of the samples we could have drawn. As a result, we are 95 percent confident that this confidence interval contains the true percentage of contracts expected to include whistleblower clause(s); however, to assess legal compliance we would have to make a case by case determination, which we did not do. We conducted data reliability checks on the FPDS-NG dataset by comparing it to contract documentation obtained from contract files and determined it was sufficiently reliable for our purposes. Additionally, we conducted interviews with NASA procurement officials and contracting officers at multiple locations including NASA Headquarters, NSSC and JSC to discuss any additional measures NASA takes to communicate whistleblower protections to its contractors and their contractor employees. To further assess internal communication, we reviewed relevant documentation, including guidance, and conducted interviews with procurement officials, NASA's Office of General Counsel, and Chief Counsels at JSC, NSSC, and Marshall Space Flight Center.

To assess the extent to which NASA communicated the applicable whistleblower reprisal protections with grantees, we reviewed a non-generalizable sample of grants awarded by NASA in fiscal year 2016 to determine whether NASA grants included a mechanism notifying grantees of their employees' whistleblower rights and reprisal protections. We used FPDS-NG to identify a non-generalizable random sample of 10 grants awarded by NASA in fiscal year 2016 for review to determine whether any of the selected grants included a mechanism to communicate whistleblower reprisal protections to grantee employees.[24] We conducted data reliability checks on the FPDS-NG data by comparing it to grant documentation obtained from grant awards and determined it was sufficiently reliable for our purposes. Additionally, we conducted interviews with NASA grant making officials to discuss any additional measures NASA takes to communicate whistleblower reprisal protections to its grantees and their grantee employees.

Finally, in order to learn about contractor and grantee experiences during NASA's implementation of enhanced whistleblower protections, we conducted interviews with or received written answers to questions from a selected group of NASA contractors and grantees. Using FPDS-NG data, we selected institutions with the highest and lowest contracts (including small business contracts) and grants by obligations in 2016.[25] Using these selection criteria, we selected three contractors and three grantees to meet with based on the amount of funds obligated in 2016. We ultimately interviewed or obtained written answers from all selected contractors and grantees. Additionally, we spoke with two advocacy groups, one about grants and one about contracts.

We conducted this performance audit from March 2017 to March 2018 in accordance with generally accepted government auditing standards. Those standards require that we plan and perform the audit to obtain sufficient, appropriate evidence to provide a reasonable basis for our findings and conclusions based on our audit objectives. We believe that the evidence obtained provides a reasonable basis for our findings and conclusions based on our audit objectives.

---

[24] We selected 10 random grants from grants awarded in 2016, with positive dollar values to avoid grants captured in FPDS-NG as negative numbers due to deobligations.

[25] "Low" grant obligations starts at $150,000. We selected a figure that is consistent with the simplified acquisition threshold. This number was also selected because it reflects an organization that still has some significant spending, and would therefore benefit more from being aware of these protections.

APPENDIX II: COMMENTS FROM THE NATIONAL AERONAUTICS AND SPACE ADMINISTRATION

National Aeronautics and Space Administration
Office of the Administrator
Washington, DC 20546-0001

February 13, 2018

Ms. Shelby S. Oakley
Director
Contracting and National Security Acquisitions
United States Government Accountability Office
Washington, DC 20548

Dear Ms. Oakley:

The National Aeronautics and Space Administration (NASA) appreciates the opportunity to review and comment on the Government Accountability Office (GAO) draft report entitled, "NASA Contractor Whistleblowers: Steps Taken to Implement Program but Improvements to Timeliness and Guidance Needed" (GAO-18-262), dated January 18, 2018.

In the draft report, GAO makes three recommendations to the NASA Administrator intended to improve NASA's implementation of its contractor and grantee employee whistleblower program. Specifically, GAO recommends the following:

Recommendation 1: The Administrator should monitor, evaluate, and make appropriate corrective actions, such as a documented process, to ensure it reviews reprisal complaints in a timely manner.

Management's Response: Concur. NASA will develop a documented process to ensure it reviews reprisal complaints in a timely manner that ensure all parties due process rights are protected.

Estimated Completion Date: March 31, 2019

Recommendation 2: The Administrator should review NASA's guidance or develop other guidance, including defining major modification, to clarify when whistleblower protections are conveyed.

Management's Response: Concur. NASA will review existing procurement policy relative to when whistleblower protections are conveyed and provide clarifying guidance as appropriate.

Estimated Completion Date: October 31, 2018

Recommendation 3: The Administrator should communicate whistleblower protections to grantees and sub-grantees and their employees.

Management's Response: Concur. NASA will update the NASA Grant and Cooperative Agreement Manual to communicate whistleblower protections to grantees and sub-grantees and their employees.

Estimated Completion Date: October 31, 2018

Sincerely,

Robert M. Lightfoot, Jr.
Administrator (Acting)

Appendix III: ACCESSIBLE DATA

Data Tables

Data Table for Highlights figure, Figure: Timeline for NASA Administrator's Response for 5 Investigated Reprisal Cases Subject to Statutory 30-Day Final Determination from 2008 through June 2017

Statute requirements	Total time elapsed for Administrator response to OIG findings		Agency response to OIG findings not documented
Reprisal case 5	30	80	NA
Reprisal case 4	30	80	NA
Reprisal case 3	30	35	NA
Reprisal case 2	30	239	NA
Reprisal case 1	30	NA	243

Data Table for Figure 1: Disclosure and Reprisal Complaint Investigation and Review Processes for NASA Contractor and Grantee Employees

Employee of a contractor, subcontractor, grantee or subgrantee files initial disclosure of potential wrongdoing with one of the following:

- A Member of Congress or a representative of a committee of Congress
- Office of Inspector General (OIG) for the National Aeronautics and Space Administration (NASA)
- GAO
- A NASA employee responsible for contract or grant oversight or management
- An authorized official of the Department of Justice or other law enforcement agency
- A court or grand jury
- A management official or other employee of the contractor, subcontractor, r grantee who has the responsibility to investigate, discover, or address misconduct
-

If an employee believes that he or she has been subjected to a reprisal for the disclosure, he or she may file a reprisal complaint with the NASA OIGa

OIG determines whether an investigation is needed

If No

OIG determines the complaint is:

- Frivolous
- Fails to allege a violation of a prohibition under the statute
- Previously addressed by another federal or state judicial or administrative forum

IF No investigation is required OIG notifies complainant that no further action will be taken

If Yes

OIG initiates an investigation

OIG has 180 days to submit its report to the head of agency but can request an extension of up to 180 days with agreement from the complainant

OIG submits a report to:

- Head of agency
- Complainant
- Contractor, subcontractor, grantee or subgrantee

Head of agency determines:

- No reprisal
- Issues an order denying relief
- Reprisal

May issue an order granting relief

Head of agency has 30 days to make a determination and may request additional information

Data Table for Figure 2: NASA Office of Inspector General (OIG) Process for Investigating Reprisal Complaints

Reprisal complaint received

Complainant fills out whistleblower form to be identified as a whistleblower. This begins the 180 days investigation period. If complainant does not complete the form required, chooses not to continue the complaint, or the complaint otherwise does not qualify for protections, the investigation is closed

If complaint is NOT investigated OIG notifies complainant of decision not to investigate

If Complaint is investigated

- Over the course of 180 days, investigators gather evidence from the contractor or grantee which may include emails, human resource records, and interviews
- If the OIG determines the investiation will likely go longer than 180 days, the OIG asks for written agreement from complainant for an additional 180 days

- OIG transmits report of findings to agency head, contractor, and complainant

Data Table for Figure 3: Disposition of Reprisal Complaints Received by NASA's Office of Inspector General (OIG) from 2008 through June 2017

1) OIG reported whistleblower disclosures 277
2) Whistleblower reported experiencing reprisal, such as demotion Reprisal Complaints 48

   a) Ongoing investigations 5

   b) Investigated reprisal complaints 6

      i. Reprisal complaints substantiated by OIG 3

      ii. Reprisal complaints not substantiated by OIG 3

   c) Not Investigated, 37

      i. Determined disclosure not covered by statute 7

      ii. Determined the complaint was frivolous 27

      iii. Complaint addressed through other forum 3

Data Table for Figure 4: Timeline for NASA Administrator's Response for 5 Investigated Reprisal Cases Subject to Statutory 30-Day Final Determination from 2008 through June 2017

	Statute requirements	Total time elapsed for Administrator response to OIG findings	Agency response to OIG findings not documented
.eprisal case 5	30	80	
eprisal case 4	30	80	
eprisal case 3	30	35	
.eprisal case 2	30	239	
.eprisal case 1	30		243

In: Whistleblowers
Editor: Isabelle Guertin
ISBN: 978-1-53616-310-0

Chapter 6

OFFICE OF SPECIAL COUNSEL: ACTIONS NEEDED TO IMPROVE PROCESSING OF PROHIBITED PERSONNEL PRACTICE AND WHISTLEBLOWER DISCLOSURE CASES*

United States Government Accountability Office

ABBREVIATIONS

ADR	Alternative Dispute Resolution Unit
Army	Department of the Army
CEU	Complaints Examining Unit
CIGIE	Council of Inspectors General on Integrity and Efficiency
DHS	Department of Homeland Security
DU	Disclosure Unit
eCMS	Electronic Case Management System

* This is an edited, reformatted and augmented version of the United States Government Accountability Office Report to Congressional Committees, Publication No. GAO-18-400, dated June 2018.

IPD	Investigation and Prosecution Division
IPD-Field	Investigation and Prosecution Division-OSC field offices
IPD-HQ	Investigation and Prosecution Division-OSC headquarters
IG	inspector general
MSPB	Merit Systems Protection Board
NSF-OIG	National Science Foundation Office of Inspector General
OSC	Office of Special Counsel
OSC 2000	OSC's electronic case management system
PPP	Prohibited Personnel Practice
RDU	Retaliation and Disclosure Unit
VA	Department of Veterans Affairs

WHY GAO DID THIS STUDY

OSC is responsible for safeguarding the merit system in federal employment by protecting employees and applicants, including whistleblowers. Consequently, OSC must ensure its case processes are adequate to protect the federal workforce, including its own employees.

GAO was asked to review OSC case processes and procedures for whistleblower disclosures and PPPs. For both types of cases, this chapter among other things (1) examines trends in cases received and closed from fiscal year 2011 to 2016, (2) examines timeliness of cases closed from fiscal year 2011 to 2016, and (3) assesses the extent to which safeguards are in place for OSC employees who make allegations.

GAO reviewed OSC case guidance, processes, controls, and the latest available OSC data from fiscal year 2016. GAO also assessed whether OSC's processes adhered to *Standards for Internal Control in the Federal Government*; and surveyed and interviewed OSC employees.

WHAT GAO RECOMMENDS

GAO is making seven recommendations, including that OSC communicate timelines to whistleblowers and finalize a time frame for obtaining an independent internal review process for OSC employees. OSC agreed with GAO's recommendations.

WHAT GAO FOUND

Between fiscal years 2011 and 2016, the number of prohibited personnel practice (PPP) and whistleblower disclosure cases the Office of Special Counsel (OSC) received from employees of other federal agencies increased by 66 percent. Although the number of cases OSC closed increased by 62 percent during this period, the pace at which cases were closed did not keep pace with the number of cases received. As a result, the backlog also grew. OSC closed the vast majority of cases it received for various reasons, including a lack of sufficient evidence or lack of OSC jurisdiction.

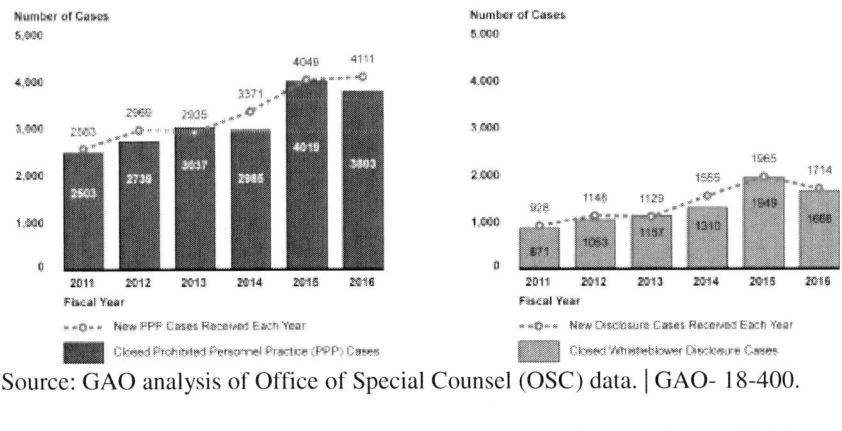

Source: GAO analysis of Office of Special Counsel (OSC) data. | GAO- 18-400.

Trends in PPP and Whistleblower Disclosure Cases, Fiscal Years 2011 to 2016

OSC's processing time increased for both types of cases from fiscal year 2011 to 2016, but the time for processing whistleblower disclosure cases experienced a significantly greater increase, from a median of 10 days to 29 days. Because processing times for whistleblower disclosures include the time that agencies take to conduct investigations and respond to OSC, they can be significant, especially if an agency requests an extension from OSC for additional time. GAO found that in fiscal year 2016, OSC approved on average 2.7 extensions per whistleblower referral, and that the average time to process these cases was 1.8 years. However, OSC does not provide whistleblowers specific information on timelines for agency responses to OSC referrals; as a result these individuals may not know how long the process could potentially take.

OSC's process for reviewing and referring allegations submitted by its own employees includes the involvement of officials and staff. This involvement was identified as a key concern by OSC employees. Specifically, 17 of the 87 OSC employees who responded to GAO's survey reported that they considered filing internal allegations against another OSC employee but chose not to do so in part because they feared losing anonymity, feared management reprisal, or were uncertain how to file an internal OSC complaint. Congress recently enacted statutory changes to provide additional safeguards to OSC employees who file internal complaints, including establishing an agreement with an agency inspector general to review internal OSC cases. However, OSC has not yet fully implemented such an agreement.

June 14, 2018
Congressional Committees

The U.S. Office of Special Counsel (OSC) is an independent federal investigative and prosecutorial agency. Its primary mission is to safeguard the merit system in federal employment by protecting employees and applicants for federal employment from prohibited personnel practices (PPP), including reprisal for whistleblowing. OSC also reviews claims of wrongdoing within the federal government from current federal employees, former employees, and applicants for federal employment. These individuals, known as whistleblowers, report to OSC potential fraud, waste, and abuse in the federal government and threats to public safety or health.

You asked us to review OSC's processes and procedures for PPP and whistleblower disclosures cases. This chapter examines (1) the number of PPP and whistleblower disclosure cases OSC received and closed from fiscal year 2011 to 2016 and the effect on its existing caseload, (2) the timeliness of PPP and whistleblower disclosure cases closed from fiscal year 2011 to 2016, (3) the extent to which OSC's PPP and whistleblower disclosure case processes adhere to selected internal control principles, and (4) the extent to which safeguards are in place for OSC employees who file PPP and whistleblower disclosure complaints against OSC.

For the first objective, we reviewed case-level data from OSC's electronic case management system, OSC 2000, on PPP and whistleblower disclosure cases that OSC closed from fiscal years 2011 to 2016 (the most recent full fiscal year available at the time of our analysis). We identified and analyzed the number of PPP and whistleblower disclosure cases closed, the federal agencies from which they were received, the types of case resolutions, and the effect of case receipts and closures on OSC's existing caseload.

For the second objective, we analyzed OSC 2000 case-level data on the median number of days cases were open. We also analyzed OSC data and documents on agency extension requests granted for whistleblower disclosure cases and compared the median number of days whistleblower cases were open to relevant statutory requirements. We assessed the reliability of the OSC 2000 data, by reviewing relevant documentation, interviewing knowledgeable OSC officials, and electronically testing the data to identify obvious errors or outliers. We determined that the OSC 2000 data used in our analysis were sufficiently reliable for our reporting purposes. For both objectives 1 and 2, we also interviewed OSC officials, federal agency liaisons, whistleblower advocacy organizations, and an employment law firm to obtain their views on the number of cases received and closed by OSC.

For the third objective, we reviewed OSC procedures, reports, and related guidance intended to help OSC implement its case processes for PPP and whistleblower disclosure cases. We also interviewed relevant OSC officials concerning their understanding of OSC's case processes and procedures. To obtain their respective views on OSC's PPP and whistleblower disclosure case processes, we interviewed OSC liaison officials from the three federal agencies that most frequently were the subject of PPP complaints and whistleblower disclosures in cases closed in fiscal year 2016, and interviewed officials from two whistleblower advocacy organizations and one law firm that specializes in federal employment law. We assessed whether OSC's procedures and related guidance adhered to relevant Standards for Internal Control in the Federal Government.[1]

To obtain OSC staff's perspective on the extent to which OSC adhered to relevant internal control principles related to processing PPP and whistleblower disclosure cases, we held small group discussions with employees from the six OSC work units involved in the PPP and whistleblower disclosure processes. For four of the six units, we held these discussions with a random, nongeneralizable selection of nonmanagement staff in those units. For the remaining two units, given their small size, we held discussions with all nonmanagement staff in those units. A GAO analyst reviewed all six write-ups of our small group discussions to code identified themes from the discussions. Another GAO analyst reviewed the coding. If there was a disagreement, the two analysts reviewed and discussed until they reached agreement. As a result of the analysis, we identified the major themes that covered the relevant internal control principles we discussed with the participants.

To assess how well OSC implemented its PPP and whistleblower disclosure case procedures and processes, we reviewed five distinct groups of PPP and whistleblower disclosure cases closed in fiscal year 2016.[2]

---

[1] GAO, *Internal Control: Standards for Internal Control in the Federal Government*, GAO-14-704G (Washington, D.C.: Sept. 10, 2014).

[2] These included (1) whistleblower disclosure cases referred to an agency, (2) whistleblower disclosure cases not referred to an agency, (3) PPP cases with a favorable action taken in the

Given the larger size of case populations for two of these groups, we examined randomly selected, generalizable samples of cases. For the remaining three groups, none of which totaled more than 84 cases, we reviewed all cases of that case type. We selected these groups to include the various types of case outcomes for PPP and whistleblower disclosure cases. We used uniform data collection instruments for our file reviews to help ensure we consistently captured information on the completeness of required documentation for PPP and whistleblower disclosure cases. OSC officials reviewed and verified the elements of the data collection instruments we used to review case files. To ensure the accuracy of our reviews, two GAO analysts reviewed each case file and reconciled any differences between responses. We then identified common themes from our reviews.

For the fourth objective, we examined OSC procedures for its employees to file PPP and whistleblower disclosure allegations. We interviewed officials from OSC, the National Science Foundation Office of the Inspector General (NSF-OIG), and the Council of Inspectors General for Integrity and Efficiency (CIGIE). We interviewed officials from these entities because they review certain complaints and disclosures from OSC employees. In addition, we assessed whether OSC's procedures aligned with relevant Standards for Internal Control in the Federal Government.

We also sent a survey to all 132 OSC employees to obtain their views on processes by which they could file PPP complaints and make whistleblower disclosures. The survey questions and subsequent responses helped us identify OSC employees who had filed or considered filing an allegation against another OSC employee. We conducted in-person and phone interviews with this group of OSC employees to allow them to discuss their views and experiences with OSC's internal allegations procedures in more detail. We supplemented these views with information from OSC's Federal Employee Viewpoint Surveys from fiscal years 2012 to 2017. Finally, we reviewed all PPP complaints and whistleblower

---

Complaints Examining Unit (CEU), (4) PPP cases referred for investigation, and (5) cases closed in CEU without a favorable action.

disclosures from fiscal years 2011 through 2016 that OSC submitted to the CIGIE Integrity Committee and the NSFOIG, as well as all OSC PPP complaints and whistleblower disclosures where OSC reviewed allegations against OSC employees. For additional details on our scope and methodology, see appendix I.

We conducted this performance audit from March 2017 to June 2018 in accordance with generally accepted government auditing standards. Those standards require that we plan and perform the audit to obtain sufficient, appropriate evidence to provide a reasonable basis for our findings and conclusions based on our audit objectives. We believe that the evidence obtained provides a reasonable basis for our findings and conclusions based on our audit objectives.

BACKGROUND

Office of Special Counsel

Individuals who believe that a prohibited personnel practice (PPP), such as nepotism, has been committed may file complaints with OSC.[3] OSC has a number of other responsibilities as well. It operates as a secure channel for federal whistleblowing disclosures of violations of law, rule, or regulation; gross mismanagement; gross waste of funds; abuse of authority; and substantial and specific dangers to public health or safety. OSC also provides advisory opinions and enforces Hatch Act restrictions on political activities of individuals employed by the federal government as well as certain state and local government employees employed in connection with programs financed by federal funds. Finally, the agency enforces the rights of federal employees and applicants for federal employment under the Uniformed Services Employment and Reemployment Rights Act of 1994.[4]

---

[3] Nepotism is the hiring, promotion, or advocating the hiring or promotion of relatives. See 5 U.S.C. § 2302(b)(7).

[4] Pub. L. No. 103-353, 108 Stat. 3149 (Oct. 13, 1994), *codified* at 38 U.S.C. §§ 4301-4335.

OSC is led by the Special Counsel, who is appointed by the President and later confirmed by the Senate to serve a 5-year term.[5] The current Special Counsel was confirmed on October 16, 2017. OSC is headquartered in Washington, D.C., with three field offices in Dallas, Detroit, and Oakland. As of fiscal year 2017, OSC had 135 full-time equivalent employees.[6]

OSC tracks its workload across case types through its computerized system, known as OSC 2000. OSC 2000 is designed to store case status updates on all case types, from the initial filing of the complaint, whistleblower disclosure, or request for advisory opinion until closure and archiving of the file. OSC staff also maintain paper case files. OSC is transitioning to a new data tracking system, the electronic Case Management System (eCMS). According to OSC, eCMS will allow OSC to track and maintain electronic cases, as well as provide capacity to deliver customizable reports.

Prohibited Personnel Practices

Federal law designates 14 PPPs.[7] If a federal employee, applicant, or former employee believes he or she has been subjected to 1 or more of these PPPs, he or she can file a complaint with OSC using OSC Form 11—Complaint of Possible Prohibited Personnel Practice or Other Prohibited Activity—or submit a correspondence. In fiscal year 2016, OSC received 4,111 PPP complaints, about 68 percent of its total cases received that year. See figure 1 for OSC's PPP process.

PPP complaints are received by OSC's Complaints Examining Unit (CEU). The CEU Chief assigns cases to CEU examiners based on the following: case complexity, case priority, examiner's case preferences,

[5] 5 U.S.C. § 1211(b).

[6] Full-time equivalent employees equal the number of employees on full-time schedules plus the number of employees on part-time schedules converted to a full-time basis.

[7] 5 U.S.C. § 2302(b).

examiner position, examiner availability, and the examiner's current caseload.

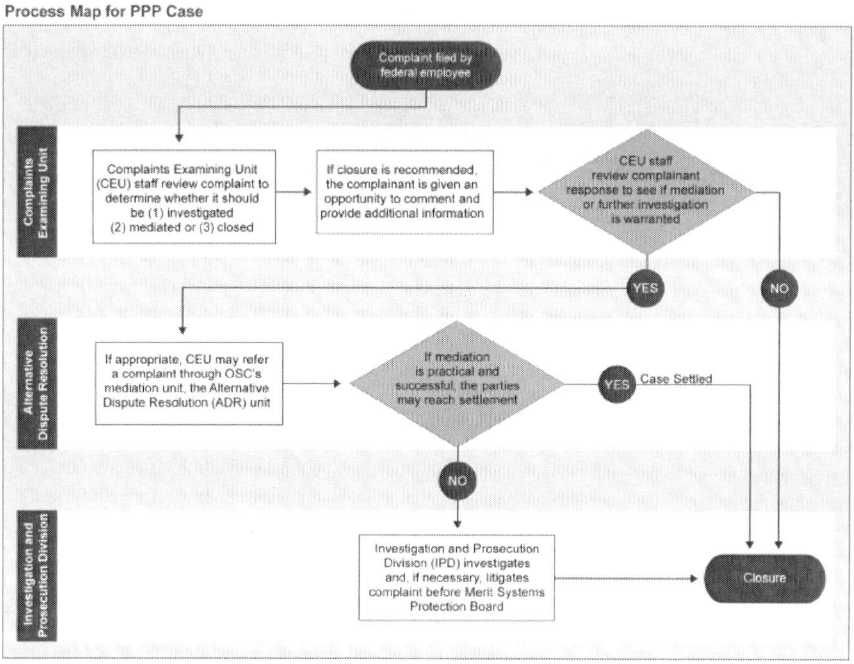

Source: GAO analysis of Office of Special Counsel (OSC) documentation. | GAO- 18-400.

Note: CEU may also forward cases to the Retaliation and Disclosure Unit (RDU) for hybrid cases that involve both a whistleblower disclosure and an allegation of retaliation. In addition, CEU may directly refer some cases to ADR and some directly to IPD. IPD or RDU may also refer cases back to ADR.

Figure 1. Office of Special Counsel (OSC) Prohibited Personnel Practice (PPP) Process.

A CEU examiner may determine a complaint contains evidence of a PPP or other prohibited activity, which warrants further investigation by OSC. To make this determination, the examiner reviews the information contained in the complaint, speaks with the complainant, and may also contact liaison officials at the federal agency in question. The examiner may also request information from those parties. After CEU's review is complete, CEU could: (1) close the case, (2) refer the case to the

Alternative Dispute Resolution (ADR) Unit for evaluation for potential mediation, or (3) refer the case to the Investigation and Prosecution Division (IPD) for further investigation. When referring a case to either office, CEU has determined that there are reasonable grounds to believe that a PPP has occurred, exists, or will occur.

ADR reviews complaints to determine whether they are appropriate for mediation after CEU has referred them for investigation, but before any investigation has occurred. If the mediation is successful, both parties agree to settlement terms and the agreement is put into writing. If settlement is not reached, the complaint will proceed to IPD for investigation.

IPD investigates PPP allegations for OSC. When IPD receives a case, an attorney or investigator is assigned who may request additional documentation and also interview the parties involved. Attorneys are assigned based on their current caseload and the complexity of cases. After the IPD attorney completes the investigation, IPD management discusses the case evidence and applicable law and recommends an outcome that is subject to review by OSC management. Depending on the recommendation, IPD will (1) close the complaint because no further action is warranted, or (2) pursue corrective or disciplinary action (or both) against the subject officials.[8]

OSC allows complainants 13 days to comment on preliminary determinations and the reason for the determinations made in a case. After reviewing any response from the complainant, IPD or CEU will decide whether further investigation is warranted or the complaint should be closed.[9]

At any time during the PPP complaint process, OSC units may pursue favorable actions on cases. A favorable action is an outcome in a case that could result in a specific benefit to the complainant, an outcome aimed at disciplining the subject official and deterring future bad conduct, or an

---

[8] In some instances where there is evidence that supports the allegations in a complaint, IPD may attempt to settle a complaint with the agency or refer the case to ADR if the investigator deems it appropriate.

[9] Complainants can request that OSC reconsider the closure. At this point, OSC management reviews both the complainant's submission and the case.

improvement to agency processes. OSC tracks the following types of favorable actions that result from its involvement in PPP cases:

- stays (e.g., delay in an agency decision to demote the employee),
- corrective actions (e.g., agency rescinds a suspension),
- systemic corrective actions (e.g., subject agency changes deficient regulation), and
- disciplinary actions (e.g., agency official is suspended).[10]

If the agency does not take the corrective or disciplinary action requested or grant the stay within a reasonable period, OSC can file a petition with the Merit System Protection Board (MSPB).[11]

Whistleblower Disclosures

OSC also responds to employees', former employees', and applicants' disclosures of alleged wrongdoing (termed "whistleblower disclosures") within federal agencies. In fiscal year 2016, OSC received 1,714 whistleblower disclosures, about 28 percent of its total caseload received that year.[12] OSC has jurisdiction and may take further action if the whistleblower disclosure alleges a violation of law, rule, or regulation; gross mismanagement; gross waste of funds; abuse of authority; or a substantial and specific danger to public health or safety.[13] Figure 2 illustrates OSC's process for reviewing these cases, and a more detailed description of each step follows below.

---

[10] OSC tracks stays of personnel action, settlements, corrective actions, and disciplinary actions as performance metrics based on its Strategic Plan.

[11] MSPB's mission is to protect the merit system principles and promote an effective federal workforce free of prohibited personnel practices. MSPB's primary role is to adjudicate the cases brought to the Board. 5 U.S.C. §§ 1204.

[12] The remaining cases closed by OSC in fiscal year 2016 were Hatch Act and Uniformed Services Employment and Reemployment Rights Act of 1994 cases.

[13] 5 U.S.C. § 1213(a).

Process Map for Whistleblower Disclosure

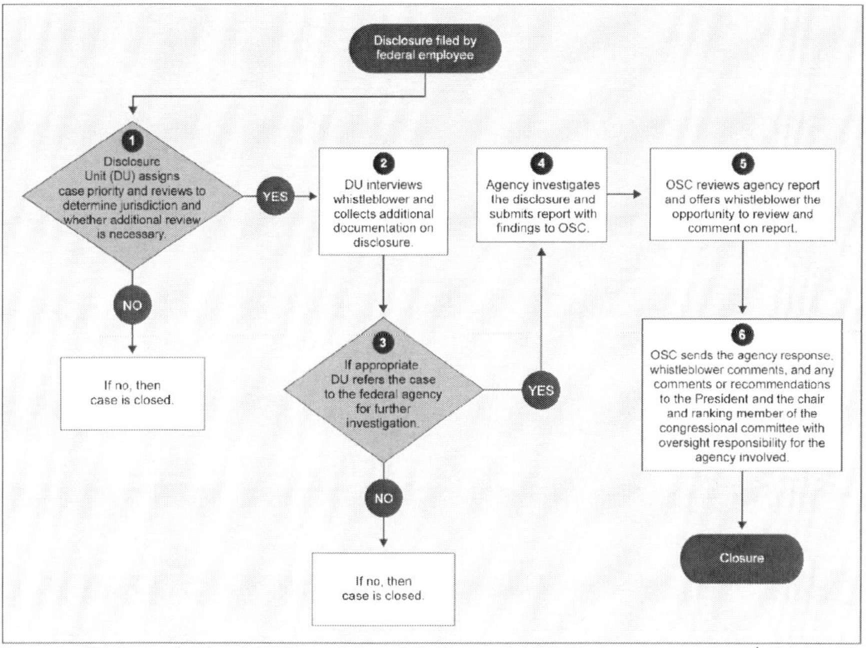

Source: GAO analysis of Office of Special Counsel (OSC) documentation. | GAO- 18-400.

Figure 2. Office of Special Counsel (OSC) Whistleblower Disclosure Process.

OSC takes the following steps in the whistleblower disclosure process:

1. OSC management reviews the case to determine whether it constitutes a whistleblower disclosure as defined by statute and if OSC has jurisdiction over the matter. If not, OSC closes the case.
2. If OSC determines the case constitutes a whistleblower disclosure, an attorney in the Disclosure Unit (DU) is assigned. He or she examines the material forwarded by the whistleblower, interviews the whistleblower, and requests additional information if needed. Attorneys are assigned cases based on their current caseload and the complexity of the case. The assigned attorney determines whether there is a substantial likelihood that the information discloses one of the types of wrongdoing described above. Prior to December 2017, OSC was required by law to make this

determination within 15 days of receiving the whistleblower disclosure. Because of a statutory change in December 2017, OSC now has 45 days to make this determination.[14]

3. If OSC determines that the substantial likelihood threshold is met, it formally refers the allegations to the head of the subject agency.[15] OSC will close a case if it determines that there is not a substantial likelihood that the alleged action occurred. Prior to referring a whistleblower disclosure, OSC must ask whether the whistleblower consents to the release of his or her name to the agency.[16] If the whistleblower declines, OSC is to inform the whistleblower that it may be possible for agency officials to identify the whistleblower based on the information disclosed, and that anonymity may affect the agency investigation. In referred cases, when OSC submits a referral letter to the agency head, the agency head is required to investigate the allegations and provide a written report to OSC in 60 days or within any longer period agreed to in writing by the Special Counsel. OSC also notifies the whistleblower of the referral to the agency. OSC can grant multiple time extensions if the agency requests additional time to respond. Each extension could provide 60 or more additional days for the agency to respond to the referral. OSC also can informally refer the allegations to the subject agency's general counsel office if the allegations do not meet the substantial likelihood threshold and are less egregious in nature.[17]

---

[14] National Defense Authorization Act for Fiscal Year 2018, Pub. L. No. 115-91, § 1097(c)(2)(A), 131 Stat. 1283, 1618 (Dec. 12, 2017), amending 5 U.S.C. § 1213(b).

[15] 5 U.S.C. § 1213(c). In cases where OSC does not make a positive substantial likelihood determination, OSC may, with the consent of the whistleblower, transmit the information to the head of the agency concerned. The agency head is required to inform OSC in writing, within a reasonable time, of what action has been or is being taken, and when such action will be completed. OSC is required to inform the whistleblower of the agency's report. 5 U.S.C. § 1213(g)(2).

[16] OSC may determine that the whistleblower disclosure of the individual's identity is necessary because of an imminent danger to public health or safety or imminent violation of any criminal law. 5 U.S.C. § 1213(h).

[17] OSC also has the discretionary authority to refer information to the agency head from a whistleblower who reasonably believes the information evidences wrongdoing within an agency other than the one where the individual is, was employed by, or has applied to, or

4. The agency is to investigate the whistleblower disclosure and submit a report to OSC with its findings. The report is required to include the agency's findings and a description of any action taken or planned as a result of the investigation, including policy changes the agency has implemented in response to the whistleblower disclosure.[18]
5. When OSC receives the agency's report, OSC's assigned attorney is to review the report to determine whether it contains the information required and whether the report's findings appear to be reasonable. OSC may request a supplemental agency report if it believes the agency did not include the necessary information or the findings do not appear reasonable. OSC is then to share the agency response with the whistleblower, who may provide comments.
6. Finally, OSC is to submit the agency report and any supplemental reports, the whistleblower's comments, and any comments or recommendations from OSC to the President and the chairmen and ranking members of the congressional committees with oversight responsibility for the involved agency. OSC also sends the involved agency and the whistleblower a closure letter and posts the case information on OSC's public website.[19]

---

where the information is obtained outside the performance of the individual's duties. The agency must inform OSC of the actions taken, or to be taken, in response to the referral, and when such action shall be completed. OSC is required to inform the whistleblower of the agency's response. 5 U.S.C. § 1213(g)(1).

[18] 5 U.S.C. § 1213(c), (d).

[19] See www.osc.gov. Whistleblowers may request that OSC reconsider its review of a case. Generally, a whistleblower is limited to two requests for reconsideration. Upon receipt of a request for reconsideration, the attorney is to review the request and contact the whistleblower to determine if any additional information has been provided. If there is no information presented that reverses the initial determination, the attorney is to prepare a closure letter for review and signature by OSC management.

OSC's Data Show a Higher Number of Cases Received and Cases Closed from 2011 to 2016, although the Backlog Has Increased

Number of Cases Received and Cases Closed Increased More than 60 Percent between Fiscal Years 2011 and 2016

OSC reported that it received a total of 5,825 PPP and whistleblower disclosure cases in 2016, an increase of 66 percent over the 3,511 cases it received in fiscal year 2011. (See figure 3.) OSC and agency officials believe that the passage of the Whistleblower Protection Enhancement Act of 2012 likely contributed to the increase. The act amended federal personnel law to, among other things, clarify the breadth of disclosures that are afforded protection, expand the right to bring reprisal claims for certain protected activities, and enhance the remedies available to federal whistleblowers who have suffered retaliation.[20]

OSC's previous Special Counsel attributed some of the increase in cases received to OSC's expanded educational outreach efforts to federal employees. For example, in fiscal years 2015 and 2016, OSC reported it completed over 300 outreach events to agencies and certified 69 new agencies under its 2302(c) Certification Program. According to OSC, this program helps agencies meet their statutory requirements for informing employees of their whistleblowing rights.[21] Additionally, on its website, OSC promotes favorable actions received for individuals in PPP and whistleblower cases. OSC also issues various press releases regarding case closures, and posts favorable results on social media. According to OSC, these actions promote greater awareness among federal employees of the services OSC provides.

---

[20] Pub. L. No. 112-199, 126 Stat. 1465 (Nov. 27, 2012).

[21] Agency heads are required to ensure, in consultation with OSC, that employees are informed of the rights and remedies available to them under the Whistleblower Protection Act, as amended. 5 U.S.C. § 2302(c)(1)(B), (2)(C). In 2002, OSC established a "2302(c) Certification Program" to provide agencies and agency components with a process for meeting this statutory requirement.

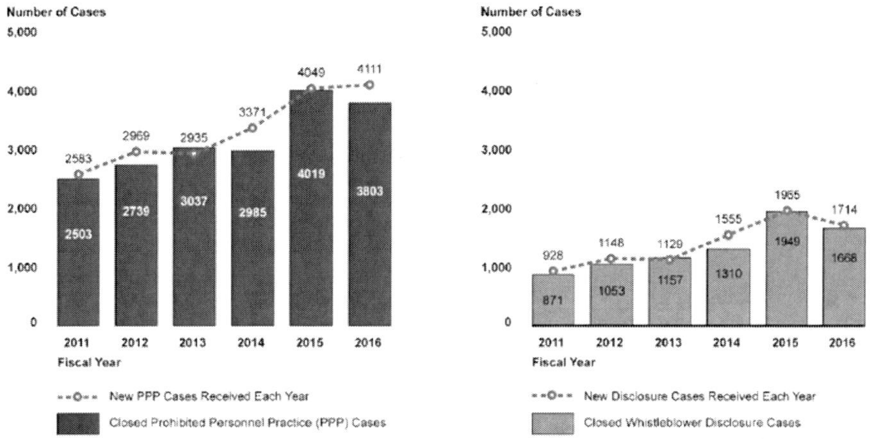

Source: GAO analysis of Office of Special Counsel (OSC) documentation. | GAO- 18-400.

Figure 3. Numbers of PPP and Whistleblower Disclosure Cases Received and Closed from Fiscal Years 2011 through 2016.

OSC also reported that the number of cases closed increased between fiscal years 2011 and 2016. As shown in figure 3 above, the total number of closed PPP and whistleblower disclosure cases increased from 3,374 in fiscal year 2011 to 5,471 in fiscal year 2016, a 62 percent increase. In 2016, the number of closed PPP cases (3,803) was about 50 percent more than in 2011 (2,503), and the number of closed whistleblower disclosure cases nearly doubled from 871 in 2011 to 1,668 in 2016. During this time, staff available to work on these cases full time increased by 29 percent, from 76 employees in 2011 to 98 employees in 2016.

During the period we reviewed, OSC did not refer the majority of cases it ultimately closed to either IPD (in PPP cases) or the subject agency (in whistleblower disclosure cases) for additional investigation. OSC closed these cases for at least one of the following reasons:

1. The case lacked sufficient evidence to warrant further investigation.
2. OSC lacked jurisdiction over the case, which happens if the whistleblower in question is not a current, former, or prospective

federal employee, or if the individual has the basis of an Equal Employment Opportunity complaint.[22]

3. The case had been misfiled, meaning complainants incorrectly filed PPPs as whistleblower disclosures.

From fiscal years 2011 through 2016, at least 80 percent of OSC's case closures were the result of one these OSC determinations. According to OSC staff, many federal workers and applicants for the federal workforce incorrectly submit PPP allegations as whistleblower disclosure allegations because they do not understand the difference between PPPs and whistleblower disclosures and their respective filing systems (i.e., Form 11 for PPPs and Form 12 for whistleblower disclosures). Such misfiling in turn delays OSC's processing of the case. Once correctly identified, DU closes the whistleblower disclosure case, and notifies CEU staff to open a PPP case, then CEU staff process the cases in accordance with CEU procedures.

OSC has undertaken efforts to replace the separate filing systems with a one-stop filing system, known as Form 14, for both types of cases. OSC staff believe Form 14 could reduce misfiling because the single form should remove the need for filers to distinguish between PPP and whistleblower disclosure allegations. OSC promulgated a final rule adopting Form 14 effective July 2017 but has since encountered delays.[23] OSC officials told us that they are looking to implement this system in tandem with the rollout of OSC's new electronic case management system, which is still in testing.

We also found that OSC's caseload, in terms of case closures, is not spread evenly across federal agencies. In fiscal year 2016, 51 percent of all OSC case closures involved cases at three agencies, the Department of Veterans Affairs (VA), the Department of the Army (Army), and the Department of Homeland Security (DHS). The percentage of closed PPP and whistleblower disclosure cases that involved VA increased from 20

---

[22] OSC also has no jurisdiction over allegations filed by employees of intelligence agencies, the armed forces, ourselves, the Postal Rate Commission, and the Federal Bureau of Investigation.

[23] 82 Fed. Reg. 26,739 (June 9, 2017).

percent (678 cases) in 2011 to 34 percent (1,853 cases) in 2016. During the same period, the percentage of cases that involved DHS and Army remained stable. In fiscal year 2011, DHS and Army represented 18 percent of OSC's closed PPP and whistleblower disclosure cases and 17 percent in fiscal year 2016. Thus, VA's caseload can account for much of the increase in OSC's closed cases during the period of our review. VA officials attributed the higher number of VA cases to increased publicity stemming from congressional hearings and media attention surrounding lengthy patient wait times at VA.

OSC reported having taken several actions to help process the higher caseload. OSC officials said that, starting in 2013, incoming PPP cases were assigned to nonCEU staff across the agency, including employees in the Hatch Act Unit, which normally processes cases involving alleged illegal political activities. In addition, OSC revised its review process in 2014 to help process the higher number of cases originating from VA. This process included a focus on expedited settlements for whistleblower retaliation cases. Finally, in fiscal year 2016, OSC established its Retaliation and Disclosure Unit (RDU) as a permanent unit to process hybrid cases that involve both a whistleblower disclosure and an allegation of retaliation. Previously, CEU, DU, and IPD reviewed these cases separately.

OSC Case Backlog Persists despite OSC' s Efforts

Heading into fiscal year 2011, OSC already had a PPP and whistleblower disclosure case backlog of 953 cases. As previously discussed, OSC has received an increased number of PPP and whistleblower disclosure cases every year except 1 since 2011, including approximately 2,000 more cases in fiscal year 2016 than it received in fiscal year 2011. This resulted in nearly doubling backlogged cases from fiscal years 2011 to 2016 and an increase in the proportion of total caseload backlogged each year except 2012 and 2014. As shown in table 1, OSC's case backlog at end of fiscal year 2016 was over 1,850 PPP and whistleblower disclosure cases and represented over 24 percent of the PPP and whistleblower disclosure caseload. The trend of an increasing backlog was particularly evident in whistleblower disclosure cases, where the number of cases carried over as a percentage of total whistleblower caseload increased from 8.4 percent in fiscal year 2011 to 20.8 percent in fiscal year 2016.

A sustained backlog puts OSC's ability to fulfill its mission of protecting federal employees at risk. As OSC noted in its fiscal year 2017 Performance and Accountability Report, a longer backlog risks further delay for processing newly received cases. Further, lengthy processing times delays attaining desired favorable actions and remedying

Table 1. Number and Percentage of Prohibited Personnel Practice and Whistleblower Disclosure Case Backlog from Fiscal Years 2011-2016

	Fiscal Year					
	2011	2012	2013	2014	2015	2016
Cases remaining from prior years	953	1,074	1,381	1,241	1,851	1,858
New cases received	3,511	4,117	4,064	4,926	6,014	5,825
Total caseload	4,464	5,191	5,445	6,167	7,865	7,683
Percent of caseload backlogged	21.3	20.7	25.4	20.1	23.5	24.2

Source: GAO analysis of Office of Special Counsel data. | GAO-18-400.

OSC's Time to Close Both Types of Cases Increased from Fiscal Year 2011 to 2016, but Review Times for Referred Whistleblower Disclosure Cases Increased the Most

OSC is Taking Longer to Process Cases

As discussed above, the majority of OSC's case closures do not require full investigation. However, overall OSC is taking longer to review and close PPP and whistleblower disclosure cases (measured as the median number of days from when OSC receives a case).[24] According to OSC management, processing times are affected by the complexity of a particular case, the cooperation level of involved parties, and agency requests for additional time. Figure 4 shows the median number of days OSC took to close all PPP and whistleblower disclosures cases from fiscal year 2011 through fiscal year 2016. Median closure times for whistleblower disclosure cases showed a greater relative increase over this time than PPP cases, increasing from 10 days in 2011 to 29 days in 2016.

Cases Referred to Agencies Often Take the Longest to Process

The increase in the median number of days to close all whistleblower disclosure cases, from 10 to 29 days, was also influenced by the time it took OSC to close the small subset of cases that it referred to agencies for investigation. While these cases represented only 5 percent of the whistleblower disclosure cases OSC closed in fiscal year 2016, they took significantly longer to close. The median lifespan of whistleblower disclosure cases that OSC referred to agencies for investigation increased from 450 days to 668 days from fiscal years 2011 to 2016, a 48 percent increase, with some cases taking as long as 1,523 days (or almost 4.2 years) to close.[25]

Referred whistleblower disclosure cases have lengthy review times across multiple stages of the case review process. The 2018 OSC Reauthorization, part of the National Defense Authorization Act for 2018, grants OSC 45 days, instead of 15, to determine whether there is a substantial likelihood that the information disclosed one or more of the categories of wrongdoing.[26]

---

[24] We report case processing times in terms of medians because some cases that are referred for further investigation can have extremely long processing times. Despite being generally rare, these cases can distort averages that are described in terms of means.

[25] Some whistleblower disclosure referrals are closed out quickly in OSC's case management system because they are anonymous and are thus referred directly to the agencies' Inspector General instead of the agencies themselves. The median closure time for these referrals ranged from 2 to 7 days. As a result, we omitted them from this analysis.

[26] 5 U.S.C. § 1213(b) and Pub. L. No: 115-91, § 1097, 131 Stat. 1283, 1618 (Dec. 12, 2017).

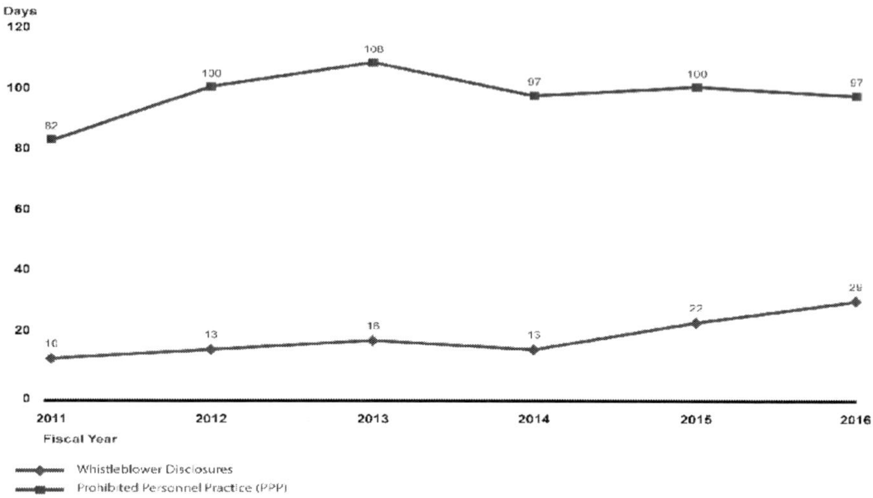

Source: GAO analysis of Office of Special Counsel (OSC) documentation. | GAO- 18-400.

Figure 4. The Median Number of Days to Close All PPP and Whistleblower Disclosure Cases from Fiscal Years 2011 to 2016.

Even though this change gives OSC increased processing flexibility, OSC may not be able to meet these revised standards. Of the 71 referrals under subsection 1213(c) we reviewed that were closed in fiscal year 2016, 55 would not have met the 45-day requirement. In contrast, 16 would have met the 45-day requirement, with 8 of the 16 referred to an agency within 15 days. Among the closed cases that we reviewed in fiscal year 2016, the median number of days OSC took between opening and referring a case was 91 days. Between fiscal years 2011 and 2016, prior to the change in law, OSC made referrals within 45 days less than half the time in every year except for fiscal year 2012.[27]

A major factor contributing to the lengthy processing times for referred whistleblower disclosure cases is the length of time it takes agencies to conduct their investigations in response to OSC. By law, the subject agency is required to respond to the allegations within 60 days.[28] OSC may grant one or more extensions of this timeline to agencies that request them, and

[27] See table 8 in appendix II for more information.

[28] 5 U.S.C. § 1213(c)(1)(B). The time the agency has to respond can be longer than 60 days if agreed to in writing by the Special Counsel.

OSC did so in most cases we reviewed. From fiscal year 2011 through fiscal year 2016, OSC granted on average 88 percent of all extension requests received from agencies. In any given year during this period, OSC granted at least 83 percent of extension requests. While OSC procedures normally allow up to two extensions, the disclosure worksheet included in case files has slots for up to five extensions. We found that OSC granted between 2.7 and 4 agency extension requests per case on average from fiscal years 2011 through 2016.

Our review of cases closed in fiscal year 2016 also showed similar results. OSC did not receive agencies' responses within 60 days for any of the 71 referrals under subsection 1213(c) it closed in fiscal year 2016 that we reviewed. The median number of days between when the referral letter was sent to the agency and when the initial agency response was received by OSC was 169 days, and 33.8 percent (23 of 68) took more than 200 days.[29] In certain instances OSC may ask the agency for a supplemental report if OSC believes the agency's report was insufficient. The median number of days between when the referral letter was sent to the agency and when OSC received the final supplemental report response was 289 days and 69.6 percent (48 of 69) took more than 200 days.[30] Two agencies, VA and DHS, accounted for 56 of the 71 referrals made under section 1213(c). For those referrals, the median number of days for VA's initial responses to the referrals was 168, and DHS's was 165 days. The median number of days for OSC to receive a final supplemental report from VA was 266 days, and from DHS was 370 days.

Agency officials we interviewed told us that they routinely request extensions and OSC rarely or never rejects their initial requests. They explained that in most cases they need extensions to compile the necessary information to respond to the referral and to have the investigation approved internally. Because OSC information requests can be quite expansive, according to agency officials, agencies have to spend more time identifying the specific issues at the root of any allegations.

---

[29] Three of the referrals we reviewed did not have data on timeframes for agencies' initial responses.

[30] Two of the referrals we reviewed did not have data on timeframes for agencies' final responses.

OSC has discretion in approving these requests, however, and whistleblower advocacy representatives told us that OSC could use its case closure letters to the President and Congress to apply pressure on agencies to respond more timely to allegations. OSC officials told us that their preference is to give agencies the needed time to complete investigations. They explained that if they have to close a case because an agency did not conduct a full investigation in a timely manner, the whistleblower is ultimately disadvantaged because he or she will have to refile the allegations if he or she wants them fully investigated. OSC's strategic plan for fiscal years 2017 to 2022 includes an objective for OSC to ensure agencies provide timely and appropriate outcomes for referred whistleblower disclosures. To achieve this objective, OSC says it plans to undertake strategies that include engaging agencies in the development of investigation plans of referred whistleblower disclosures and maintaining communications with agencies before, during, and after agencies' investigations of referred whistleblower disclosures, among others. Until OSC reviews and determines whether its policy for extensions is appropriate, it will be unable to meet its strategic goal for timely and appropriate outcomes.

OSC Does Not Communicate Potential Processing Timelines to Whistleblowers

OSC's procedures for notifying whistleblowers initially and when their cases are referred to the agency do not require OSC to communicate time frames for the referral and agency response. The referral notification letter to whistleblowers notes that agencies may ask for an extension and that the investigation may take longer than 60 days. In March 2018, OSC revised its referral letter template for whistleblowers to inform the whistleblower that agency investigations may take longer than 60 days and that agencies frequently request and receive extensions beyond the initial 60 days. This language, however, does not include agency-specific information on typical length of time a whistleblower could expect in their case.

Standards for Internal Control in the Federal Government notes that it is important for an agency to communicate quality information to external parties in order to achieve the agency's objectives.[31] However, given that disclosure cases that were referred and closed in fiscal year 2016 took on average almost 1.8 years to resolve, whistleblowers are waiting a long time for cases to close. As whistleblower representatives noted, whistleblowers may be subject to retaliatory work environments during these extended processing times. In some instances whistleblowers may have changed positions, left the agency, or otherwise given up on a remedy, which presents uncertainty for all involved. Similarly, agency liaisons noted that officials who are the subject of allegations may have also changed positions during the interim, which limits the corrective or disciplinary actions an agency can take. By not providing sufficient transparency on realistic time frames for the referral and agency referral response process, OSC risks and limits whistleblowers' ability to adequately plan for the whistleblower disclosure case process and have a better understanding of the potential timeline for case closure.

Some Aspects of OSC Case Processing Procedures Generally Adhere to Internal Control Principles, but Others Do Not

We identified eight internal control principles that are relevant to ensuring that OSC has an effective process in place so that its objective will be achieved for resolving PPP and whistleblower disclosure cases. These eight internal control principles include (1) establishing a structure, responsibility, and authority; (2) defining objectives and risk tolerances; (3) identifying, analyzing, and responding to change; (4) communicating internally; (5) performing monitoring activities; (6) implementing control activities through policies; (7) design control activities; and (8) committing

[31] GAO-14-704G.

to competence. Based on our review, OSC generally adhered to five of the relevant internal control principles, but did not fully adhere to three.

OSC Generally Adhered to Five Relevant Internal Control Principles

Establish Structure, Responsibility, and Authority

We believe that OSC has established a structure for PPP and whistleblower case processing, and assigned responsibilities and authorities. Specifically, CEU guidance outlines criteria for when to refer cases to IPD for investigation. The guidance includes a checklist of factors to aid the ADR Unit in evaluating whether a case is suitable for mediation. OSC's units have established and documented the key roles needed to carry out unit responsibilities. OSC also has documentation that assigns units responsibilities for working with external stakeholders, such as complainants, whistleblowers, and federal agencies, and that establishes reporting lines for OSC to communicate with these parties. OSC also provides training to federal agencies on whistleblower disclosures and PPPs and certifies that federal agencies have informed their employees about the PPP and whistleblower disclosure processes.

Define Objectives and Risk Tolerances

We believe that OSC has defined program objectives and risk tolerances for PPP and whistleblower case processing. Specifically, OSC's most recent two strategic plans outline program objectives as well as implementation strategies, and specify PPP and whistleblower disclosure case metrics to track. OSC unit mangers, via staff meeting minutes, notes, and various reports, document how they communicate objectives and track progress towards achieving those objectives.

Identify, Analyze, and Respond to Change

We believe that OSC has identified, analyzed, and responded to changes that could affect its case processing. Specifically, OSC's agency-wide Enterprise Risk Management process, established in early 2017, documents OSC's key risk identification and management process. According to the risk management profile and meeting minutes, the Enterprise Risk Management group has met twice since being established to identify risks, develop responses, and follow up on previous responses and risks identified.

Communicate Internally

We believe that OSC has established a process to communicate internally. Specifically, OSC management communicates information about PPP and whistleblower case processes using internal communication channels such as mass emails, employee newsletters, one-on-one meetings, and meeting agendas. OSC staff also told us they utilize informal communication channels and that OSC management are available to discuss PPP and whistleblower case processes. OSC management also provided policy memos and procedures that communicate certain PPP and whistleblower disclosure case processes.

Perform Monitoring Activities

We believe that OSC has established a process to monitor case activities. Specifically, OSC's monitoring of case operations include a variety of reports that track cases received, pending cases, and case resolutions to assess the effectiveness of OSC's PPP and whistleblower disclosure operations. Key pieces of information from these reports are shared via the internal meeting structures with staff and management. IPD, DU and RDU management also conduct docket reviews of cases with their staffs. OSC management provided examples of monitoring the caseloads of staff as well as how they discussed and monitored the status of open cases at meetings. For example, CEU tracks which staff are assigned certain cases and whether the cases were closed or referred to another unit.

OSC Generally Did Not Adhere to Three Relevant Internal Control Principles

Implementation of Control Activities through Policies

We believe that for the PPP and whistleblower disclosure processes OSC did not implement its control activities through policies.

Prohibited Personnel Practices

CEU receives and processes PPP cases and is OSC's largest unit in terms of staff and caseload. However, CEU lacks documented, complete procedures for processing cases, such as a comprehensive guide or manual describing procedures for reviewing and resolving PPP cases. We identified the following specific procedures, for which CEU lacks documentation: (1) case priorities, (2) obtaining favorable actions, (3) staff productivity expectations, and (4) supervisory review.

First, regarding case priorities, CEU management described to us seven different types of cases that should be prioritized but did not provide documentation for them. OSC cases files also lacked documentation regarding case prioritization. In May 2016, CEU conducted a "Best Practice Survey," in which CEU staff were asked their views on CEU's case processes. One of the many themes identified was that CEU needs to clarify its case priorities.

Second, concerning favorable actions, CEU lacks procedures for how staff should determine when a favorable action is warranted, how to obtain and negotiate favorable actions with agencies, and how to document favorable actions in case files. A favorable action is an outcome in a case that could result in a specific benefit to the complainant, an outcome aimed at disciplining the subject official and deterring future bad conduct, or an improvement to agency processes. OSC lists the number of favorable actions as a key performance metric in its budget and performance documents. CEU, in particular since 2014, has sought favorable actions, especially in cases that do not merit referral to its investigative unit or mediation unit. According to OSC officials, this initiative was part of an effort by the prior Special Counsel to expand CEU's investigative role beyond that of an intake unit. CEU increased its share of OSC's favorable actions from approximately 1 percent in fiscal year 2011(1 of 75) to 31 percent in fiscal year 2016 (77 of 251). However, without documentation of procedures, OSC staff may not consistently perform required steps to attain favorable actions. For example, we found that 18 of the 61 cases (29.5 percent) where CEU claimed a favorable action lacked documentation of OSC's involvement in obtaining the favorable action, the agencies' implementation of the favorable action, whether the favorable action was achieved in another OSC unit but claimed by CEU, or some other discrepancy. The "Best Practice Survey" results noted that CEU staff would like written procedures for obtaining favorable actions.

Third, CEU lacked documentation for staff productivity expectations. In August 2017, according to an OSC official, CEU staff were expected, though not required, to resolve at least 36 PPP cases per quarter. CEU officials were unable to provide documentation on how the goal was communicated to staff. Another finding from OSC's "Best Practice Survey" was that CEU staff need clarity regarding case resolution requirements. In addition, during our small group discussion with CEU staff in September 2017, the staff raised concerns regarding OSC's case resolution expectations. They said that productivity expectations are unwritten and vary depending on whether staff telework or not. One staff person was concerned that management had an unwritten expectation for staff to close significantly more than the 36 cases per quarter. OSC shared documentation in April 2018 clarifying staff expectations for case productivity. The expectations, which are effective June 1, 2018, and vary depending on the grade level of the OSC employee, were emailed to all CEU staff. However, while OSC has documented and communicated CEU staff productivity expectations, the expectations did not include guidance on how staff should balance resolving a certain number of cases over a specified time period and obtaining favorable actions, which OSC has also emphasized for CEU staff.

Fourth, CEU does not have written procedures specifying supervisory review of CEU cases. CEU management officials told us they are required to review (1) PPP closure letters; (2) all cases that allege reprisal for whistleblowing; and (3) all cases referred to other units, such as those referred for mediation and investigation. However, OSC lacked procedures for these review processes. As a result, OSC staff has not followed some steps in case files consistently. For example, of the 61 cases we reviewed with a corrective action taken in CEU, 45 alleged reprisal for whistleblowing. We found that 15 of these 45 cases did not have a CEU management review. Also, of those cases without a corrective action that were not referred for investigation, we estimate that 58.8 percent did not include CEU managerial review of the closure letter.[32] For cases referred for investigation, we found that 44.7 percent did not include CEU managerial review of the referral memorandum.[33] The OSC "Best Practice Survey" results also indicated that CEU staff would like to standardize the unit's review procedures.

Standards for Internal Control in the Federal Government states that management should implement control activities through policies by documenting them. CEU management said these specific steps, though not documented, could be discussed during staff's initial training, at midterm and annual reviews, when assigning cases, and at OSC meetings. CEU management officials said they are formalizing guidance and have orally communicated these case processes to staff during off-site training and informal communications. Without documented procedures, there is an increased risk that employees will not consistently follow management's directives.

Whistleblower Disclosures

OSC has written procedures for processing whistleblower disclosure cases. These procedures, among other things, describe case productivity requirements for staff, specify managerial involvement for cases, and outline the case prioritization process, as well as other case processes. However, these procedures also include outdated processes. For example, OSC's case prioritization process specifies three priority levels but we

---

[32] The margin of error of the estimates is no larger than +/- 10.8 percentage points. We reviewed a sample of 85 cases and our estimates apply to the 3,168 cases in population.

[33] The margin of error of the estimates is no larger than +/- 11.1 percentage points. We reviewed a sample of 47 cases and our estimates apply to the 106 cases in population.

found whistleblower disclosure priority worksheets in case files that specify four priority levels. In addition, OSC's written procedures outline an informal referral process to agencies' respective inspector general (IG) offices. According to OSC's procedures, OSC uses this referral process in cases where the whistleblower disclosure is less egregious in nature and does not warrant a referral to the head of the federal agency. However, according to OSC officials, OSC no longer refers whistleblower disclosures informally to IG offices, but instead refers whistleblower disclosures informally to agencies' respective general counsel offices.

Standards for Internal Control in the Federal Government states that management should periodically review policies, procedures, and related control activities for continued relevance and effectiveness. An OSC official told us OSC had not updated its procedures due to OSC's high caseload for whistleblower disclosures. In April 2018, OSC provided us with updated case procedures for case prioritization and informal referrals. OSC officials said they will communicate the updated procedures to the appropriate staff during a staff meeting and will make the procedures available on OSC's intranet page. The updated procedures should help OSC staff implement case processes as intended by OSC management.

Design Control Activities

To conduct our case file review, we asked OSC to locate and retrieve 396 PPP and whistleblower disclosure paper case files that were closed in fiscal year 2016. OSC told us after several months, that it was unable to locate 18 files (4.5 percent) and was still retrieving 36 case files (9 percent). Ultimately, OSC could not locate 20 case files and told us 13 cases would be unavailable within the course of our review. These 33 cases were opened by OSC in fiscal years 2012 to 2016, although a majority were opened in fiscal years 2015 and 2016. Based on our estimates, OSC would not be able to locate 8.3 percent of closed case files.[34]

[34] The margin of error of the estimates is no larger than +/- 3.03 percentage points.

According to OSC officials, some of the difficulty of finding their files is because they are maintained in paper files. OSC officials said that one full-time OSC employee oversees the maintenance and retrieval of closed OSC paper case files. They explained that records are stored at multiple locations: OSC headquarters, OSC's field offices, and at federal record and archive centers. OSC officials told us that, if given additional time beyond our January 2018 deadline, then they could locate the remaining cases files but could not provide us a time frame for doing so.

OSC is planning to implement a new electronic case management system (eCMS), which is designed to mitigate the need to maintain physical case files. According to OSC, staff could then retrieve electronic case files as needed. OSC documentation indicated that eCMS will allow OSC to take an electronically filed Form 14 and create an electronic case file.[35] Based on OSC's functional requirements for eCMS, the system should also allow staff to quickly locate case files that may be connected to other cases. This system would also allow staff to search e-mails and documents based on a particular filter, among other capabilities. OSC's original time frame was to have eCMS operational in October 2017.

However, OSC has had issues migrating data from OSC 2000 to eCMS, has not implemented the new system, and continues to maintain paper files. As of March 2018, OSC was determining whether its contracted vendor would be able to migrate the OSC 2000 data to eCMS. In addition, OSC was examining (1) whether eCMS as constructed can reach full functionality so that OSC can eliminate paper case files, and (2) if so, what further system development is required to accomplish this. OSC officials said their tentative goal is to transition from OSC 2000 to eCMS at the beginning of fiscal year 2019.

Under *Standards for Internal Control in the Federal Government*, management should clearly document internal control and all transactions and other significant events in a manner that allows the documentation to be readily available for examination. In addition, according to OSC regulations, OSC is to maintain records to (1) document how OSC handled

---

[35] As of March 2018, OSC said that it plans to roll out Form 14 in line with its implementation of eCMS at the beginning of fiscal year 2019.

each matter; (2) provide a resource for consistency in interpretation and application of the law; and (3) allow for statistical reports and analysis of matters processed at OSC.[36] Until OSC develops an electronic case management system that would allow individual staff to perform customizable case history searches and manage their caseloads, it cannot ensure that cases related to a specific individual or agency will be located in a timely manner, which could also delay the work of OSC staff.

Commitment to Competence

OSC does not have a systematic, standardized training program for OSC employees who review and process PPP and whistleblower disclosure cases. CEU and DU, OSC's two largest units in terms of cases closed, described a number of aspects of training for entry level employees. For example, OSC officials said both units provide a training manual to new staff. The training manuals cover a number of topics, such as unit and OSC policies, case processes, and relevant case law, and include examples. In DU, OSC officials said new staff receive some training on PPPs, and are assigned less difficult cases although they did not provide documentation. They explained that new staff become familiar with DU's procedures through on-the-job training. In CEU, OSC officials described a 2-week training course, but could not provide documentation of the training, such as a syllabus or a list of course participants. OSC officials said the 2-week training course was being updated and formalized. They added that the guidance currently used for the training is informal and not regularly available for staff to access.

In April 2018, OSC provided us with additional documentation regarding training provided in CEU. The documentation included an outline of PPP topics and the CEU training manual we had previously received. As we discussed earlier, to help manage OSC's caseload, PPP cases were assigned to staff to outside of CEU as part of the CEU project. Staff not accustomed to working PPP cases on a regular basis were asked

---

[36] Notice of a modified system of records, 82 Fed. Reg. 45,076 (Sept. 27, 2017).

to do so. However, OSC officials said that no formal training was provided to these staff as part of this project.

OSC nonmanagement staff told us they would like more regular, standardized training. During our small group discussions, OSC staff discussed two consistent themes related to training: (1) on-the-job training at OSC is emphasized, and (2) existing training for entry-level employees could be enhanced. For example, one participant in our small group discussions stated that although the nature of their work requires that much is learned via on-the-job training, OSC could do better by providing a systematic approach for new hires that helps them understand the life of a case (e.g., documenting case lifecycle or formalizing checklists). Also, as part of the OSC's "Best Practice Survey" CEU staff identified the need for regular quarterly training meetings to discuss OSC policy issues, developments in case law, and changes and clarifications on CEU case processing procedures.

Standards for Internal Control in Federal Government state that management should demonstrate a commitment to recruit, develop, and retain competent individuals. This includes tailoring training based on the needs of the role. In addition, OSC's strategic plan for fiscal years 2017 to 2022 has an objective on recruiting, developing, and retaining a highly talented, engaged, and diverse workforce. OSC officials noted that given OSC's small size, OSC does not have a regular, standardized training program. OSC officials did explain and provide documentation regarding continuous training provided to staff, such as external training staff attended. They also told us that efforts to find staff external training opportunities depend on the extent to which funding is available.

As OSC's caseload continues to increase, efficiently recruiting and onboarding staff may help OSC better manage its caseload. The lack of standardized training poses a risk to the consistency with which cases are worked, reviewed, and closed, especially since staff not accustomed to working PPP cases as part of the CEU project were not provided training because OSC lacks standardized training based on the documentation we reviewed. Ensuring consistent training among staff could help alleviate any issues created by absences and employee turnover. Such training would also help OSC manage its caseload if nonPPP staff are again asked to work PPP cases.

OSC'S INTERNAL COMPLAINT AND WHISTLEBLOWER DISCLOSURE PROCESS IN SOME CASES DOES NOT PROVIDE OSC EMPLOYEES PROTECTIONS AFFORDED TO OTHER FEDERAL EMPLOYEES

OSC Processes for Reviewing and Referring Internal Allegations Involve OSC Officials and Staff

OSC's policy for reviewing of internal PPP and whistleblower disclosure allegations involves OSC officials and staff at various points in the process depending on the complainants, whistleblowers, and subject officials involved. Table 2 summarizes the various review scenarios for both PPP and whistleblower disclosure cases at OSC.

According to OSC Directive 57, OSC's policy document that explains the internal allegations process, the Principal Deputy Special Counsel reviews allegations against CEU, IPD, or DU non–senior management staff. CEU and DU chiefs review their respective categories of allegations made against employees outside of those units who are not senior managers. The Special Counsel can either refer internal whistleblower disclosure allegations against employees other than senior managers to the NSF-OIG or appoint OSC investigators from another office location. However, it is unclear how this selection process works in practice because, of the five cases in our case file review in which OSC played an investigative role, OSC could only locate one of the cases, which was a PPP instead of a whistleblower disclosure case. For allegations against political appointees, senior executives, and senior managers other than the Special Counsel and Principal Deputy Special Counsel, OSC employees must first submit allegations with either the Special Counsel or with OSC's Authorized Individual—an employee elected by OSC's workforce—before

NSF-OIG can decide to provide investigative services. If NSF-OIG declines to provide such services, Directive 57 notes that OSC reviews the allegations in question.

An OSC employee can choose to file with the Authorized Individual or file directly with a third party when the allegations are against either the Special Counsel or Principal Deputy Special Counsel. Pursuant to the Inspector General Reform Act of 2008, the Council of Inspectors General for Integrity and Efficiency (CIGIE) Integrity Committee reviews allegations made against IGs, their designated Office of Inspector General staff members, and OSC's Special Counsel and Principal Deputy Special Counsel.[37] Until 2016, the Special Counsel was also a member of this committee.[38] Per OSC Directive 57, OSC employees may file directly with this committee.

OSC officials noted that, in their opinion, the internal allegations process available to OSC staff has challenges and is not ideal. Officials had concerns that partnering with an agency IG that is large or that may frequently have employees that file allegations for OSC to review could create conflicts of interest if the agency IG in turn has to review OSC employee allegations. According to officials, OSC has actively tried to strengthen its internal allegation process by securing an agreement with the NSF-OIG.

OSC's memorandum of understanding with NSF-OIG specified that NSFOIG staff would determine whether to provide investigative services for allegations that OSC referred to them either via the Special Counsel or the Authorized Individual. NSF-OIG is to present a summary of facts to the Special Counsel after it concludes its investigation, but does not exercise enforcement authority in these matters. The Special Counsel is responsible for initiating corrective or disciplinary action.

---

[37] Pub. L. No. 110-409, § 7, 122 Stat. 4302, 4306 (Oct. 14, 2008).

[38] Until December 2016, the Special Counsel was a sitting member of the committee. Our review of CIGIE Integrity Committee meeting minutes showed that then-Special Counsel Carolyn Lerner recused herself from committee proceedings involving all five cases filed by OSC employees against OSC leadership.

Table 2. Different Entities Investigate Prohibited Personnel Practice (PPP) and Whistleblower Disclosure Cases Depending on Which Type of Office of Special Counsel (OSC) Employee Is the Subject Official

Type of case	Allegations involving Special Counsel or Principal Deputy Special Counsel	Allegations involving other political appointees and senior managers	Allegations involving nonleadership employees who review PPP or whistleblower disclosure cases, respectively	Allegations involving all other employees
PPP Complaint	Council of the Inspectors General for Integrity and Efficiency (CIGIE) receives case from complainant directly or from OSC Authorized Individual, then reviews case.	National Science Foundation Office of Inspector General (NSF-OIG) receives case from OSC Authorized Individual or Special Counsel, then reviews case.[a]	Complaints Examining Unit receives and reviews case (same as external process).	Principal Deputy Special Counsel receives and reviews case.
Whistle-blower Disclosure	CIGIE receives case from whistleblower directly or from OSC Authorized Individual, then reviews case.	NSF-OIG receives case from OSC Authorized Individual or Special Counsel, then reviews case.[a]	Disclosure Unit receives and reviews case and may make referral determination to Special Counsel. If referred, the case would be investigated by either the NSF-OIG or OSC investigators from a different location than the subject official.	Principal Deputy Special Counsel receives and reviews case and may make referral determination to Special Counsel. If referred, the case would be investigated by either the NSF-OIG or OSC investigators from a different location than the subject official.

Source: GAO analysis of OSC and NSF-OIG documentation. I GAO-18-400.

[a] The NSF-OIG may decline to review the allegations, in which case OSC conducts the review.

According to OSC officials familiar with the negotiations that resulted in the initial 2014 agreement, NSF-OIG was concerned with the resources that would be involved if it were charged with independently undertaking investigations of allegations made against OSC without an authorization from OSC. The result of these concerns, via Directive 57, was to have either the Special Counsel or the Authorized Individual route allegations to NSF-OIG before NSF-OIG staff decided whether to accept the case.

One-Fifth of OSC Employee Survey Respondents Have Considered Filing Allegations but Cited Clarity and Reprisal Concerns

Of the 87 (of 132) OSC employees who responded to our survey (representing a 66 percent response rate), 17 told us that they either had filed or had considered filing a PPP or whistleblower disclosure allegation against another OSC employee over the course of their careers.[39] Five of these 17 employees said they ultimately filed allegations. These 5 also said they had considered filing additional allegations but ultimately chose not to do so.[40] Table 3 shows that concerns about the integrity of OSC's process for internal allegations played significant roles in the 17 respondents' decisions not to file. These employees, in follow-up discussions with us, cited similar themes. While a majority of these employees said they were able to resolve their issues informally, this was the least common reason to contribute either moderately or very much to an employee's decision not to file.

---

[39] Response rates were higher than average in the Investigation and Prosecution Division and Complaints Examining Unit. Nonmanagement staff responded at higher rates than did management staff. Among respondents, per-question response rates for all of the questions summarized in this report were at or above 85 percent.

[40] OSC employees were given the ability to file allegations against political appointees, senior executives, and other senior managers apart from the Special Counsel and Principal Deputy Special Counsel in 2014 with the signing of a memorandum of understanding with NSF-OIG. While we reviewed available information on cases filed with NSF-OIG since 2014, our survey asked employees about their experiences both before and after 2014.

Table 3. Some Procedural Concerns Contributed to Office of Special Counsel (OSC) Employees, Who Considered Filing Complaints, Deciding Not to File Those Complaints

Concern	Number of respondents who considered filing but said concern either moderately or very much contributed to decision not to file
Ability to resolve issue informally	9 of 17
Fear of reprisal from within OSC	15 of 17
Not sure how to file	9 of 17
Concern about objectivity or conflict of interest within complaint process	16 of 17
Concern about length of process	10 of 17
Fear that anonymity would be compromised	16 of 17

Source: GAO survey of OSC employees. | GAO-18-400.

Table 4. Employees Have a Range of Views on How the Office of Special Counsel's (OSC) Policy Addresses Several Components of Process for Internal Allegations

Concern	Employees who said OSC's policy addressed concern not at all well or somewhat well	Employees who said OSC's policy addressed concern very well or moderately well
Address all stages of the process of filing	31 of 87	44 of 87
Explain employee appeal rights	36 of 87	38 of 87
Identify the entities who will review the allegations	25 of 87	49 of 87
Protect against a conflict of interest in responding to allegations	30 of 87	45 of 87
Identify Authorized Individual who refers allegations for investigation	28 of 87	48 of 87
Protect the anonymity of the employee	33 of 87	41 of 87

Source: GAO survey of OSC employees. | GAO-18-400.

Some OSC employees, regardless of whether they had previously considered filing an allegation, expressed concerns about OSC's process for internal PPP and whistleblower disclosure allegations, as shown in table 4.[41]

We found that OSC employees had expressed similar concerns in recent editions of the Federal Employee Viewpoint Survey. From 2012 to 2015, OSC experienced increases in negative responses on questions concerning whether PPPs are tolerated, whether employees feel they can disclose violations of law without fear, and on the honesty and integrity of their leaders. In particular, the percentage of negative responses on the question of whether employees felt they could disclose violations of law without fear rose from 10 percent in 2012 to 37 percent in 2015. Scores on these questions generally improved beginning in 2016, and the agency-wide response rate rebounded significantly from 2015 to 2016.[42]

During our follow-up discussions with survey respondents, a theme emerged that anonymity is difficult to maintain, in part owing to the perception that OSC has a culture of informal discussion. Given the roles that OSC leadership and other officials currently play in this process, these concerns may be valid. Having an authorized individual and multiple OSC managers responsible for examining case files against OSC employees cannot assure employees that their claims can be reviewed anonymously and independently. Consequently, employees told us they are reluctant to report their workplace concerns in part because OSC management and the Authorized Individual are involved in the review process for certain cases. This in turn increases OSC's risk that workplace violations go unreported.

Standards for Internal Control in the Federal Government states that agencies should segregate management authority and oversight duties to reduce the risk of fraud, waste, and abuse.[43] We found no instances in which top OSC leadership were directly involved in the review of allegations made against them. However, OSC is a small agency of only

---

[41] Nonresponse rates for subparts of this survey question ranged from 13 to 15 percent.

[42] The OSC-wide response rate was 85 percent in 2014 before declining to 61 percent in 2015 and increasing to 92 percent in 2016.

[43] GAO-14-704G.

135 employees. Without separating management authority and oversight from the review of OSC allegations, the likelihood of an allegation involving someone closely related to or frequently in contact with agency management—even if not involving a member of management directly—is greater and could promote a perception of a conflict of interest.

Statutory Changes Increase Safeguards for OSC Employees, but OSC Has Not Yet Taken All Steps to Implement Changes

Congress has taken multiple actions to increase the independence of reviews of internal PPP and whistleblower disclosure allegations at OSC. As previously noted, the Inspector General Reform Act of 2008 and subsequent CIGIE procedures provided the CIGIE Integrity Committee as an avenue where OSC employees could directly file allegations against either the Special Counsel or Principal Deputy Special Counsel. The Inspector General Empowerment Act of 2016 further bolstered the independence of CIGIE Integrity Committee reviews of OSC cases by removing OSC officials from the committee in these cases.[44] More recently, the 2018 OSC Reauthorization requires OSC to establish an agreement with at least one agency. Under such an agreement, an IG can receive allegations for investigation directly without the need for an OSC Authorized Individual.[45] The legislation authorizes OSC to reimburse the third party IG for any expenses related to their investigations.

In March 2018, OSC officials told us OSC extended the existing agreement with NSF-OIG, with a revised expiration date of August 2018. OSC officials said they are working with CIGIE and other agencies to secure a new IG arrangement, though they had not finalized one. Officials added that they intend to adopt language as part of a future arrangement that will allow OSC employees to contact the IG directly. However, it is

---

[44] Pub. L. No. 114-317, § 3(3)(A)(i), 130 Stat. 1595, 1596 (Dec. 16, 2016).

[45] Pub. L. No: 115-91, § 1097(g), 131 Stat. 1283, 1683 (Dec. 12, 2017) *codified* at 5 U.S.C. § 1212(i). The OSC reauthorization enacted additional changes for OSC unrelated to OSC's internal allegation process.

still unclear who will provide these investigative services. Given the concerns stated above, it is important that OSC employees have a resource that can receive allegations directly, independently investigate allegations, and pursue favorable actions when appropriate. These features of PPP and whistleblower disclosure investigations are protections that federal employees and applicants currently are afforded by OSC and the IG community. The impending expiration of OSC's current agreement with NSF-OIG presents an opportunity for OSC to secure a fully independent review for internal OSC allegations.

Uncertainty over How to File Also Inhibits Some Employees from Reporting Concerns

We also found that there is some uncertainty among OSC staff of OSC's policy for making these allegations. Of the 17 employees who responded to our survey and said that they ultimately chose not to file allegations, 9 said that uncertainty about how to file either moderately or very much contributed to their respective decisions. Moreover, while 44 of 87 employees surveyed said that they were both familiar with and had read OSC's policies for internal allegations, 19 of 87 said they either could not locate OSC's policies or did not know they existed. OSC management told us that OSC has not routinely included information on its internal allegations process as part of its new employee orientation program nor included this information as part of all-staff meetings. The OSC employee newsletter includes an announcement that OSC employees can file allegations and have them reviewed by NSF-OIG. However, in the two most recent examples provided to us, the announcement language did not provide information on the Authorized Individual and did not directly address other types of cases that may not fall under NSF-OIG's jurisdiction.

Regardless of the nature of employees' concerns with their workplace or with the process for investigating allegations, it is important that employees have the information they need to report those concerns.

Standards for Internal Control in the Federal Government emphasizes that agency management needs to communicate quality information throughout all levels of an organization.[46] Moreover, management should take opportunities to evaluate how it is communicating information in light of its audience, the legal and regulatory environment, and the nature of the information. Implementing recent statutory changes, if successful, may prompt fundamental alterations in how OSC employees' PPP and whistleblower disclosure allegations are investigated. Given the timing of these changes and the sensitivities of employees with workplace concerns, OSC has an opportunity to bolster its information outreach in this area and help promote a greater awareness of OSC internal complaint policies and procedures. In March 2018, after we discussed our preliminary findings, the Special Counsel notified all OSC employees of their rights to disclose wrongdoing at OSC, and officials reported displaying posters with the revised information. OSC officials also said that, in May 2018, OSC started to include a copy of the poster explaining how to make disclosures in every new employee orientation packet.

Continuing this type of outreach periodically may help notify OSC employees of their rights going forward.

CONCLUSION

The position that OSC occupies in the defense of merit system principles in the federal government carries great weight, but it also presents many challenges. OSC's increased caseload has led to a continuing backlog of unresolved cases, both in absolute numbers and in terms of their proportion of total caseload. Alongside this trend has been an increase in the time OSC takes to close individual PPP and whistleblower disclosure cases, with a particularly significant increase for whistleblower disclosure cases that OSC refers to other agencies. OSC's strategic plan for fiscal years 2017 to 2022 includes objectives for OSC to ensure agencies

---

[46] GAO-14-704G.

provide timely and appropriate outcomes for referred whistleblower disclosures. However, as cases linger in OSC, there is a greater chance that the individual making the allegations and officials in question may have changed positions, moved jobs, or given up seeking a remedy altogether. OSC has not undertaken a review of its practice of approving multiple extensions at the request of agencies conducting investigations. These extensions have resulted in longer processing times, which have not been transparently communicated to whistleblowers. Whistleblowers therefore have limited understanding of OSC's review process and cannot adequately plan for the complete disclosure case process.

OSC's practices are generally consistent with certain internal control standards for internal communication, risk management, and monitoring. However, it has not fully adhered to internal control principles with regard to fully documenting its policies, particularly within CEU, and ensuring staff receive consistent training. Moreover, the lack of an effective electronic case file management and storage capability limits OSC's ability to quickly retrieve cases as needed for its work and thus improve its efficiency.

OSC's lack of a fully independent internal complaints filing process has reduced the confidence some OSC employees have in its process for reviewing PPP and whistleblower disclosure allegations. Although Congress has taken steps to mitigate potential conflicts of interest, challenges at OSC include a review process that continues to involve OSC staff and officials, uncertainty among employees about how to file cases, and uncertainty about the future of obtaining permanent investigative services. Leveraging existing resources with CIGIE, NSFOIG, and others as needed would help OSC ensure that its employees can voice their concerns free from OSC involvement. Once such a process is established, it will be important for OSC to continue to provide its employees outreach and information so they are fully aware of how the process works.

RECOMMENDATIONS FOR EXECUTIVE ACTION

We are making the following seven recommendations to OSC:

The Special Counsel should review and revise as appropriate, its policy for agency extension requests. (Recommendation 1)

The Special Counsel should communicate expected processing timelines to whistleblowers. (Recommendation 2)

The Special Counsel should develop, document, and implement case processing procedures for OSC's Complaints Examining Unit, including procedures for how cases are prioritized, how to take favorable actions, how to balance obtaining favorable actions with meeting staff productivity expectations, and how cases should be reviewed by supervisors. (Recommendation 3)

The Special Counsel should identify and implement additional controls and tools needed to ensure closed case files can be tracked and located efficiently. (Recommendation 4)

The Special Counsel should develop, document, and implement a standardized training program for entry-level employees, across units. (Recommendation 5)

The Special Counsel should finalize a time frame for completing work with CIGIE and agency Inspectors General to obtain a fully independent review process for internal OSC allegations. (Recommendation 6)

The Special Counsel should increase and clarify ongoing outreach to OSC employees regarding OSC's process for handling internal PPP claims or whistleblower disclosure allegations. (Recommendation 7)

AGENCY COMMENTS AND OUR EVALUATION

We provided a draft of this chapter to the Special Counsel. In its comments, reproduced in appendix III, OSC agreed with all seven of our recommendations and said it is already taking steps to implement them.

We also received technical comments from OSC, which we incorporated where appropriate.

As agreed with your offices, unless you publicly announce the contents of this chapter earlier, we plan no further distribution until 30 days from the report date. At that time, we will send copies to the appropriate congressional committees, the Special Counsel, and other interested parties.

Yvonne D. Jones
Director
Strategic Issues

List of Committees

The Honorable Ron Johnson
Chairman

The Honorable Claire McCaskill
Ranking Member
Committee on Homeland Security and Governmental Affairs
United States Senate

The Honorable Charles E. Grassley
Chairman
Committee on the Judiciary
United States Senate

Appendix I: Objectives, Scope, and Methodology

The objectives of this engagement were to examine (1) the trends in the number of Prohibited Personnel Practice (PPP) and whistleblower disclosure cases Office of Special Counsel (OSC) received and closed from fiscal year 2011 to 2016 and the effect on its existing caseload, (2) the trends in the timeliness of PPP and whistleblower disclosure cases closed from fiscal year 2011 to 2016, (3) the extent to which OSC's PPP and whistleblower disclosure case processes adhere to relevant internal control principles, and (4) the extent to which safeguards are in place for OSC employees who file PPP and whistleblower disclosure complaints against OSC.

To examine PPP and whistleblower disclosure cases received and closed from fiscal years 2011 to 2016, we requested and obtained all case-level data from OSC's electronic case management system (OSC 2000) for the PPP and whistleblower disclosure cases closed from fiscal years 2011 through 2016 (the most recent full fiscal year available). We identified unique cases (i.e., case type, fiscal year case is opened, and four-digit identification number) to analyze case receipts and closures (by OSC unit of closure, type of resolutions, number of allegations per case, allegation type, federal agency, and referral type). To analyze by allegation type, we grouped 36 allegation codes into the 13 PPP allegation types and had OSC officials verify those groupings. Because a case filed with OSC can contain multiple allegations, we used the unique case identifiers to analyze allegations without over counting the number of cases. When we discuss the types of case closures, we are doing so by the types of allegations closures because different allegations of the same case could be closed in different ways. We also requested and reviewed relevant OSC 2000 documentation, including the data dictionary and reference files to identify appropriate data tables and variables. We also analyzed publicly available data on OSC's website as well as data from OSC 2000 to determine how PPP and whistleblower disclosure case receipts and closures have affected OSC's existing caseload.

To examine PPP and whistleblower disclosure timelines from fiscal years 2011 to 2016 and the effect on OSC's existing caseload, we requested and obtained OSC 2000 data for the PPP and whistleblower disclosure cases closed from fiscal years 2011 through 2016. We analyzed OSC 2000 data on the median number of days cases were open, including by federal agency from which cases were received. We also analyzed OSC 2000 data on agency extension requests granted for whistleblower disclosure cases and compared the median number of days whistleblower cases were open to select statutory requirements. Our analysis included presenting information from our review of closed case files, which is discussed below.

For both of the OSC 2000 data objectives above, we also interviewed OSC officials, federal agency liaisons, whistleblower advocacy organizations, and a law firm to obtain their views on changes in the OSC data, which are also discussed in more detail below.

For the purposes of this review, we determined that the OSC 2000 data used in our analysis were reliable. Our data reliability assessment included reviewing relevant documentation, conducting interviews with knowledgeable OSC officials, such as OSC's Chief Information Officer, and electronic testing for missing data, outliers, and obvious errors.

To evaluate the extent to which OSC's case management processes and procedures for PPP and whistleblower disclosures adhere to relevant internal control standards, we compared documentation for OSC's PPP and whistleblower disclosure processes to selected standards in the *Standards for Internal Control in the Federal Government*.[47] We also reviewed OSC's case processing documentation including case procedures, checklists, fact sheets, training manuals, case reports, example templates documents, and OSC's strategic plan, as well as other documentation. We then assessed whether these documents adhered to the relevant standards for internal control in the federal government. To determine which internal control standards were most relevant, we utilized our Internal Control Management and Evaluation Tool, in conjunction with observations based on our preliminary audit work, to select the standards that most closely related to OSC activities.[48] We then focused our assessment of OSC internal controls around our selected standards by interviewing OSC officials in each of the units and divisions responsible for PPP and whistleblower disclosures case

---

[47] GAO, *Internal Control: Standards for Internal Control in the Federal Government*, GAO-14-704G (Washington, D.C.: Sept. 10, 2014).

[48] GAO, *Internal Control Management and Evaluation Tool*, GAO-01-1008G (Washington, D.C.: Aug. 1, 2001).

processes, and reviewing available documentation. We interviewed OSC officials from the following units and divisions: the Complaints Examining Unit (CEU), Investigation and Prosecution Division (IPD), Disclosure Unit (DU), and Retaliation and Disclosure Unit (RDU). Because IPD is overseen by different managers in OSC's Washington, D.C. headquarters and in Methodology OSC's field offices in Detroit, Oakland, and Dallas, for our internal control evaluation we considered IPD-HQ and IPD-Field separately. Similarly, for much our audit, we were unable to interview the Alternative Dispute Resolution (ADR) unit manager due to personal reasons. Thus, we were unable to complete our internal control evaluation because a new manager was not put in place by the time we completed our evaluation.

We also interviewed the OSC liaison officials from the three federal agencies that most frequently were the subject of PPP complaints and whistleblower disclosures in cases closed in fiscal year 2016, to discuss their views on working with OSC. We held similar discussions with two whistleblower advocacy organizations and one law firm that specializes in federal employment law. To obtain the views of nonmanagement OSC staff on our selected internal controls, we held small group discussions with each of the six units responsible for PPP and whistleblower disclosure case processing (CEU, IPD-HQ, IPD-Field, ADR, RDU, and DU). For DU, IPD-Field, CEU, and IPD-HQ, we held the small group discussions with a random selection of six staff in each of those units. In RDU and ADR, since those units have fewer than six staff, we held small group discussions with all staff. We asked questions on internal control– related topics, such as their understanding of key case processes, training, and internal communication in OSC. The IPD-Field discussions were held over the phone while the remaining discussions were held in person at our headquarters. We used NVivo qualitative data analysis software to analyze and summarize the small group discussions. An analyst examined all six write-ups of our small group discussions to code and quantify identified themes from them. Another analyst reviewed the coding. If there was a disagreement, the two analysts reviewed and discussed until they reached an agreement. As a result of the analysis, we identified the major themes that covered the five internal control principles we discussed with the participants.

To assess how well OSC implemented its PPP and whistleblower disclosure case procedures and processes, we reviewed five groups of cases closed in fiscal year 2016. For three of these groups, we examined randomly selected, generalizable samples of cases. For the remaining two groups, we attempted to review all cases of that case type. We selected those groups to include the various resolutions for PPP and whistleblower disclosure cases. We used uniform data collection instruments for our file reviews to consistently capture information on the completeness of required documentation related to PPP and whistleblower disclosure cases. OSC reviewed and verified the elements of the data collection instruments we used to review case files.

Table 5. Office of Special Counsel (OSC) Prohibited Personnel Practice (PPP) and Whistleblower Disclosure Case Outcome Types

Case outcome type	Case type	Population size	Sample size	Cases not reviewed[a]
Referred to the agency	Whistleblower Disclosures	84	84	4
Not referred to the agency	Whistleblower Disclosures	1,558	92	3
Complaints Examining Unit cases with a corrective action	Prohibited Personnel Practice	65	65	4
Cases referred for investigation	Prohibited Personnel Practice	106	55	8
Cases without a corrective action and not referred for investigation	Prohibited Personnel Practice	3,168	95	10
Cases where OSC is the subject of the allegations	Both	5	5	4

Source: GAO analysis of OSC documentation. I GAO-18-400.

[a] These cases were not available by our deadline in January 2018 because OSC could not locate them or they were still being retrieved when we ended our case file review.

See table 5 for case outcome types. We also reviewed a sixth group of cases where OSC was the subject of the allegations. We planned to review five of these cases, which were closed between fiscal years 2011 to 2016.

OSC officials agreed these five case outcome types covered the range of potential outcomes for PPP and whistleblower disclosure cases. Since each sample could have provided different estimates, we express our confidence in the precision of our particular sample's results as a 95 percent confidence interval (i.e., a margin of error of plus or minus 7 percentage points). This is the interval that would contain the actual population value for 95 percent of the samples we could have drawn.

There were three types of case outcomes for which we planned to review all cases: (1) cases referred to the agency; (2) CEU cases with a corrective action; and (3) cases where OSC is the subject of the allegations. Of these, four cases were unavailable to be reviewed by us for each case group. For the agency referral and CEU corrective action case groups, we continued to treat our case file review results as a census. For the remaining group, where OSC was the subject of the allegations, we did not speak about the one case we reviewed due to concerns about disclosing the individual who filed the allegations.

For the case file review, we developed a data collection instrument for PPPs and whistleblower disclosures for each case outcome type. The steps we planned to review were based on OSC guidance as well as testimonial evidence from OSC officials and steps we would expect to find in the closed case files. We shared the data collection instruments with OSC for its review and incorporated its comments as appropriate. To ensure accuracy, two analysts reviewed each case file and reconciled any differences in responses. We then analyzed the results of these data collection efforts to identify main themes and develop summary findings.

For the fourth objective on OSC's internal allegations process, we reviewed OSC procedures for OSC employees to file PPP complaints and make whistleblower disclosures specifically found in OSC Directive 57. We also interviewed OSC officials, National Science Foundation Office of the Inspector General (NSF-OIG) officials, and Council of the Inspectors General on Integrity and Efficiency (CIGIE) officials on how these procedures are carried out and, at a high level, what experiences these entities had with cases they have investigated. We interviewed officials from these entities because they review certain complaints and disclosures from OSC employees. To assess how OSC and third-party entities were carrying out the documented procedures, we reviewed all PPP complaints and whistleblower disclosures submitted to the CIGIE Integrity Committee and NSF-OIG by OSC. We also reviewed all OSC PPP complaints and whistleblower disclosures where OSC was the subject agency from fiscal years 2011 to 2016. As discussed above, OSC was only able to locate one of the five complaints or whistleblower disclosures filed with OSC where OSC was the subject of the allegations. Finally, we reviewed the 2018 OSC reauthorization enacted during the course of our audit, and interviewed OSC officials on its potential effects on OSC's internal allegation process.[49] We reviewed OSC's overall process for internal PPP and whistleblower disclosure allegations to determine whether it adhered to selected Standards for Internal Control in the Federal Government—specifically standards for internal communication and segregation of duties within an agency.

To obtain OSC employees' views on how their agency's internal PPP and whistleblower disclosure allegations processes are designed and implemented, we fielded a Microsoft Word-based survey of all 132 OSC employees on board as of July 31, 2017, from August through September 2017. We pretested this survey with five separate individuals in July 2017 to verify that the questions were clear and accurately addressed the relevant terms and concepts. Employees' emailed submissions were coded and saved anonymously, with original submissions saved only for the purposes of following up with respondents as needed to clarify responses. We received submissions from 87 of 132 employees for a response rate of 66 percent. We also analyzed the response rates by unit and supervisory status to account for any potential nonresponse bias.

---

[49] National Defense Authorization Act for Fiscal Year 2018, Pub. L. No. 115-91, § 1097, 131 Stat. 1283, 1618 (Dec. 12, 2017).

In addition, we also incorporated the aggregated responses of OSC employees to relevant questions on the Federal Employee Viewpoint Survey—particularly those concerning PPPs, workplace environment, organizational leadership, and workload—from years 2012 through 2017 to supplement the survey responses we received.

To better understand employees' views and any concerns expressed in the survey about OSC's internal processes and workplace environment, we offered to hold short interviews with each survey respondent who indicated that he or she either had filed an allegation against another OSC employee or had considered doing so but ultimately chose not to. We interviewed 12 respondents who said they had considered or filed allegations. We also interviewed individual OSC employees who reached out to us to discuss their views of the OSC workplace culture independent of the survey. We offered these interviews as either in-person at our headquarters or phone-based discussions. At multiple points during our engagement, we also offered OSC employees the ability to contact us and our Fraudnet hotline. Fraudnet is an anonymous service whereby concerned employees can report waste, fraud, or abuse to our investigators. Our investigators then may offer to meet and interview the employee(s) in question. We then reviewed these interviews and follow-up discussions using the qualitative analytical software NVivo to code for common themes. Once aggregated, these responses formed the basis for how we presented what were the most frequent testimonial observations and concerns of OSC employees about the internal allegations process.

We conducted this performance audit from March 2017 to June 2018 in accordance with generally accepted government auditing standards. Those standards require that we plan and perform the audit to obtain sufficient, appropriate evidence to provide a reasonable basis for our findings and conclusions based on our audit objectives. We believe that the evidence obtained provides a reasonable basis for our findings and conclusions based on our audit objectives.

Appendix II: Additional Data on Office of Special Counsel Prohibited Personnel Practice and Whistleblower Disclosure Cases

Table 6. Favorable Actions Claimed by Complaints Examining Unit (CEU), Fiscal Years 2011 to 2016

Fiscal Year	Number of favorable actions claimed agency-wide in prohibited personnel practice (PPP) cases	Number of favorable actions claimed by CEU in PPP cases	Percent of agency's favorable actions claimed by CEU in PPP cases
2011	75	1	1.3
2012	150	6	4.0
2013	151	9	6.0
2014	175	33	18.9
2015	269	58	21.6
2016	251	77	30.7

Source: GAO analysis of Office of Special Counsel data. | GAO-18-400.

Table 7. Office of Special Counsel Is Generally Unable to Refer Whistleblower Disclosure Cases to Agencies within 45 Days

Fiscal Year	Number of whistleblower disclosure cases referred for investigation under 1213(c)	Number of referrals made within 45 days	Percent of referrals made within 45days
2011	21	5	23.8
2012	24	12	50.0
2013	56	3	5.4
2014	25	3	12.0
2015	76	27	35.5
2016	84	18	21.4

Source: GAO analysis of Office of Special Counsel data. | GAO-18-400.

Table 8. Average Whistleblower Disclosure Case Complexity Shows Steady Trend amid Increasing Caseload

Fiscal Year	Total number of whistleblower disclosure cases	Average number of types of alleged wrongdoing per whistleblower disclosure case
2011	871	2.67
2012	1053	2.51
2013	1157	2.57
2014	1310	2.61
2015	1949	2.43
2016	1668	2.52

Source: GAO analysis of Office of Special Counsel data. | GAO-18-400.

Table 9. Federal Agencies That Submit the Most Prohibited Personnel Practice Complaints to the Office of Special Counsel, Fiscal Year 2016

Federal Agency	Total number of PPP complaints
Department of Veterans Affairs	1225
Department of Homeland Security	333
Department of the Army	288
Department of Defense	225
Department of the Navy	206
Department of Justice	153
Department of Agriculture	124
Department of Health and Human Services	110
Department of The Air Force	89
Social Security Administration	78
Other	972

Source: GAO analysis of Office of Special data. | GAO-18-400.

Table 10. Federal Agencies That Submit the Most Whistleblower Disclosures to the Office of Special Counsel, Fiscal Year 2016

Federal Agency	Total number of whistleblower disclosures
Department of Veterans Affairs	628
Department of Homeland Security	188
Department of the Army	125
Department of the Navy	84
Department of Justice	78
Department of Agriculture	58
Department of Defense	58
Department of Health and Human Services	57
Department of The Air Force	43
Department of Transportation	37
Other	312

Source: GAO analysis of Office of Special Counsel data. | GAO-18-400.

Appendix III: Comments from the Office of Special Counsel

U.S. OFFICE OF SPECIAL COUNSEL
1730 M Street, N.W., Suite 218
Washington, D.C. 20036-4505
202-804-7000

May 30, 2018

Ms. Yvonne Jones
Director, Strategic Issues
United States Government Accountability Office
441 G Street, N.W.
Washington, D.C. 20548

Dear Ms. Jones:

The Office of Special Counsel (OSC) appreciates the opportunity to review and comment on the Government Accountability Office (GAO) draft report entitled *Office of Special Counsel: Actions Needed to Improve Processing of Prohibited Personnel Practice and Whistleblower Disclosure Cases* (GAO-18-400). In the report, GAO makes seven recommendations for improving case processing at OSC. We concur in all seven recommendations and, in fact, have already undertaken steps to implement them.

OSC appreciates the significant time and effort GAO expended reviewing our processes and generating this thoughtful report. I especially want to acknowledge and thank the GAO team for their professionalism, diligence, and commitment to understanding fully the challenges OSC faces in carrying out its dual mission to safeguard the merit system in federal employment and to provide a safe channel for employees, applicants and former employees for disclosing wrongdoing in their federal government agencies. I trust that GAO's recommendations, along with additional changes that I am instituting at OSC, will ensure OSC's robust enforcement of the laws entrusted to us, now and into the future.

We look forward to receiving the final report.

Sincerely,

Henry J. Kerner
Special Counsel

In: Whistleblowers
Editor: Isabelle Guertin
ISBN: 978-1-53616-310-0

Chapter 7

WHISTLEBLOWER PROGRAM: IRS NEEDS TO IMPROVE DATA CONTROLS FOR SOME AWARD DETERMINATIONS*

United States Government Accountability Office

ABBREVIATIONS

FATCA	Foreign Account Tax Compliance Act
FBAR	Report of Foreign Bank and Financial Accounts
FinCEN	Financial Crimes Enforcement Network
FISMA	Federal Information Security Modernization
Act of 2014	Federal Information Security Management Act of 2002
IRM	Internal Revenue Manual
IRS	Internal Revenue Service
NIST	National Institute of Standards and Technology

---

* This is an edited, reformatted and augmented version of United States Government Accountability Office; Report to the Committee on Finance, U.S. Senate, Publication No. GAO-18-698, dated September 28, 2018.

OVDP	Offshore Volunteer Disclosure Program
Treasury	Department of the Treasury

WHY GAO DID THIS STUDY

Tax whistleblowers who report on the underpayment of taxes by others have helped IRS collect $3.6 billion since 2007, according to IRS. IRS pays qualifying whistleblowers between 15 and 30 percent of the proceeds it collects as a result of their information. However, until February 9, 2018, IRS did not pay whistleblowers for information that led to the collection of FBAR penalties.

GAO was asked to review how often and to what extent whistleblower claims involve cases where FBAR penalties were also assessed. Among other objectives, this chapter (1) describes the extent to which FBAR penalties were included in whistleblower awards prior to the statutory change in definition of proceeds; (2) examines how IRS used whistleblower information on FBAR noncompliance, and how IRS responded to the statutory change in definition of proceeds; and (3) describes the purposes for which IRS collects and uses FBAR penalty data, and assesses controls for ensuring data reliability. GAO reviewed the files of 132 claims closed between January 1, 2012, and July 24, 2017, that likely included FBAR allegations; analyzed IRS data; reviewed relevant laws and regulations, and IRS policies, procedures and publications; and interviewed IRS officials.

WHAT GAO RECOMMENDS

GAO recommends IRS update IRS Form 11369 and improve controls for the reliability of FBAR penalty data. IRS agreed with all of GAO's recommendations.

WHAT GAO FOUND

Prior to February 9, 2018, when Congress enacted a statutory change requiring the Internal Revenue Service (IRS) to include penalties for *Report of Foreign Bank and Financial Accounts* (FBAR) violations in calculating whistleblower awards, IRS interpreted the whistleblower law to exclude these penalties from awards. However, GAO found that some whistleblowers provided information about FBAR noncompliance to IRS. In a sample of 132 whistleblower claims closed between January 2012 and July 2017, GAO found that IRS assessed FBAR penalties in 28 cases. It is unknown whether the whistleblower's information led IRS to take action in all of these cases. These penalties totaled approximately $10.7 million. Had they been included in whistleblower awards, total awards could have increased up to $3.2 million. Over 97 percent of the FBAR penalties collected from these 28 claims came from 10 cases with willful FBAR noncompliance, for which higher penalties apply.

FBAR penalty type	Number of claims	FBAR penalty amount (dollars)	Maximum potential whistleblower award[a] (dollars)
Willful penalty	10	10,485,847	3,145,754
Non-willful & negligent	18	263,039	78,912
Total	28	10,748,886	3,224,666

Source: GAO analysis of IRS data. | GAO 18 698.

[a]Maximum potential award is defined as 30 percent of the FBAR penalty amount. Report of Foreign Bank and Financial Accounts (FBAR) Penalties and Potential Whistleblower Awards for Selected IRS Whistleblower Claims Closed between January 1, 2012, and July 24, 2017.

IRS forwards whistleblower allegations of FBAR noncompliance to its operating divisions for further examination. However, IRS Form 11369, a key form used for making award determinations, does not require examiners to include information about the usefulness of a whistleblower's information FBAR and other non-tax issues. After Congress enacted the statutory change, IRS suspended award determinations for 1 week, but resumed the program before updating the form or its instructions, or issuing internal guidance on new information required on the Form. As of

June 28, 2018, IRS had not begun updating the Form 11369 or its instructions. The lack of clear instructions on the form for examiners to include information on FBAR and other non-tax enforcement collections may result in relevant information being excluded from whistleblower award decisions.

IRS maintains FBAR penalty data in a standalone database. It uses these data for internal and external reporting and to make management decisions. Because of the change in statute, IRS will need these data for determining whistleblower awards. GAO found that IRS does not have sufficient quality controls to ensure the reliability of FBAR penalty data. For example, IRS staff enter data into the database manually but there are no secondary checks to make sure the data entered are accurate. Without additional controls for data reliability, IRS risks making decisions, including award determinations, with incomplete or inaccurate data.

This is a public version of a sensitive report issued in August 2018. Information on the FBAR Database that IRS deemed to be sensitive has been omitted.

September 28, 2018

The Honorable Orrin G. Hatch
Chairman

The Honorable Ron Wyden
Ranking Member
Committee on Finance United States Senate

Tax whistleblowers—individuals who report the underpayment of taxes or the violation of tax laws by others—could help the Internal Revenue Service (IRS) collect potentially billions of dollars in revenue that may otherwise go uncollected. According to IRS, whistleblower information has assisted IRS in collecting almost $3.6 billion since 2007. This information can help reduce the tax gap—the difference between the amount of taxes owed by taxpayers and the amount voluntarily paid on time.[1] The Tax Relief and Health Care Act of 2006 included an expansion of IRS's whistleblower program by establishing the IRS Whistleblower Office and requiring IRS to pay qualifying whistleblowers between 15 and 30 percent of the proceeds IRS collects as a result of the whistleblower's information.[2]

The Bank Secrecy Act and its implementing regulations require certain individuals with offshore bank accounts to file an annual *Report of Foreign Bank and Financial Accounts* (FBAR). FBARs help the government identify and prevent tax evasion, money laundering, terrorist financing, and other crimes. IRS enforces FBAR filing requirements. Individuals who fail to disclose these accounts and pay appropriate taxes on them contribute to the tax gap. If IRS identifies these unreported accounts and income, it can assess taxes, interest, and penalties. For each FBAR violation, the penalty for willful violations can be as high as the larger of $100,000 (adjusted for inflation) or half of the value of the unreported account at the time of the violation. Some estimates put the value of offshore accounts in the hundreds of billions to over a trillion dollars.[3]

In an August 2014 regulation, IRS interpreted the tax whistleblower law as applying only to collections made under Title 26, the U.S. Tax

---

[1] IRS estimated the average annual gross tax gap for tax years 2008-2010 (the most recent estimate available) to be $458 billion. IRS expects it will ultimately collect $52 billion annually, making the estimated annual net tax gap $406 billion.

[2] Pub. L. No. 109-432, div. A, title IV, § 406, 120 Stat. 2922, 2958 (Dec. 20, 2006). This expanded program, codified in the U.S. Tax Code at §7623(b), requires IRS to pay an award between 15 and 30 percent of collected proceeds when IRS takes action based on the whistleblower's information for claims when the amount in dispute is greater than $2 million in tax underpayments and when the individual's gross income exceeds $200,000 for any taxable year subject to the action. Claims that meet the criteria laid out in the expanded program are referred to as 7623(b) claims. 26 U.S.C. § 7623(b)(1); 26 U.S.C. § 7623(b)(5).

[3] Gabriel Zucman, "Taxing across Borders: Tracking Personal Wealth and Corporate Profits," *Journal of Economic Perspectives* vol. 28 no.4: 121–48 (2014). Zucman (2014) estimates that U.S. residents possessed approximately $1.2 trillion in offshore financial assets in 2013. It is uncertain what proportion of these offshore assets are undisclosed. The Boston Consulting Group, *Global Wealth 2017: Transforming the Client Experience* (2014). The Boston Consulting Group (2014) estimates that offshore wealth for the United States and Canada was $0.7 trillion in 2016. In 2013, we reported that there were no official estimates, but that in 2002, the IRS commissioner estimated offshore tax noncompliance was likely in the several tens of billions of dollars. See GAO, *Offshore Tax Evasion: IRS Has Collected Billions of Dollars, but May be Missing Continued Evasion*, GAO-13-318 (Washington, D.C.: Mar. 27, 2013).

Code. Because penalties assessed and collected by IRS for FBAR violations are collected under Title 31, the Bank Secrecy Act, IRS did not include these penalties in whistleblower award calculations. Similarly, criminal fines, which are collected under Title 18, were excluded from whistleblower award calculations.

Some whistleblowers have challenged these exclusions in the courts. Also, in 2015, the IRS Taxpayer Advocate Service included a legislative recommendation in its annual report that Congress amend the tax whistleblower law to specifically include FBAR penalties in proceeds. On February 9, 2018, Congress passed legislation that replaced the term "collected proceeds" with the word "proceeds" and defined proceeds as "penalties, interest, additions to tax, and additional amounts provided under the internal revenue laws and any proceeds arising from laws for which the Internal Revenue Service is authorized to administer, enforce, or investigate, including criminal fines and civil forfeitures, and violations of reporting requirements."

Prior to the statutory change in the definition of proceeds, you asked us to review how often and to what extent whistleblower claims involve cases where FBAR penalties were also assessed. This chapter (1) describes the extent to which the Whistleblower Office included FBAR penalties in whistleblower awards prior to the change in the definition of proceeds; (2) examines how IRS used whistleblower information on FBAR noncompliance and how IRS responded to the statutory change in the definition of proceeds; (3) describes the purposes for which IRS collects and uses data from the FBAR Database and assesses the controls for ensuring data reliability; and (4) summarizes what is known about the potential effect that exclusions from whistleblower awards, including FBAR penalties, may have had on whistleblowers bringing claims to IRS.

This chapter is a public version of a sensitive report that we issued in August 2018. IRS deemed some of the information in our August report to be sensitive, which must be protected from public disclosure. Therefore, this chapter omits sensitive information about the information security safeguards of IRS's FBAR Database as well as an associated recommendation. Although the information provided in this chapter is more limited, the report addresses the same objectives as the sensitive report and uses the same methodology.

To address our first objective, we reviewed a generalizable stratified sample of 132 whistleblower claim files closed between January 1, 2012, and July 24, 2017, (the time of our analysis) to identify how often these claims included allegations related to offshore accounts and FBAR violations and how often these claims led to IRS assessing FBAR penalties. The sample included (1) all 92 claims where the taxpayer identified by the whistleblower was also included in IRS's FBAR Database, IRS's database of FBAR enforcement actions; (2) all 10 claims that the Whistleblower Office closed as having no Title 26 collected proceeds; and (3) a sample of 30 claims randomly selected from 299 claims identified as having one or more key words indicating offshore account activity in E-TRAK, the Whistleblower Office's electronic claims management information system.[4] We compared information gathered from our file review with data on FBAR enforcement actions from the FBAR Database. We also interviewed IRS officials.

We assessed the reliability of the FBAR Database and E-TRAK to use limited data from these databases for our own analysis. We reviewed agency documents, electronically tested data for missing data and outliers, and interviewed IRS officials about these databases. These two databases are the only sources of data within IRS for whistleblower claims information and FBAR enforcement actions and outcomes. We used data from E-TRAK to identify whistleblower claims that were likely to involve allegations of FBAR noncompliance. We compared data from ETRAK and the FBAR Database to identify individuals that were named by a whistleblower and also subject to FBAR enforcement actions and any related enforcement actions taken by IRS. We also reviewed data on the amount of FBAR penalties assessed, if any, to the individuals included in our sample. We discuss the limitations of these databases in this chapter, but concluded that the elements we used in our analyses were sufficiently reliable for our purposes.

---

[4] See appendix I for more details on the population we identified and the sampling methodology we used.

To address our second objective, we reviewed relevant portions of the Internal Revenue Manual (IRM) and other IRS internal guidance. We interviewed IRS Whistleblower Office and IRS operating division officials about what IRS did with information received from whistleblowers about FBAR allegations prior to the statutory change in the definition of proceeds. In addition, we reviewed the February 2018 statutory provisions concerning the definition of proceeds on which whistleblower awards are based.

To address our third objective, we evaluated IRS's FBAR Database to identify any control deficiencies, using as criteria principles on design activities for information systems and use of quality information from *Standards for Internal Control in the Federal Government*; the Federal Information Security Modernization Act of 2014, and National Institute of Standards and Technology Special Publication 800-53.[5] We electronically tested the FBAR Database for missing data, outliers, and obvious errors, and reviewed IRS documentation on the database. We also interviewed IRS officials responsible for maintaining and using the database to determine how IRS uses the data, existing controls, any known limitations of the database, and any planned changes or improvements for the database. While we determined that the data we used from the FBAR Database were sufficiently reliable for the purposes of identifying individuals also named in whistleblower claims as well as FBAR enforcement outcomes, we identified risks to the reliability of the data, as discussed later in the report.

For our fourth objective, we interviewed a nonprobability sample of 11 attorneys from nine law firms that represent multiple clients who have submitted claims to the IRS Whistleblower Office under Section 7623(b). The views expressed in these interviews represented only those of the attorneys who participated and are not generalizable to all whistleblower attorneys or law firms. These attorneys also have a financial interest in IRS's treatment of whistleblower claims; however, interviewing these attorneys allowed us to gather broad viewpoints on how whistleblower

---

[5] GAO, *Standards for Internal Control in the Federal Government,* GAO-14-704G (Washington, D.C.: September 2014).

award exclusions may affect their professional decisions and the decisions of their clients and prospective clients. We also analyzed FBAR penalty data from the FBAR Database, and tax assessment data. In addition, we interviewed IRS Whistleblower Office and operating division officials.

The performance audit upon which this chapter is based was conducted from March 2017 to August 2018 in accordance with generally accepted government auditing standards. Those standards require that we plan and perform the audit to obtain sufficient, appropriate evidence to provide a reasonable basis for our findings and conclusions based on our audit objectives. We believe that the evidence obtained provides a reasonable basis for our findings and conclusions based on our audit objectives. We subsequently worked with IRS from August 2018 to September 2018 to prepare this public version of the original sensitive report for public release. This public version was also prepared in accordance with these standards.

BACKGROUND

Since 1867, the internal revenue laws have allowed the government to pay awards to individuals who provided information that aided in detecting and punishing those guilty of violating tax laws. In 1996, Congress increased the scope of the program to also provide awards for detecting underpayments of tax. It also changed the source of awards to money IRS collects as a result of information whistleblowers provide rather than appropriated funds. The Tax Relief and Health Care Act of 2006 created a mandatory whistleblower award program which made fundamental changes to IRS's existing informant awards program. The 2006 act also established the IRS Whistleblower Office.[6]

[6] The Tax Relief and Health Care Act of 2006 established the Whistleblower Office which is responsible for managing and tracking whistleblower claims from the time IRS receives them to the time it closes them either through a rejection or denial letter or an award payment. The Secretary of the Treasury is required to submit an annual report to Congress on the activities and outcomes of both the original and expanded whistleblower programs.

The Whistleblower Office processes claims that allege a tax noncompliance of more than $2 million as potential 7623(b) claims. If these claims meet the requirements for an award, the whistleblower receives a mandatory award of between 15 and 30 percent of collected proceeds, with the exact percentage determined by IRS's Whistleblower Office based on the extent of the whistleblower's contributions. Claims not meeting the criteria for a 7623(b) claim are referred to as 7623(a) claims and are subject to procedural steps similar to those of 7623(b) claims. However, 7623(a) claims are neither eligible for appeals to the U.S. Tax Court nor subject to mandatory award payments.

For claims processed as 7623(b) claims, the whistleblower claims process involves multiple steps, starting with a whistleblower's initial application and ending with a rejection, a denial, or an award payment.[7] The process begins when a whistleblower submits a signed Form 211, *Application for Award for Original Information*, to the Whistleblower Office. The Initial Claim Evaluation unit, which is part of the Small Business/Self-Employed operating division, performs an administrative review of the incoming applications. The Initial Claim Evaluation unit examines the submission for completeness and logs it into E-TRAK. They may reject claims because the tax noncompliance allegation is unclear, no taxpayer is identified, or the whistleblower is ineligible for an award.[8] Claims that are not rejected are sent to classification to determine which operating division should review the claim.[9]

---

[7] While the claim review process for 7623(a) claims is similar to that of 7623(b) claims, 7623(a) claims are afforded less administrative processes and are subject to more limited judicial review.

[8] A whistleblower may be ineligible for an award for reasons which include, but are not limited to, if he or she is an employee of the Department of Treasury, or is acting within the scope of his or her duties as an employee of any federal, state, or local government or the individual obtained or was furnished the information while acting in his or her official capacity as a member of a state body or commission having access to such materials as federal returns, copies, or abstracts.

[9] IRS has four operating divisions. These operating divisions are divided by the types of taxpayers they service. The operating divisions are Small Business/Self-Employed, Large Business & International, Wage & Investment, and Tax Exempt/Government Entities. IRS also has the Criminal Investigation division which handles criminal tax matters. Whistleblower claims are generally referred to Small Business/Self-Employed, Large Business & International, and Criminal Investigation.

Claims are then generally sent to subject matter experts in the various operating divisions—usually the Small Business/Self-Employed or Large Business & International division—where they are reviewed to determine whether the claims merit further consideration by the operating division, should be referred to Criminal Investigation for investigation, or should be sent back to the Whistleblower Office as denied. Claims can be denied if there is limited audit potential or if there is limited time left on the statute of limitations, among other reasons. Claims that are not denied are generally added to the operating division's inventory for potential examination. If a claim is selected for examination, the examiner completes and returns to the Whistleblower Office a Form 11369, *Confidential Evaluation Report on Claim for Award*, at the conclusion of the examination. The Whistleblower Office uses the information on this form when making an award determination. Figure 1 summarizes the full claim review process for 7623(b) claims.

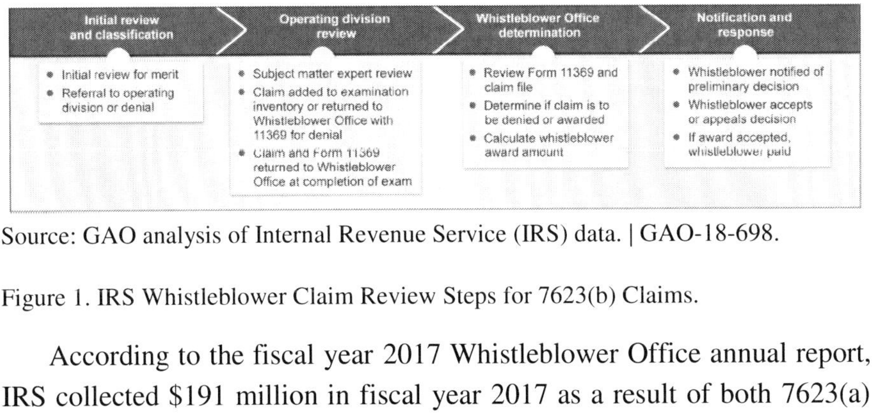

Source: GAO analysis of Internal Revenue Service (IRS) data. | GAO-18-698.

Figure 1. IRS Whistleblower Claim Review Steps for 7623(b) Claims.

According to the fiscal year 2017 Whistleblower Office annual report, IRS collected $191 million in fiscal year 2017 as a result of both 7623(a) and 7623(b) whistleblower claims. IRS also paid out $34 million on 367 claims to 242 whistleblowers. The average whistleblower award for fiscal year 2017 was over $140,000. Figure 2 below shows the collection and payout amounts for fiscal years 2012 through 2017.

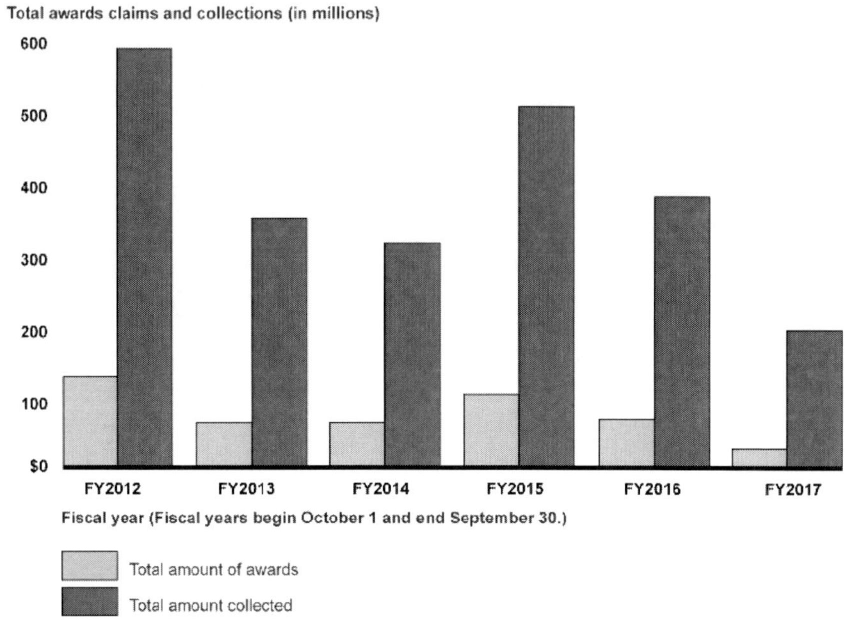

Source: GAO analysis of Internal Revenue Service (IRS) Whistleblower Office Annual Report to Congress, FY2013-2017. | GAO-18-698.

Figure 2. Total Collections Attributed to Whistleblower Information and Awards Paid to Whistleblowers, Fiscal Years 2012 through 2017, as Reported by IRS.

Collected Proceeds

Prior to February 9, 2018, section 7623(b) of Title 26 required the Whistleblower Office to calculate whistleblower award amounts as a percent of "collected proceeds (including penalties, interest, additions to tax, and additional amounts)."[10] On August 12, 2014, IRS issued a final rule to implement section 7623 (the whistleblower law) that clarified that certain penalties—those collected under Title 31 for FBAR violations, and those collected under Title 18 for criminal and civil penalties for tax law violations—do not constitute collected proceeds for calculating

[10] The award can be between 15 and 30 percent of proceeds if the whistleblower's information substantially contributed to the IRS action but no more than 10 percent of the proceeds collected if the action was based primarily on other information. The Whistleblower Office may reduce or deny awards under certain circumstances. 26 U.S.C. § 7623(b)(3).

whistleblower awards. IRS received comments on the proposed rule contending that excluding money collected under Title 18 and Title 31 eliminates a whistleblower's incentive to provide information on violations under these titles and would reduce the number of whistleblowers willing to provide information to IRS. IRS stated in its final rule that section 7623 only authorizes awards for amounts collected under Title 26. IRS also noted that under the Victims of Crime Act, criminal fines paid for tax law violations must go into the Crime Victims Fund and are unavailable for payment to whistleblowers.

Whistleblowers challenged IRS's definition of collected proceeds in court. In August 2016, the U.S. Tax Court issued a ruling in response to a petition filed by a married couple who, as whistleblowers, had provided information leading to a conviction related to a tax fraud scheme and then disputed the award determination made by the Whistleblower Office. The U.S. Tax Court ruled that criminal fines and civil forfeitures were collected proceeds for purposes of an award under Section 7623(b). In its ruling, the court held that "the term 'collected proceeds' means all proceeds collected by the Government from the taxpayer" and that "...the term is broad and sweeping; it is not limited to amounts assessed and collected under title 26."[11] On April 24, 2017, IRS filed an appeal of the Tax Court's decision with the U.S. Court of Appeals for the District of Columbia Circuit.

Before the U.S. Court of Appeals made a final ruling, Congress replaced the term "collected proceeds" with the term "proceeds" and provided a definition of "proceeds" on February 9, 2018, in the Bipartisan Budget Act of 2018.[12] The act's definition of proceeds includes: (1) penalties, interest, additions to tax, and additional amounts provided under the internal revenue laws; and (2) any proceeds arising from laws for which the IRS is authorized to administer, enforce, or investigate including criminal fines and civil forfeitures, and violations of reporting requirements. This includes FBAR penalties in the definition of proceeds,

---

[11] U.S. Tax Court, *Whistleblower 21276-13W, v. Commissioner of Internal Revenue* and *Whistleblower 21277-13W, v. Commissioner of Internal Revenue* (August 3, 2016).

[12] Bipartisan Budget Act of 2018, 132 Stat. 64 (2018).

as well as criminal fines and civil forfeitures.[13] This definition of proceeds applies to cases for which a final determination for an award was not made prior to enactment. On March 26, 2018, IRS withdrew its appeal before the U.S. Court of Appeals.

Reporting of Foreign Bank and Financial Accounts

Under the Bank Secrecy Act of 1970, and in particular those sections incorporated into Title 31 of the U.S. Code, U.S. persons with a financial interest in, or signature or other authority over a bank, securities, or other financial account in a foreign country are required to keep records and file reports on transactions with foreign financial institutions.[14] Persons with a financial interest or signature authority over one or more foreign financial accounts with a total value of more than $10,000 must file an FBAR with the Department of the Treasury (Treasury). If an FBAR is required, it must be filed each year for the previous calendar year on or before April 15 (or other date as prescribed by the IRS) to coincide with the tax filing deadline. Administration of this statute has been delegated by Treasury to the Financial Crimes Enforcement Network (FinCEN). In April 2003, FinCEN delegated its authority to IRS to enforce the FBAR requirements. These requirements include conducting examinations of FBAR compliance and taking such enforcement actions as assessing penalties, as appropriate.

A person's civil penalty for each FBAR violation can be up to $500 for a negligent FBAR violation and up to $10,000 for non-willful violation. In addition, a person with a willful FBAR violation may be subject to a civil monetary penalty equal to the greater of $100,000 or 50 percent of the amount in the account at the time of the violation, and also be subject to

---

[13] In addition, whistleblower awards are to be determined without regard to whether such proceeds are available to the Secretary.

[14] Bank Secrecy Act, titles I and II of Pub. L No 91-508, 84 Stat. 1114 (1970), as amended, codified as 12 U.S.C. §§ 1829b, 1951-1959, and 31 U.S.C. §§ 5311-5322.4. Persons includes corporations, companies, etc., as well as individuals, as defined in law.1 U.S.C. § 1.

possible criminal sanctions.[15] These penalties are per person, per account, and per year. According to the Internal Revenue Manual (IRM), FBAR penalties assessed by IRS are collected and tracked separately from tax assessments.

PRIOR TO FEBRUARY 2018, IRS DID NOT CONSIDER WHISTLEBLOWER INFORMATION THAT MAY HAVE LED TO FBAR ENFORCEMENT ACTIONS IN AWARD DETERMINATIONS

Whistleblowers Likely Identified Millions in FBAR Noncompliance for Which They Were Not Awarded

IRS assessed approximately $10.7 million in FBAR penalties to taxpayers who were identified in our sample of whistleblower claims. We reviewed 92 whistleblower claims closed between January 1, 2012, and July 24, 2017, where the identified taxpayer was also subject to an IRS FBAR examination.[16] IRS assessed FBAR penalties in 28 of these 92 cases.[17] In none of these instances was the FBAR penalty included in the

---

[15] For penalties assessed after August 1, 2016, whose associated violations occurred after November 2, 2015, the maximum penalties for negligent, non-willful, and willful violations are adjusted for inflation. 31 CFR § 1010.821.

[16] We limited our review to whistleblower claims that the Whistleblower Office processed under section 7623(b). This included having an allegation where the tax, penalties, interest, additions to tax, and additional amounts in dispute exceed $2 million, and if the taxpayer is an individual with a gross income of more than $200,000 for any taxable year. We limited our review to claims closed between January 1, 2012 and July 24, 2017. IRS retains whistleblower files at its Ogden, Utah location, where we performed our review, for 5 calendar years after closure. The oldest claim files available for review dated back to January 1, 2012 or later. July 24, 2017 was the date IRS downloaded E-TRAK data for our use to identify claims for review.

[17] These cases are included in our calculations of the potential increase in whistleblower awards if FBAR penalties had been included in collected proceeds. However, we make no claim that all whistleblowers would have received an award or that they were eligible for one, only that there was the potential for an award. In addition, because of the limitations of information retained in whistleblower files, we were unable to determine whether the whistleblower's allegation directly led to IRS opening an FBAR examination on the

collected proceeds used to calculate whistleblower awards. Our analysis of these 28 claims suggests that if IRS had included FBAR penalties in the awards, the whistleblowers involved could have received an additional $1.6 million to $3.2 million, assuming an award of between 15 and 30 percent.[18]

Examples of Whistleblower Claims
A whistleblower claim may provide IRS information on the undisclosed offshore account of a single individual (such as a business partner, former spouse, or family member), while other whistleblowers, such as bank insiders, may provide IRS a list of individuals with undisclosed offshore accounts.

Source: Internal Revenue Service. | GAO-18-698.

The exclusion of FBAR penalties from whistleblower awards is consistent with IRS's August 2014 regulation outlining the whistleblower award process. The final regulation describes the process for determining whistleblower awards and includes a definition of collected proceeds. Specifically, the regulation defines collected proceeds as "limited to amounts collected under the provisions of Title 26, United States Code." This definition excluded FBAR penalties assessed under Title 31 and criminal fines assessed under Title 18. This regulation's definition of collected proceeds, however, has been superseded by the replacement of "collected proceeds" with "proceeds" and a definition of "proceeds" in the Bipartisan Budget Act of 2018, effective February 9, 2018. The new law defines proceeds as including "penalties, interest, additions to tax, and additional amounts provided under the internal revenue laws and any proceeds arising from laws for which the Internal Revenue Service is authorized to administer, enforce, or investigate, including criminal fines and civil forfeitures, and violations of reporting requirements."

taxpayer in all 92 of these instances. Of our 92 reviewed claims, we found evidence in some claim files and related IRS data that IRS used whistleblower information for taking some FBAR enforcement actions, including assessing penalties and sending warning letters. We could not determine whether the whistleblower information was directly related to the examination for all files.

[18] For the purposes of our report, we assumed award rates of 15 percent to 30 percent in our calculations. These are the mandatory minimum and maximum rates for whistleblower awards outside of specific scenarios where a rate of less than 15 percent may be used. 26 U.S.C. § 7623(b)(2)-(3).

While no whistleblowers were paid for any FBAR penalties collected as a result of the information they provided to the Whistleblower Office, our analysis found that IRS took FBAR enforcement actions against at least 10 taxpayers based on whistleblowers' information.[19] Table 1 shows the FBAR enforcement outcomes for the 92 claims we reviewed.

Table 1. Report of Foreign Bank and Financial Accounts (FBAR) Enforcement Outcomes for Taxpayers Named in Selected IRS Whistleblower Claims Closed between January 1, 2012, and July 24, 2017

FBAR enforcement action	Number of claims
FBAR penalty assessed	28
Taxpayer entered Offshore Voluntary Disclosure Program	39
FBAR warning letter sent to taxpayer	9
No FBAR enforcement action taken	14
Unknown outcome	2
Total claims reviewed	92

Source: GAO analysis of Internal Revenue Service (IRS) data. | GAO-18-698.

No FBAR Enforcement Action

Some Report of Foreign Bank and Financial Accounts (FBAR) exams do not result in an enforcement action. This may happen when IRS opens an exam for FBAR violations but finds no FBAR violation or the violation was due to reasonable cause and the taxpayer submits any late FBARs.

Source: Internal Revenue Service. | GAO-18-698.

Of these 92 whistleblower claims we reviewed where the identified taxpayer was subject to an FBAR enforcement effort, 39 involved taxpayers accepted into IRS's Offshore Voluntary Disclosure Programs (OVDP).[20] OVDP enables taxpayers with tax noncompliance from

[19] For the purposes of this report, we define an FBAR enforcement action as the assessment of an FBAR penalty, entry into the OVDP, or the issuance of an FBAR warning letter.

[20] For more information on OVDP, see GAO-13-318. IRS initiated the first of four voluntary disclosure programs in 2003. According to IRS, IRS has collected more than $11 billion in revenue from these programs since 2009. On March 13, 2018, IRS announced the 2014 OVDP will close on September 28, 2018.

undisclosed offshore accounts to avoid prosecution and resolve their past noncompliance by paying limited civil penalties. As one of a number of required actions for OVDP, IRS assesses taxpayers accepted into the program a miscellaneous Title 26 offshore penalty in lieu of all other penalties for undisclosed foreign accounts, including FBAR penalties. According to IRS officials, because the OVDP penalty is a Title 26 penalty, these collections were included in collected proceeds for the purposes of whistleblower award calculations even before the new definition of proceeds took effect on February 9, 2018. The case files we reviewed included some examples of whistleblowers receiving an award based in part on the miscellaneous Title 26 OVDP penalty in addition to tax, interest, and other penalties.[21] If the taxpayer had not participated in OVDP, the whistleblower would not have received an award on the part of the collected proceeds that came from the FBAR penalty.[22]

FBAR Warning Letters

At the conclusion of a Report of Foreign Bank and Financial Accounts (FBAR) examination, an examiner can either assess a penalty or can use a warning letter (Letter 3800, *Warning Letter Respecting Foreign Bank and Financial Accounts Report Apparent Violations*) to notify taxpayers that they are not in compliance with FBAR reporting requirements. The examiner can use their discretion to issue a warning letter if they determine that the taxpayer would improve their FBAR reporting compliance in the future. A taxpayer's failure to file an FBAR after receiving a warning letter supports a determination of a willful FBAR violation.

Source: Internal Revenue Service. | GAO-18-698.

The new definition of proceeds establishes a policy of including FBAR penalties in whistleblower awards regardless of whether the identified

---

[21] The case files we reviewed included some examples of taxpayers being denied entry to OVDP due to whistleblowers' claims, making the taxpayer ineligible for reduced penalty rates. However, there may be instances where a whistleblower has provided information on the taxpayer to IRS, but, because of timing issues, IRS was not aware of this information when approving entry into the program. There may also be limited circumstances where a whistleblower's information led to the taxpayer entering OVDP, and the whistleblower may receive an award for OVDP penalty collections.

[22] IRS records did not enable us to determine what portion of the miscellaneous Title 26 offshore penalty was due to FBAR noncompliance versus other potential penalties for not reporting an offshore account.

taxpayer enters OVDP or is assessed an FBAR penalty as a result of an FBAR exam. It also creates consistency with the treatment of penalties assessed under the Foreign Account Tax Compliance Act (FATCA). FATCA, enacted in 2010 under Title 26, assesses penalties for failure to report foreign financial accounts and assets.[23] Because FATCA is under Title 26, any penalties assessed stemming from a whistleblower's information were already eligible for inclusion in whistleblower awards.

Of the total revenue collected from the 28 whistleblower claims we reviewed with an FBAR penalty assessed, more than 97 percent came from 10 cases with willful FBAR penalties. Willful FBAR penalties, which are up to 50 percent of the value of the account, represent a small portion (less than 0.1 percent) of all whistleblower claims closed in our time frame, and less than half of the 28 FBAR penalty cases we reviewed. However, we calculated that had these willful penalties been included in awards, the whistleblower awards would have increased by up to $3,145,754. In contrast, the 18 cases that had a non-willful or negligent FBAR penalty would have led to an increase in whistleblower awards of up to $78,912 based on our calculations.[24] Table 2 shows the number of cases and total amount of FBAR penalties collected by the type of FBAR penalty.

Whistleblowers may play an important role in bringing willfully noncompliant taxpayers to the attention of IRS. These taxpayers may be purposefully hiding their assets from IRS detection. To highlight the difference in the magnitude of FBAR penalties between willful and non-willful or negligent taxpayers, Figure 3 shows the range of potential whistleblower awards had FBAR penalties been included in award determinations.

---

[23] Unlike FBAR, FATCA has a third-party reporting provision which requires the foreign financial institutions holding the investments of U.S. taxpayers to report such accounts to IRS. Penalties assessed under FATCA had been included in the definition of collected proceeds for the purposes of IRS whistleblower awards before and after the 2018 change to the definition of proceeds.

[24] While IRS considers a negligent FBAR penalty to be a separate category of penalty that may be assessed against firms, for the purposes of reporting data in this report, we combined negligent with non-willful noncompliance.

Table 2. Number and Total Amount of Report of Foreign Bank and Financial Accounts (FBAR) Penalty Cases by Penalty Type in IRS Whistleblower Claims Closed between January 1, 2012, and July 24, 2017

FBAR penalty type	Number of cases	Total FBAR penalty amount (dollars)
Willful failure to report	10	10,485,847
Non-willful & negligent failure to meet recordkeeping requirements	18	263,039
Total	28	10,748,886

Source: GAO analysis of Internal Revenue Service (IRS) data. | GAO-18-698.

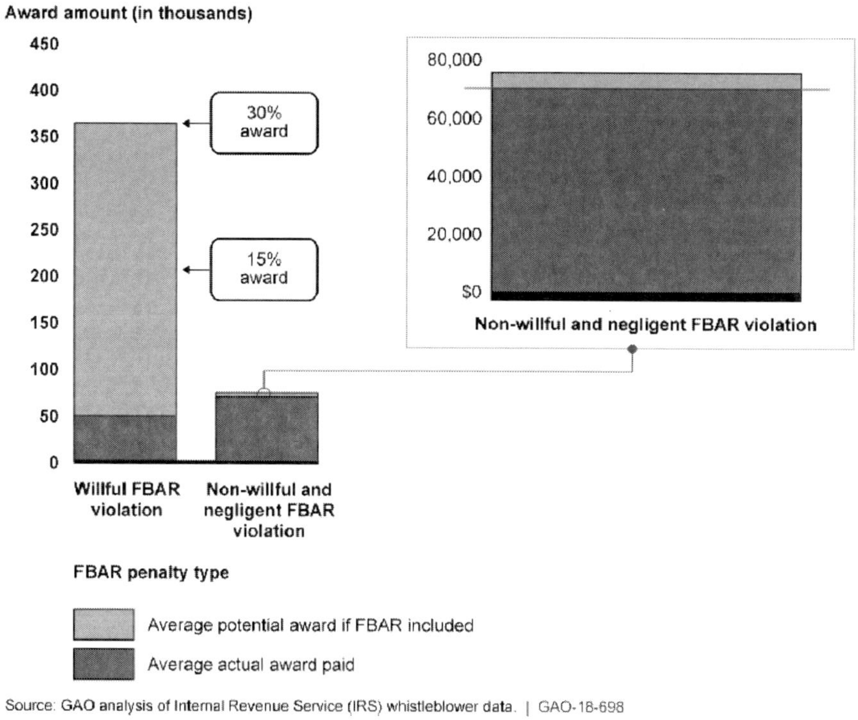

Source: GAO analysis of Internal Revenue Service (IRS) whistleblower data. | GAO-18-698.

Figure 3. Potential Average Award Amounts If *Report of Foreign Bank and Financial Accounts* (FBAR) Penalties Were Included in Collected Proceeds, by FBAR Penalty Type, for Claims Closed between January 1, 2012, and July 24, 2017.

Some Whistleblower Claims Closed between January 2012 and July 2017 Included FBAR Allegations

There is no way to estimate how many whistleblowers would have come forward had IRS included FBAR penalties in whistleblower awards. However, we found a small number of whistleblower claims that included FBAR information anyway. To look for how often whistleblowers submitted claims with allegations of FBAR noncompliance, we identified 401 of the 10,306 IRS whistleblower claims closed between January 1, 2012, and July 24, 2017, as likely to contain allegations of FBAR noncompliance by an identified taxpayer.[25] We identified three groups of claims as being most likely to contain allegations of FBAR noncompliance: 92 claims where the identified taxpayer was subject to an FBAR enforcement action (population discussed above); 299 claims that included key terms in E-TRAK indicating offshore assets; and 10 claims that were closed with "no Title 26 collected proceeds," which could indicate FBAR noncompliance since FBAR penalties are Title 31 penalties.[26] Since FBAR penalties were excluded from whistleblower proceeds, IRS did not track FBAR allegation data in E-TRAK. Therefore, our numbers might underrepresent the total population of claims likely to include

---

[25] The Whistleblower Office assigns a claim number to each individual taxpayer identified by a whistleblower. The unit of analysis that we sampled was the claim number. Therefore, the number of claims in our sample may be greater than the total number of whistleblowers involved in these claims to the extent a whistleblower provided information to IRS on more than one taxpayer in one or more submissions.

[26] To identify how often whistleblowers make allegations of FBAR noncompliance, we searched E-TRAK to identify the universe of closed 7623(b) claims that included any of the following terms across relevant fields, including free text fields: FBAR, Report of Foreign Bank and Financial Accounts, FinCEN, Form 114, offshore, foreign account, Title 31, bank secrecy, or Bank Secrecy Act. We also identified any claims with the "claim issue" field marked as any of the following: offshore accounts, failure to file, foreign tax credits, tax shelter, and unreported income.

Table 3. Allegations of Report of Foreign Bank and Financial Accounts (FBAR) Noncompliance in Selected IRS Whistleblower Claims Closed between January 1, 2012, and July 24, 2017

Type of claim	Number of claims In population	Number of claims reviewed by GAO	Number of reviewed claims containing alleged FBAR noncompliance
Matched claims	92	92	85
Key terms claims	299	30a	11
No Title 26 collected proceeds claims	10	10	1
Total	401	132	97

Source: GAO analysis of Internal Revenue Service data. | GAO-18-698.

[a]Random sample of key terms claims generalizable to the population of 299 claims identified as having key terms included in the electronic claim file. The key terms we used were: FBAR, Report of Foreign Bank and Financial Accounts, FinCEN, Form 114, offshore, foreign account, Title 31, bank secrecy, or Bank Secrecy Act. We also identified any claims with the "claim issue" field marked as any of the following: offshore accounts, failure to file, foreign tax credits, tax shelter, and unreported income. allegations of FBAR noncompliance.

We reviewed all 92 of the claims that included taxpayers that were also present in IRS's FBAR Database (matched claims) and found that 85 of them included allegations of FBAR noncompliance on IRS Form 211, the form used to submit a claim to the Whistleblower Office. We reviewed a random sample of 30 claims from the 299 claims we identified as being likely to include FBAR information based on key terms in the E-TRAK database (key terms claims)—11 of them included allegations of FBAR noncompliance. We also reviewed all 10 of the claims that were closed with "no Title 26 collected proceeds" and found one allegation of FBAR noncompliance. This was not unusual because IRS uses the "no Title 26 collected proceeds" code for closures other than those with FBAR penalties, such as claims with Title 18 criminal fines. Table 3 shows our three populations and how often we found claims with allegations of FBAR noncompliance in each.

Based on our stratified sample of selected whistleblower claims, we estimate that at least 1.4 percent (or at least 146 claims) of all large-dollar (7623(b)) whistleblower claims closed between January 1, 2012, and July

24, 2017, involved allegations of FBAR noncompliance.[27] Because the Whistleblower Office did not require data in E-TRAK to indicate the nature of the violation the whistleblower is reporting, the actual number of claims that include allegations of FBAR noncompliance may be higher. While our estimate represents a small proportion of all whistleblower claims, this may be because of the prior policy of excluding FBAR penalties from awards. However, the analysis suggests that despite being ineligible for award payment, some whistleblowers provided information on FBAR noncompliance to IRS that may have helped improve FBAR's effectiveness as a tool for anti-money laundering and tax enforcement. With the statutory change in award basis, IRS may see more whistleblowers come forward with better information about FBAR noncompliance, according to whistleblower attorneys we interviewed.

IRS Historically Used FBAR Information from Whistleblower Claims for Enforcement Efforts, but the Statutory Change in Award Basis Increases the Importance of Reporting Full Information

The Whistleblower Office Forwarded FBAR Information to Other IRS Divisions for Exam Purposes, Even Before FBAR Information Was Required to Be Included in Award Determinations

Even though FBAR penalties were not considered for whistleblower awards until the February 9, 2018 legislative change, the Whistleblower Office forwarded allegations it received of FBAR noncompliance to IRS's

[27] The estimated 146 claims is the one-sided lower bound of the 95 percent confidence interval and represents a margin of error of less than 12 percentage points relative to the sample frame of 401 selected whistleblower claims. See appendix I for more detail on how we selected claims for this analysis.

operating divisions for further examination. Whistleblower Office officials told us that if a whistleblower provides information concerning offshore accounts held by a taxpayer, including specific allegations of FBAR noncompliance, IRS evaluates it as it does any other information. The presence of information on possible FBAR noncompliance does not change the process for evaluating the claim. Whistleblower Office instructions for the initial review of a claim specify that, if the claim merits further consideration, it will be referred to the appropriate operating division for review.

According to officials from the Small Business/Self-Employed and Large Business & International operating divisions, during their review process information dealing with offshore accounts and possible FBAR violations is treated just as all other information provided by a whistleblower. Once a claim is referred to an operating division, it is generally reviewed by a subject matter expert who then determines whether the claim has sufficient audit potential to warrant adding it to the division's inventory of possible returns for audit. If the subject matter expert concludes that the claim does not have sufficient audit potential, or the division later decides not to proceed with an examination, the claim is returned to the Whistleblower Office. If the subject matter expert forwards a whistleblower claim for possible audit and an examination takes place, the examiners will establish an audit file for the tax examination. If evidence of FBAR noncompliance is found, a separate audit file is to be created. Most often, both files are maintained and updated by the same examiners. According to IRS officials and procedures laid out in the IRM, the outcome of the examination is based on the quality of the evidence and is not influenced by the presence of a whistleblower or the source of the information.

Information on FBAR noncompliance developed by examiners may or may not be provided to the Whistleblower Office. At the conclusion of the examination process, the examiner provides the Whistleblower Office with a Form 11369, *Confidential Evaluation Report on Claim for Award*. On this form, examiners are required to answer a series of detailed questions about the whistleblower's contribution to the investigation, such as whether the whistleblower identified specific issues or provided analysis that saved IRS time and resources. According to the IRM, the purpose of the Form 11369 is to inform the Whistleblower Office of the whistleblower's contribution, if any, to an examination, investigation, or other action.[28]

According to the instructions on the Form 11369 as well as the IRM, the Whistleblower Office bases its award determinations in large part on the form and information provided to supplement it. There is no specific space set aside on the Form 11369 for information dealing specifically with FBAR noncompliance. In addition, there are no instructions on or accompanying the form to require examiners to provide documentation relating to FBAR noncompliance.

Prior to the legislative change in February 2018 to include FBAR penalties in awards, the Whistleblower Office retained in its files any FBAR-related information provided by the operating division but did not use it for the award determination process. According to Whistleblower Office officials, any information about FBAR noncompliance in its claim files was there incidentally and not collected or retained for any specific tracking purposes. These officials told us, and we found in our review, that some claim files had information about FBAR violations or penalties because the operating division examiner chose to include it in the Form 11369 narrative or in supplemental information, even though the examiner was not required to do so. Because providing FBAR information with the Form 11369 was discretionary prior to the legislative change in February 2018, Whistleblower Office officials told us that if FBAR information existed in the files at the time of the interview, it may not be complete.

While having complete information about FBAR exams on the Form 11369 was not needed when IRS did not consider FBAR noncompliance as part of award determinations, now that it is defined as such by statute, the Whistleblower Office will need such information on FBAR noncompliance on Form 11369 to properly determine whistleblower awards in accordance with the new legal requirements. As of June 28, 2018, the Whistleblower

---

[28] IRM Chapter 25, Part 2, Section 2.6.

Office had not updated Form 11369 or its accompanying instructions. Whistleblower Office officials told us they were reviewing and commenting on draft guidance from the Office of Chief Counsel on how to implement the new provision but had not yet updated the Form 11369 or its instructions. IRS officials did not provide a timeline for when IRS expects to update the form.

Because this form asks questions specific to Title 26 tax noncompliance examiners may not have clear guidance indicating that non-Title 26 issues should be included in these answers. According to the IRM, the Form 11369 should assist the Whistleblower Office in making an award determination by explaining how the whistleblower and their information assisted IRS in taking action. By not using an updated form that reflects the technical language distinguishing between tax issues and non-Title 26 issues that IRS also enforces, the Whistleblower Office may not be able to ensure the information it collects for determining whistleblower awards that includes non-Title 26 violations is complete and accurate.

IRS Has Taken Some Steps to Communicate Change in Whistleblower Award Basis

When enacted on February 9, 2018, the new law immediately required information concerning FBAR violations to be included in the awards determination process. Subsequently, the Whistleblower Office and IRS started to make changes to policies and procedures to ensure award determination decisions are made fairly and with full information. The day the new statutory definition became law, IRS placed a hold on whistleblower award determinations while the Whistleblower Office developed new procedures. On February 15, 2018, IRS lifted the hold, instructing Whistleblower Office analysts to check with their managers prior to making award determinations on any claims that may include non-Title 26 proceeds. However, the Whistleblower Office did not issue any additional specific guidance to Whistleblower Office staff on how to review claims for any non-Title 26 issues until April 19, 2018. According to IRS officials, the Whistleblower Office closed 2,096 whistleblower claims between the date the law changed and April 19, 2018 when IRS issued the internal guidance.

In the April 19, 2018 policy alert, later reissued as a memo on May 8, 2018, Whistleblower Office staff were instructed to look over the Form 211 for indications of FBAR or criminal activity when reviewing a Form 11369 or making award determinations. The policy alert also instructs staff to contact the FBAR Penalty Coordinator and review Special Agent's Reports and Judgement Documents for non-Title 26 proceeds and to document the results of these reviews in E-TRAK.

Issuing complete and final guidance will take time; however the Whistleblower Office did not issue any interim guidance to IRS units outside the Whistleblower Office for more than 2 months after the enactment of the statute redefining proceeds. On April 12, 2018, the Director of the Whistleblower Office issued a memo to the commissioners of the operating divisions and chief of the Criminal Investigation division. This memo stated that those working on whistleblower claims need to provide the Whistleblower Office with details of how whistleblower information was used in any actions taken regardless of whether they were Title 26 issues or not. The Whistleblower Office emailed a communication similar to the memo to other IRS employees working on whistleblower claims on April 18, 2018. The initial memo did not provide specific instructions as to how to provide such information, such as specifying to use Form 11369, but the email said additional guidance and training would be forthcoming. According to Whistleblower Office officials, the timing of the internal communication about the change in whistleblower award basis was because the Whistleblower Office was waiting on draft guidance from the IRS Office of Chief Counsel. The Whistleblower Office received this draft guidance on April 19, 2018.

In late April and early May, the Whistleblower Office posted information about these changes in internal IRS media, including IRS-wide web pages and pages for individual IRS operating divisions. The Whistleblower Office specified information should be included with the

Form 11369 in these later communications. However, as noted above, the Form 11369 itself and its accompanying instructions had not been updated to reflect these new requirements.

The current regulations on whistleblower claims, issued in August 2014, exclude non-Title 26 proceeds from the basis for determining whistleblower awards. According to IRS officials, as of June 20, 2018, IRS had not yet started to take action on making the regulatory change. IRS, however, is in the process of updating the IRM, which serves as the primary guidance for IRS employees. Section 25.2.2 of the IRM, which provides procedures and instructions for the whistleblower award programs, defines collected proceeds for the purpose of awards as tax, penalties, interest, and additions to tax limited to amounts collected only under the provisions of Title 26. According to IRS officials, while IRM updates take time to complete, generally the IRM can be updated quicker than a regulation. The officials could not provide a timeline for when these changes would be complete.

IRS can communicate to the public about statutory changes to the whistleblower program through its various external communication channels, such as its website and social media accounts. Such communications are important because whistleblowers have a limited 30-day period to appeal certain award determinations. On May 9, 2018, IRS posted an announcement about the statutory change on the Whistleblower Office page of its web site. The announcement noted the enactment of the provision redefining proceeds for the purpose of whistleblower awards and provided a link to the May 8, 2018 Whistleblower Office memorandum. This information was posted 3 months after the statutory change went into effect and a month after we notified IRS that IRS had not yet announced the change through a press release, its web site, or its Twitter account.

IRS USES ITS FBAR DATABASE FOR INTERNAL AND EXTERNAL REPORTING BUT LACKS SUFFICIENT CONTROLS

IRS Uses Data from Its FBAR Database to Manage Workflow and for Internal and External Reporting

IRS collects and maintains FBAR penalty data in a stand-alone database. According to IRS officials, they use these data to carry out IRS's delegated duties to assess and collect such penalties.[29] For example, the data are used for sending demand notice letters to taxpayers and tracking cases referred to the Department of Justice. According to these officials, IRS also uses information on FBAR penalty assessments and payments for a variety of related purposes including reporting FBAR data to the Financial Crimes Enforcement Network (FinCEN) and for use in annual reports to Congress.[30] IRS also uses the database for internal management. Specifically, IRS officials stated that they use reports on inventory, penalties, and appeals for decision making. Given the February 2018 legislative change to include FBAR penalties in the definition of proceeds, the Whistleblower Office will also use FBAR penalty data for calculating some whistleblower award determinations.

While FinCEN retains the rule-making authority for FBAR and is the repository of FBAR filings, IRS assesses and collects FBAR penalties from taxpayers who violate the FBAR reporting requirements. IRS also maintains the FBAR Database. While individuals file their FBAR forms through FinCEN's online Bank Secrecy Act E-filing portal, IRS enforces these filing requirements. Following procedures laid out in the IRM, IRS

---

[29] IRS solicits payment and processes voluntary payments received from taxpayers, but has no further collection authority for FBAR penalties. As required by law, collection enforcement action is referred to the Bureau of Fiscal Services, the Department of Justice, or both.

[30] The 2003 *Memorandum of Agreement and Delegation of Authority for Enforcement of FBAR Requirements* requires IRS to supply to FinCEN annually the number and amounts of FBAR penalties as well as a count of cases categorized by outcome. This agreement lays out responsibilities of FinCEN and IRS in enforcing FBAR requirements and preceded the development of the FBAR Database.

examiners can access FBAR filing data from FinCEN's database during the course of a tax examination.[31] Information on the taxpayers' FBAR filings is available to examiners through IRS's Integrated Data Retrieval System, including data from filed tax and information returns.

Data on FBAR enforcement actions, including penalties, are only housed in the FBAR Database. The FBAR Database is a stand-alone database maintained by the FBAR team within the Small Business/Self-Employed operating division. The FBAR Database does not interface or connect with any other IRS data sources or systems. Therefore, there is currently no mechanism for any data to automatically feed into or from the FBAR Database to cross-check with taxpayer information in other databases. When examiners open an FBAR exam, the IRM directs them to report exam and exam-outcome information to the FBAR team. Examiners fax, mail, or e-mail FBAR examination and penalty assessment information to the FBAR team which then transcribes the data into the FBAR Database manually. Within IRS, only the FBAR team has access to the database. Because the stand-alone FBAR Database is the only data source within IRS that tracks FBAR penalty assessments and payments, the FBAR team is responsible for completing all data entry as well as generating and circulating reports on FBAR enforcement actions to others within IRS.

IRS Has Insufficient Controls for the Reliability of FBAR Penalty Data

We assessed the reliability of the FBAR Database for the purposes of using limited data from this database for our own analysis. We determined that the data fields we used were sufficiently reliable for our purposes. Specifically, we matched taxpayer identification numbers in the FBAR Database to those in E-TRAK and reported on enforcement outcomes,

[31] IRM, Part 4, Chapter 10, Section 5.9.

including a limited number of penalty payments, as discussed previously.[32] These data were the only available data within IRS on FBAR penalties and enforcement actions. Even though we found the data that we used to be sufficiently reliable for our purpose of identifying penalty information and selecting a sample of claims to review further, we identified some data control deficiencies related to data input and validation. We found certain elements of the database to have limited reliability. Because FBAR penalty information will be used for whistleblower award determinations, it is important for these data to be reliable.

A key principle of federal internal control is the use of quality information. Agencies should have controls in their information systems to ensure the validity, completeness, and accuracy of data.[33] Further, these controls should be documented. In addition, the Federal Information Security Modernization Act of 2014 (FISMA) provides for the development and maintenance of the minimum controls required to protect federal information and information systems.[34] Among other things, FISMA requires the National Institute of Standards and Technology (NIST) to develop standards and guidelines that include minimum information security requirements on how agencies should design, protect, and manage their respective data systems. NIST's guidance outlines appropriate data safeguards for agency data systems based on a risk-based approach. NIST guidance also states an agency's information system should have controls to check the validity of inputs. This includes checking

---

[32] See appendix I for a more detailed discussion of the steps we took to assess the reliability of the FBAR Database.

[33] GAO-14-704G. These internal control standards provide several principles that agencies should follow with respect to how data are collected, stored, and used. These principles include designing control activities, designing control activities for information systems, implementing controls, and using quality information. For example, agencies should design information systems to obtain and process information to meet information requirements and to respond to the agency's objectives and risks.

[34] *See* 44 U.S.C. § 3551 et seq. The *Federal Information Security Modernization Act of 2014* (FISMA 2014) (Pub. L. No. 113-283, Dec. 18, 2014) largely superseded the *Federal Information Security Management Act of 2002* (FISMA 2002), enacted as *Title III, E-Government Act of 2002*, Pub. L. No. 107-347, 116 Stat. 2899, 2946 (Dec. 17, 2002). As used in this report, FISMA refers to the new requirements in FISMA 2014 and to other relevant FISMA 2002 requirements that were unchanged by FISMA 2014 and continue in full force and effect.

the valid syntax of inputs to ensure they match the specified definitions for format and content. NIST guidance also recommends controls to help ensure the information system behaves predictably, even if invalid data are entered.

While FBAR team employees transcribe data manually into the database from emails or faxed or mailed paper forms, there are no procedures for data testing or validation. For example, there is no secondary check by another individual to ensure data were entered correctly and completely. The FBAR Database procedures also lack sufficient validity checks to ensure that the data entered are accurate. There are some basic data entry checks in the database, such as limiting input to alphanumeric entries and a warning if a date is more than a year from the current date. However, these checks serve only as a reminder for the employees entering the data to verify its accuracy; these checks do not prevent erroneous data from being entered and retained. Without additional controls for accuracy and validity, IRS risks relying upon inaccurate information for some of its reporting and decision making.

According to IRS officials, not all fields in the FBAR Database are mandatory. In addition, some fields are new as of January 2017 and, therefore, only contain data after this time. IRS officials also told us that they are aware there are some data missing in the database, such as incomplete records for some taxpayers, but they could not quantify how often this occurs. They also told us that such missing data can contribute to inaccurate reports of FBAR total assessments. For example, if a date field is left blank, certain reports that pull data based on these date fields will not pull the records with this missing field, thereby underreporting FBAR outcomes. We found 44 records with input errors in this date field. The officials stated that they make every effort to input complete data into the database, but sometimes complete information is unavailable from the exam team. Because the FBAR data lack some reliability controls, IRS may rely on insufficient or incomplete data for reporting and decision making, including amounts of whistleblower awards.

IRS officials did not have any documentation showing why or how the database was developed in November 2003. Further, IRS officials told us the only documentation on how the database is used is the FBAR Database desk guide. The desk guide provides instructions for data input; however, this guide does not include any information to describe or define the elements in the database. Standard data element definitions are intended to ensure that all users of the system define the same data in the same way and have a common understanding of their meaning. Such documentation is important for providing clear instructions to users to know what information should be input in each variable field to ensure that the type of data in each variable field is consistent. Without it, IRS and other users of the data may not have reasonable assurance that data in the database are input as intended.

IRS recognized the need to address the FBAR Database and established an FBAR Improvement Project Team to review the FBAR Database and records system and make recommendations for improvements. The team was established in 2016 after reviews of database-generated reports indicated missing data. The FBAR Improvement Project Team has made recommendations to improve the overall function and reliability of the dataset, including updating FBAR policies and procedures and validating data for the report to Congress. They are also exploring automating case building by pulling taxpayer data from other IRS data sources and creating a report automation tool. As of April 2018, these recommendations had not been implemented. IRS officials were reviewing the recommendations and specific plans had not been vetted by the leadership in the relevant operating divisions. IRS officials noted that because of the small size and limited use of the database, it may be a low priority for scarce information technology resources. Until IRS develops and documents improved controls for the validity, completeness, and accuracy of data in the FBAR Database, it risks using incomplete and insufficient data for decision making.

Award Exclusions May Have Negatively Affected Whistleblowers' Willingness to Bring Information to IRS

Selected Whistleblower Attorneys in Our Review Reported They Limited or Refused to Take on Clients Who Alleged FBAR Noncompliance When Penalties Were Excluded from Awards

Whistleblower attorneys we spoke with referred to the former exclusion for FBAR and other non-Title 26 collections from whistleblower awards as a significant concern for them and their clients. Their concerns are important to the success of the whistleblower program because if whistleblowers are discouraged from coming forward, IRS risks losing opportunities to identify tax fraud and abuse and ultimately reduce the tax gap. This loss of help in identifying noncompliance could be significant for IRS. According to IRS, between 2007 and 2017, whistleblower information helped IRS collect $3.6 billion in tax revenue that may have otherwise gone uncollected. According to the whistleblower attorneys we spoke with, as well as information we gathered in a search of relevant literature, the estimated value of undisclosed offshore accounts may be in the tens of billions of dollars, but could be as great as hundreds of billions of dollars.[35]

Prior to the legislative change in the definition of collected proceeds, we interviewed 11 whistleblower attorneys from nine law firms about their experiences representing tax whistleblowers who submitted allegations of FBAR noncompliance to IRS.[36] Several of these firms also had experience

---

[35] In GAO-13-318, while we reported that there were no official estimates, in 2002, the IRS commissioner estimated offshore tax noncompliance was likely in the several tens of billions of dollars.

[36] The views expressed in these interviews represented only those of the attorneys who participated and are not generalizable to all whistleblower attorneys or law firms. These attorneys have a financial interest in IRS's treatment of whistleblower claims; however, interviewing these attorneys allowed us to gather broad viewpoints on how whistleblower award exclusions may affect their professional decisions and the decision of their clients

helping whistleblowers appeal IRS award determinations. Of these nine firms, eight firms' attorneys told us they had refused or limited the number of whistleblowers alleging FBAR noncompliance they were willing to take on as clients when such collections were excluded from award determinations. For example, one attorney told us that his firm would take on whistleblower clients alleging FBAR violations only if there was strong evidence of tax noncompliance. An attorney with another firm reported that the firm was willing to take on such clients but advised these clients that the inclusion of FBAR penalties in any award may have to be litigated in court at the award determination phase. Further, attorneys with three of the nine firms reported fewer whistleblowers either approaching them for representation or following through on filing a claim once informed of the exclusion of non-Title 26 collections from awards. Attorneys with eight of the nine firms also reported that the exclusion of criminal fines from collected proceeds was a potential reason for whistleblowers not coming forward.

We spoke with attorneys at eight of the nine firms again after the passage of the statutory change in the definition of proceeds. Most said that this was a positive step for the IRS whistleblower program and expected that more whistleblowers will come forward with information on criminal and FBAR violations. Attorneys with seven of the eight firms stated they would be willing or already had started taking on clients reporting FBAR and criminal violations. However, they cited other concerns with the program that could continue to limit their willingness to represent tax whistleblowers and discourage whistleblowers. These concerns included

- limits on anonymity for whistleblowers appealing Whistleblower Office decisions to the Tax Court;
- restrictions on filing claims anonymously;
- delays in award payments during the lengthy appeals process; and

---

and prospective clients. See appendix I for our methodology for selecting and interviewing these attorneys.

- limited communication with the Whistleblower Office during the claim review process.[37]

According to these attorneys, for those whistleblowers who are offered an award that excludes FBAR penalty and criminal fine collections, many choose to forgo appealing the decision because it would delay their collection of any part of the award until the appeals process was complete, which can take years. Further, the whistleblower may risk losing their anonymity in an appeal. They added that some whistleblowers risk their lives and livelihoods to come forward and that anonymity is critical to their willingness to provide information to IRS. The attorneys generally stated that these issues can discourage whistleblowers, which then can limit the whistleblower program's effectiveness.

Our Analysis Found No Evidence That Presence of Whistleblower Alters the Mix of FBAR Penalty and Tax IRS Assesses

Some of the attorneys we interviewed indicated that whistleblowers may have been further discouraged from bringing information on offshore noncompliance to IRS if they believed that IRS was purposefully trying to limit whistleblower awards by assessing higher FBAR penalties and lower taxes when a whistleblower was involved. The IRM provides IRS examiners with some level of discretion about when to assess tax and FBAR penalties, subject to the facts and circumstances of each individual case. Attorneys at seven of the nine firms we interviewed expressed concern that IRS examiners may have used this discretion to assess higher FBAR penalties and lower taxes as a way to reduce a whistleblower's potential award. However, these attorneys did not provide specific

---

[37] See GAO, *IRS Whistleblower Program: Billions Collected, but Timeliness and Communication Concerns May Discourage Whistleblowers,* GAO-16-20 (Washington, D.C.: Oct. 29, 2015). We have previously reported on the issue of Whistleblower Office communications, timeliness, and protection of whistleblower identities and made recommendations to IRS, which it has implemented, to take appropriate steps to address these areas.

evidence of this occurring. Because of taxpayer information privacy laws, IRS limits the amount and type of information it can share with whistleblowers and their attorneys about their claims once submitted to the Whistleblower Office.

To investigate this claim, we analyzed IRS data on taxpayers that were assessed FBAR penalties from tax years 2010 to 2015. We compared the proportion of FBAR penalties assessed to the overall tax and FBAR penalties assessed to a taxpayer for exams where a whistleblower was and was not involved. Our analysis did not find any evidence of a statistically significant difference between the taxpayers identified by a whistleblower and taxpayers with no whistleblower involved.[38]

The IRM lays out the steps examiners should take when determining whether FBAR penalties are warranted and how they should be assessed.[39] These steps are independent of IRM guidance on tax examinations and assessments. IRS officials that we interviewed, including those with oversight of examiners in Small Business/SelfEmployed and Large Business & International, indicated that the Title 26 tax exams and Title 31 FBAR exams are conducted independently of each other and neither influences the outcome of the other. Further, they stated that the presence of a whistleblower has no bearing on the decision of whether to assess a tax or penalty or the amount of such assessments, as previously discussed.

CONCLUSION

For the IRS whistleblower program to be successful, whistleblowers need to have confidence in the program's processes and outcomes, including paying awards when a whistleblower's information is used. Despite IRS's prior policy of not including non-Title 26 collections, we found some whistleblowers brought such information to IRS, and IRS

---

[38] Our analysis did not control for other factors that could affect the results, such as the taxpayer being willfully noncompliant with FBAR reporting requirements, the total tax assessment of the taxpayer, or the total income of the taxpayer.

[39] IRM, Part 4, Chapter 26, Section 16.

assessed penalties on noncompliant taxpayers. However, according to whistleblower attorneys we spoke with, this policy of award exclusions may have discouraged other whistleblowers with significant information on FBAR reporting and tax noncompliance from coming forward. With the new statutory definition of proceeds enacted on February 9, 2018, that includes FBAR and other non-Title 26 collections, whistleblowers may now be more willing to submit claims.

However, IRS has not yet fully changed some of the whistleblower program's policies and procedures to reflect that FBAR penalties, as well as criminal fines and civil forfeitures, are now included in whistleblower awards. Because the change was effective for claims that had not had a final determination made as of February 9, 2018, the Whistleblower Office taking immediate steps to ensure it had full information from other offices and divisions within IRS about claims reaching the award determination phase would have helped IRS act on these determinations. While IRS has now taken steps to communicate the need for information about non-Title 26 actions to be included with the Form 11369, updating the form itself and its instructions will help to better ensure that complete and accurate information about such actions is reflected on the form to be provided to the Whistleblower Office for inclusion in award determinations.

The FBAR Database is the only comprehensive source of information within IRS about the FBAR penalties assessed and paid. If this database does not have the controls necessary to provide reasonable assurance that the data are reliable, accurate, and complete, there is a risk that the Whistleblower Office may make award determinations based on incorrect data.

Recommendations for Executive Action

We are making the following two recommendations to IRS:

The Commissioner of Internal Revenue should ensure that the Director of the Whistleblower Office modifies the Form 11369 and its accompanying instructions to clarify how to document how whistleblower information was used in any IRS actions taken, regardless of whether the laws administered, examined, or enforced are outside of Title 26, such as FBAR penalties. (Recommendation 1)

The Commissioner of Internal Revenue should ensure that the Deputy Commissioner for Services and Enforcement develops and documents improved controls for the validity, completeness, and accuracy of data on FBAR exams and enforcement actions. (Recommendation 2)

AGENCY COMMENTS AND OUR EVALUATION

We provided a draft of the sensitive version of this chapter to IRS for review and comment. IRS agreed with our recommendations and provided technical comments which we incorporated as appropriate. However, IRS deemed some of the information in their original agency comment letter pertaining to the FBAR Database to be sensitive, which must be protected from public disclosure. Therefore, we have omitted the sensitive information in the comment letter, which is reproduced in part in appendix II. These omissions did not have a material effect on the substance of IRS's comments.

As agreed with your offices, unless you publicly announce the contents of this chapter earlier, we plan no further distribution until 30 days from the report date. At that time, we will send copies to the appropriate congressional committees and the Commissioner of Internal Revenue.

James R. McTigue, Jr.
Director, Tax Issues Strategic Issues

APPENDIX I: OBJECTIVES, SCOPE, AND METHODOLOGY

Our objectives were to: (1) describe the extent to which the Internal Revenue Service's (IRS) Whistleblower Office included Report of Foreign

Bank and Financial Accounts (FBAR) penalties in whistleblower awards prior to the statutory change; (2) examine how IRS used whistleblower information on FBAR noncompliance and how IRS responded to the statutory change in definition of proceeds; (3) describe the purposes for which IRS collects and uses data from the FBAR Database and assess the controls for ensuring data reliability; and (4) summarize what is known about the potential effect exclusions from collected proceeds, including FBAR penalties, may have had on whistleblowers bringing claims to IRS.

This chapter is a public version of a sensitive report that we issued in August 2018. IRS deemed some of the information in our August report to be sensitive, which must be protected from public disclosure. Therefore, this chapter omits sensitive information about the information security safeguards of IRS's FBAR Database as well as an associated recommendation. Although the information provided in this chapter is more limited, the report addresses the same objectives as the sensitive report and uses the same methodology.

To address the first objective, we conducted a case file review of a generalizable stratified sample of closed 7623(b) whistleblower claims to identify how often and to what extent whistleblower claims included information about offshore accounts and FBAR violations. For this case file review, we started with the population of 10,306 7623(b) claims that had been closed by IRS between January 1, 2012 and July 24, 2017 (the time of our analysis).[40] We identified three subpopulations of whistleblower claims from which we selected the claims we reviewed:

1. All 92 claims involving taxpayers who were identified in a whistleblower claim and who also appeared in IRS's FBAR Database as having been subject to an FBAR examination. We designated this subpopulation as "Matched Claims."

---

[40] Whistleblower files are generally retained in IRS's Ogden, Utah facility for 5 years after the final closing action is complete. After the 5 year retention, files are then shipped to a federal records center for long-term storage. We limited the review to those claims that were not yet sent for long-term storage. This focused our case file review on the most recent determinations the IRS Whistleblower Office has made with regard to FBAR penalty award exclusions.

2. A random sample of 30 claims from a population of 299 claims that a text search within E-TRAK had identified as likely involving noncompliance with offshore account requirements, including FBAR, and that were not included in other samples. We designated this subpopulation as "Key Terms."[41]
3. All 10 denied claims closed in E-TRAK, the IRS Whistleblower Office's claim tracking system, with the closing code "Denied - No Title 26 Collected Proceeds." We designated this subpopulation as "No Title 26 Collected Proceeds."

Table 4 shows descriptive information about each of these subpopulations.

The purpose of our file review was to determine how often whistleblower claims in each of our different subpopulations involved offshore accounts and allegations of FBAR violations. We reviewed all claims in our first and third subpopulations; because of the larger number of claims in the second subpopulation, we selected a random sample for review.

For the 132 whistleblower claims in our review, two reviewers coded the content of each file into different categories, including: whether the Form 211, *Application for Award for Original Information*, included allegations of FBAR noncompliance; whether the whistleblower received a whistleblower award; and what collections were included in collected proceeds for those paid whistleblowers. To the extent there were disagreements among the reviewers' coding for a file, a third reviewer resolved the differences. We agreed on a final coding for all of the data elements collected, recorded them in a summary document, and used these for our analysis. Because whistleblower files were not required to contain information on FBAR penalty assessments or other enforcement actions,

[41] To identify how often whistleblowers make allegations of FBAR noncompliance, we searched E-TRAK to identify the universe of closed 7623(b) claims that included any of the following terms across relevant fields, including free text fields: FBAR, Report of Foreign Bank and Financial Accounts, FinCEN, Form 114, offshore, foreign account, Title 31, bank secrecy, or Bank Secrecy Act. We also identified any claims with the "claim issue" field marked as any of the following: offshore accounts, failure to file, foreign tax credits, tax shelter, and unreported income.

although some of the files we reviewed did have this information, we supplemented our file review with data on FBAR enforcement actions, such as penalties and warning letters, from the FBAR Database.

Table 4. Sample Population Descriptions

Name	Description	Number of claims in population	Number of claims reviewed	Selection method
1. Matched claims	Whistleblower claims where the identified taxpayer matches entry in database of *Report of Foreign Bank and Financial Accounts* (FBAR) penalties	92	92	Census
2. Key terms claims	Claims that contain flag in E-TRAK indicating offshore or FBAR	299	30a	Random sample[a]
3. No Title 26 collected proceeds claims	Claims closed with code "No Title 26 Collected Proceeds"	10	10	Census
Total	401	132	—[b]	

Source: GAO analysis of Internal Revenue Service data.| GAO-18-698.

[a]Generalizable random sample of key terms claims.

[b]— = cell intentionally left blank.

We assessed the reliability of the FBAR Database and E-TRAK database for the purposes of using limited data from these databases for our own analysis. We reviewed agency documents, electronically tested data for missing data and outliers, and interviewed IRS officials about these databases. These two databases are the only sources of data within IRS for whistleblower claims information and FBAR enforcement actions and outcomes. We compared data in both databases to identify individuals that were both named by a whistleblower and subject to an FBAR enforcement action. We used data from the FBAR Database for the purpose of identifying and summarizing FBAR enforcement actions taken by IRS, and we used data from the E-TRAK database to identify whistleblower claims that were likely to include allegations of FBAR noncompliance. IRS officials told us that the FBAR Database is the most reliable data source at IRS for individuals who were subject to such FBAR enforcement actions as penalty assessments. We discuss the limitations of these databases in this chapter, but we concluded that the elements we used in our analyses were sufficiently reliable for the purposes of identifying a sample of whistleblower claims likely to include allegations of FBAR noncompliance and FBAR enforcement outcomes. We also interviewed IRS officials concerning the processing of claims and the operation and maintenance of the E-TRAK and FBAR databases.

For the second objective, we reviewed relevant portions of the Internal Revenue Manual and other IRS internal guidance and documentation and interviewed officials from IRS's Whistleblower Office and operating divisions that handle whistleblower claims about what IRS does when it receives information from whistleblowers that include allegations of FBAR noncompliance. We also reviewed the recently enacted statutory provisions concerning the definition of collected proceeds on which whistleblower awards are based. In addition we spoke to IRS Whistleblower Office officials concerning any changes IRS plans to make in its policies and procedures as a result of the statutory change.

For our third objective, we evaluated IRS's FBAR Database to identify any control deficiencies, using as criteria *Standards for Internal Control in the Federal Government*, the Federal Information Security Modernization Act of 2014, and National Institute of Standards and Technology Special Publication 800-53. We electronically tested the FBAR Database for missing data, outliers, and obvious errors. We also reviewed IRS documentation on the database. In addition, we interviewed IRS officials responsible for maintaining and using the database to determine how IRS uses the data, what controls are in place, and any known limitations of the database. We also met with IRS officials and discussed the ongoing development of plans for improvement of the database.

For our fourth objective, we interviewed a nonprobability sample of attorneys who have represented multiple whistleblowers who have submitted claims to the IRS Whistleblower Office under section 7623(b). The views expressed in these interviews represented only those of the attorneys who participated and are not generalizable to all whistleblower attorneys or law firms. These attorneys have a financial interest in IRS's treatment of whistleblower claims; however, interviewing these attorneys allowed us to gather broad viewpoints on how whistleblower award exclusions may affect their professional decisions and the decision of their clients and prospective clients. We began with whistleblower attorneys whom we previously spoke with for our 2011 and 2015 reports on the IRS Whistleblower Office and requested from those attorneys names of other attorneys currently active in the IRS whistleblower community who have represented clients who submitted allegations that included FBAR noncompliance. We individually interviewed 11 attorneys from nine firms, asking the same questions of each to obtain their perspectives on the effect the exclusion of FBAR penalties and criminal fines has on the nature and volume of whistleblower complaints and on the cases they bring forward. We also attended a regularly scheduled meeting of attorneys representing whistleblowers, including some we had spoken with and several others. Following the enactment of statutory provisions defining collected proceeds for the purpose of whistleblower awards to include FBAR penalties and other non-Title 26 collections, we contacted the 11 attorneys we had previously interviewed for their views on the effect of the new legislation, and we received written responses from 8 of them. For balance, we also analyzed data on FBAR penalty and tax assessments for a sample of taxpayers who were assessed an FBAR penalty in calendar years 2010 through 2015. For all taxpayers in our sample, we identified those where a whistleblower was involved in providing IRS information about the taxpayer and those where there was no whistleblower presence. We analyzed whether there was a statistically significant difference in proportion of FBAR penalty assessments compared to tax and FBAR penalty assessments based on whether a whistleblower was involved or not using a nonparametric Wilcoxon-Mann Whitney test. This analysis did not control for other factors that could affect the results, such as the taxpayer being willfully noncompliant with FBAR reporting requirements, the total tax assessment of the taxpayer, or the total income of the taxpayer. In addition, we interviewed IRS Whistleblower Office officials and operating division officials to discuss the relative complexity of claims involving and not involving FBAR and how the exam teams use whistleblower information related to FBAR noncompliance.

The performance audit upon which this chapter is based was conducted from March 2017 to August 2018 in accordance with generally accepted government auditing standards. Those standards require that we plan and perform the audit to obtain sufficient, appropriate evidence to provide a reasonable basis for our findings and conclusions based on our audit objectives. We believe that the evidence obtained provides a reasonable basis for our findings and conclusions based on our audit objectives. We subsequently worked with IRS from August 2018 to September 2018 to prepare this public version of the original sensitive report for public release. This public version was also prepared in accordance with these standards.

APPENDIX II: COMMENTS FROM THE INTERNAL REVENUE SERVICE

DEPUTY COMMISSIONER

DEPARTMENT OF THE TREASURY
INTERNAL REVENUE SERVICE
WASHINGTON, D.C. 20224

July 16, 2018

James R. McTigue, Jr.
Director, Tax Issues, Strategic Issues Team
U.S. Government Accountability Office
Washington, DC 20548

Dear Mr. McTigue:

Thank you for the opportunity to review and comment on the draft report of the Government Accountability Office (GAO) titled "IRS Whistleblower Program – Improvements Needed in Data Controls for Award Determinations" (GAO-18-516). We generally agree with the report and its findings.

Our Whistleblower Program is an important and effective tax administration tool. Information submitted by whistleblowers to our program has led to the detection of tax compliance issues that might otherwise have gone undetected and has assisted in collecting billions of dollars in additional tax revenue.

Some taxpayers use offshore accounts to hide assets and income outside the United States in an effort to evade their federal tax obligations. Individuals with offshore bank accounts are required to file Form 114, Report of Foreign Bank and Financial Accounts (FBAR). Significant penalties may be assessed for failure to accurately file FBARs. Historically, FBAR penalties were not included when calculating a whistleblower award amount. In February 2018, Congress passed legislation that expanded the definition of what was eligible for a whistleblower award to include FBAR penalties.

Upon the change to the law, we undertook activities to assess the operational impact and to outline policy to address the changes. We placed a temporary hold on whistleblower award determinations during the initial review of the legislation. We subsequently issued guidance to our staff to review open whistleblower claims for indications of FBAR penalties, criminal fines and/or civil forfeiture activity. We also modified our external website to reflect the change.

While we have completed these and other actions, additional actions are still necessary. We use Form 11369, Confidential Evaluation Report on Claim for Award, to document the whistleblower's contribution and use it to determine whistleblower award amount. We agree that the form and its instructions could be updated further to clarify its conformance with the new law. We also recognize the need for improved controls on our FBAR database which is used to track all FBAR enforcement actions and will now play a critical role in the whistleblower award determination process. We are currently assessing a comprehensive data solution which would address concerns raised in this report.

Our comments on the specific recommendations in this report are shared in the enclosure. The IRS is committed to helping U.S. taxpayers understand and meet their tax responsibilities. We appreciate having the opportunity to review and comment on the draft report. Please do not hesitate to contact us if you have questions concerning this response or if we can be of further assistance.

Sincerely,

Kirsten B. Wielobob
Deputy Commissioner for
Services and Enforcement

Comments on the GAO 18-516 Recommendations directed to the IRS

Recommendation 1:

The Commissioner of Internal Revenue should ensure that the Director of the Whistleblower Office modifies the Form 11369 and its accompanying instructions to clarify how to document how whistleblower information was used in any actions taken, regardless of whether the laws administered, examined, or enforced are outside of Title 26, such as FBAR penalties.

Comment:

We agree with this recommendation. The Whistleblower Office will update the IRS Form 11369 and accompanying instruction however GAO's interpretation of the statute is too broad and leaves out a key component. The code states "anything the IRS is authorized to administer, enforce, or investigate. The GAO recommendation is to document "how whistleblower information was used in any actions taken, regardless of whether the laws administered, examined or enforced are outside of Title 26, such as FBAR penalties." Changes made to the Form 11369 and accompanying instructions will conform to the statute as required.

Recommendation 2:

The Commissioner of Internal Revenue should ensure that Deputy Commissioner for Services and Enforcement develops and documents improved controls for the validity, completeness, and accuracy for data on FBAR exams and enforcement actions.

Comment:

We agree with this recommendation. IRS is in the process of assessing a comprehensive FISMA compliant data solution to transition the current FBAR database to. Included will be the preparation of a Privacy and Civil Liberties Impact Assessment (PCLIA) and the creation of ELC security documents. Proficiencies of this improved system will include controls to ensure the accurate recording of FBAR case information and the availability of Service-wide management reports.

INDEX

A

B

C

D

E

F

G

H

I

P

Q

R

S